WITHDRAWN

Nadine Gordimer Revisited

Twayne's World Authors Series

African Literature

Bernth Lindfors, Editor
University of Texas at Austin

TWAS 881

NADINE GORDIMER
Jerry Bauer

Nadine Gordimer Revisited

Barbara Temple-Thurston

Pacific Lutheran University

Twayne Publishers
New York

Twayne's World Authors Series No. 881

Nadine Gordimer Revisited
Barbara Temple-Thurston

Twayne Publishers
1633 Broadway
New York, NY 10019

Library of Congress Cataloging-in-Publication Data

Temple-Thurston, Barbara.
    Nadine Gordimer revisited / Barbara Temple-Thurston.
        p.   cm. — (Twayne's world authors series ; TWAS 881. African literature)
    Includes bibliographical references and index.
    ISBN 0-8057-4608-0 (alk. paper)
    1. Gordimer, Nadine—Criticism and interpretation.   2. Women and literature—South Africa—History—20th century.   3. South Africa—In literature.   I. Title.   II. Series: Twayne's world authors series ; TWAS 881.   III. Series: Twayne's world authors series. African literature.
    PR9369.3.G6Z89   1999
    823—dc21   98-55672
                                                        CIP

This paper meets the requirements of ANSI/NISO Z3948-1992 (Permanence of Paper).

10 9 8 7 6 5 4 3 2 1

Printed in the United States of America

In memory of my mother, Aileen Taylor.
Her faith and delight in my small achievements gave me the confidence to strive.

Contents

Preface

The best way a writer can serve a revolution is to write as well as he can.

—Gabriel García Márquez

Nadine Gordimer won the Nobel Prize for Literature in 1991, shortly after Nelson Mandela's release from prison and when the dismantling of apartheid was fervently in progress. The question most generally asked of her then was, "Once apartheid is abolished entirely, do you think there will still be something for you to write about?"[1] Gordimer has long insisted that the truth about the genesis of her writing is, in fact, the other way around, that she came to it as a child out of a sense of the mystery of life. She has struggled, however, to persuade her audience of that view. Gordimer claims that her impulse to write was motivated by a need to understand life for herself, to make ontological sense of her own being there, a curiosity that in South Africa's discriminatory society inevitably catapulted her into a headlong collision with politics. Her audience's reluctance to accept her explanation stems partly from the remarkable coincidence of the span and engagement of her writing career with the rise and fall of the brutal apartheid regime, from its 1948 inception to its demise in the historic 1994 general elections, in which Mandela's African National Congress party was voted into power. Yet it is, in fact, Gordimer's body of fiction that is the best witness to her personal reasons for writing.

Written by a young woman confined in a narrow, bigoted society, Gordimer's earliest unpublished novelistic attempts exhibit a consciousness tainted by its racist environment and show no awareness of broader social issues at all. Only through deliberate scrutiny of herself, her society, and her relationship to that society did Gordimer evolve the acute political consciousness—witnessed in the progress of her novels—for which she is renowned today. Her contention that making sense of life in South Africa means somehow piecing together inextricably intertwined factors at once intensely political, sociological, and sexual epitomizes her holistic view of life. The increasing political focus of her fiction results from the apartheid regime's extreme intrusion into the private realm of the individual. But it is not politics per se that has earned Gordimer her readership; rather it is the courageous and probing search

for understanding, best attained through fiction, that underpins all her
work. Fiction is truer than nonfiction, she says,

> because it is a disguise. Fiction can encompass all things that go unsaid
> among other people, and in yourself—all the complexities that, for rea-
> sons of your own human relations, you would never bring out in conver-
> sation, in confessional even, or in a factual assessment of any situation.
> . . . Fiction is open-ended. (Future, 138)

Gordimer's international audience—largely white Americans and Euro-
peans—find relevance in her work because readers seek themselves as
well as others in their reading. Her gift of storytelling, her exacting eye
that exposes with surgical precision the telling nuance in the smallest
gesture resonate with overseas readers. They, too, live in racially troubled
societies increasingly plagued by their histories and traditions of racial
discrimination as difficult to overcome as if they were written in law. Facing paralyzing chasms of communication and the failure of the present
system to deliver equity and opportunity, these readers find stories relevant to their own lives and societies in Gordimer's work. Even her early
novels make connections. *The Lying Days* evokes the fear of blacks and
the insularity so common to many white families abroad, while *A World of
Strangers* explores with unflinching honesty the difficulties of a personal
commitment to know and befriend the "other" in a hostile or indifferent
society. Through the trauma of an interracial relationship—a challenge
still in many communities—*Occasion for Loving* poses the inadequacy of
personal commitment to deal with discrimination and forces readers to
look more critically at the impersonal system governing their lives. So,
while peculiar to South Africa because of its apartheid system, the strong
human stories endure to touch international readers whose environments
are also etched deeply with the pain and anger of racism.

Endorsed and accepted by her fellow African writers, Gordimer has
not always enjoyed the same support from some in her white, English-
speaking community in South Africa. Centered in an educational system
that as late as 1969 was arguing over the inclusion of American literature in the university English curriculum and in a community that reads
little, they have paid scant attention to local writers, at least until acknowledged by the metropolis. They—like most colonial settler communities—
have looked to the mother country for "standards" and approval. Aware
that shifting her own community would require endorsement from

abroad, Gordimer has nevertheless worked determinedly to be worthy of her claim as an African and an African artist. She has always heeded the tug of her Africanness, and she, like other African writers, has "sought the fingerprint of flesh on history."[2]

This study of her 12 novels attests to Gordimer's enduring quality as an artist beyond the confines of the politics of apartheid. It traces her resolution to use her art as honestly and ably as she can, not only to record the complexities of her society but also to envision an alternate path to the destructive trap that racism and oppression assures. It addresses the major issues that bind her work: race, history, the land, ideology, Africanness, economics, revolution and violence, sexuality and gender, and selfhood. It examines the development of her narrative technique and form and provides an overview of the major critical responses to her work. My aim is to highlight Gordimer's remarkable artistic sensibility and narrative power, the abilities that enabled her to confront the world with South Africa's political horrors, and that ensure a continuing output of powerful and enduring works.

Now, without the shackles of apartheid, Gordimer's twelfth—and first truly postapartheid—novel, *The House Gun* (1998), faces the twenty-first century. It posits a society still haunted by the violence of the past yet with a chance to become that delicious hybrid of West and South that will draw its strength from both systems. As compelling as any of her apartheid-era novels, this most recent work is a testament to Gordimer's enduring gift: her ability to catch and intuit the implication of the smallest gesture or nuance and trace its connection to the broader social and public arenas from which it emanates. Gordimer contends that in the twenty-first century the African writer must serve "the peaceful revolution of culture; . . . without talent in our work, without ourselves writing as well as we can, we shall not serve African literature as we should" (Turning, 9).

I wish to thank my friends and colleagues Jill Kelly, Megan Benton, Suzanne Rahn, Chuck Bergman, Sharon Jansen, Richard Peterson, and Jim Kovarik, whose encouragement and advice kept me going during this project. My thanks also to Ben Lindfors for his comments and his patience, and to the editors of *World Literature Written in English* and *Studies in Twentieth Century Literature* for permission to print some reworked material that first appeared in their Spring 1988 and Winter 1991 issues, respectively.

Chronology

1918   Founding of Afrikaner Broederbond ushers in an era of rising Afrikaans power, further fueled by 1922 white miners' strike.

1923   Nadine Gordimer born on November 20 in the mining town of Springs, near Johannesburg, to Isidore and Nan Gordimer.

1924   Herzog's Nationalist-Labour Pact wins elections, encouraging greater segregation and Afrikaner nationalism. The Wage Act is soon passed to help unskilled white workers and the "Colour Bar" Act passed to protect white semi-skilled workers.

1932   Gordimer writes poem about Paul Kruger. Attracted by the rhythm of words, her interest in form is developing.

Herzog allies with Smuts to form United Party. Herzog later jettisoned when he fights to keep South Africa neutral in World War II.

1934   Gordimer is diagnosed with a minor heart ailment and withdrawn from school by her mother.

1937   Gordimer's first published story appears in children's section of Sunday newspaper.

1939   Gordimer's first adult fiction is published in *The Forum* (Johannesburg).

1943   African National Congress Youth League is formed by Tambo, Sisulu, and Mandela.

1945   Gordimer attends the University of the Witwatersrand for one year.

1946   An unfinished, unpublished novel by Gordimer reveals unquestioning racial attitudes.

African mine workers' strike closes down 9 mines and paralyzes 12 others.

1947   Gordimer's only play, *The First Circle,* is published.

1948 Dr. Malan's conservative Afrikaner National party wins elections. Apartheid era begins. Twelve African leaders issue call for African unity and adopt ANC Youth League proposal to start mass struggle.

1949 Gordimer marries Dr. Gerald Gavron. She publishes her first book, *Face to Face: Short Stories.*

Prohibition of Mixed Marriages Act makes marriage between whites and other racial groups illegal.

1950 Gordimer's daughter, Oriane, is born in June.

Population Registration Act assigns everyone to a race group; Immorality Act makes interracial sex illegal; Group Areas Act restricts residential and business areas. Suppression of Communism Bill introduced. Verwoerd is made minister of Native Affairs.

1952 Gordimer and Gavron are divorced. *Soft Voice of the Serpent and Other Stories* is published.

Defiance Campaign launched by the African National Congress and South African Indian Congress, spawning a huge surge in ANC membership. All Africans, including women, must carry passes.

1953 *The Lying Days* is published.

Separate Amenities Act, Public Safety Bill with emergency powers, Criminal Law Amendment Bill, and Bantu Education Act are all passed. The Liberal Party is introduced, supporting qualified nonracial franchise.

1954 Gordimer marries Reinhold Cassirer, an art dealer.

Native Resettlement Act starts massive removals of blacks and Coloureds.

1955 Gordimer's son, Hugo, is born in March.

Congress of the People meets outside Johannesburg and adopts the Freedom Charter before police break up the rally.

1956 *Six Feet of the Country* is published.

156 Congress of the People participants of all races are arrested for high treason. Famous Treason Trial ensues—all are acquitted by 1961. Sophiatown rezoned and renamed Triomf.

1957 The Alexandra bus boycott is staged.

✓ 1958 *A World of Strangers* is published but is banned until 1970.

Verwoerd becomes prime minister and introduces homeland policy. Africanists break away from ANC to form Pan-Africanist Congress (PAC).

1959 State-Aided Institutions Act closes access to libraries for blacks, and Extension of University Education Bill deprives universities of the right to admit black students without government permission.

1960 *Friday's Footprint* is published.

PAC campaign against pass-laws ends in Sharpeville massacre with 69 unarmed Africans shot dead and 180 injured by police. Over 18,000 people are detained. African political organizations are banned; they go underground and start strategic violence plan. Ostracism of South Africa in world affairs begins.

1961 Gordimer wins the W. H. Smith Literary Award and Ford Fellowship to the United States.

South Africa becomes a republic and leaves the British Commonwealth. Military wings of the ANC, the PAC, and the white African Resistance Movement (ARM) begin sabotage campaigns against the state. The ANC and the PAC set up headquarters outside South Africa.

1962 Detention without trial and the policy of house arrest are introduced. Umkhonto we Sizwe broken after Mandela's capture in August.

✓ 1963 *Occasion for Loving* is published.

The remainder of Umkhonto's leaders are arrested in July, signaling the collapse of the sabotage movement.

1964 Mandela and Umkhonto leaders are sentenced to life imprisonment on sabotage charges. Bram Fischer is arrested, but jumps bail to continue underground struggle.

1965 Fischer is recaptured in November and sentenced to life imprisonment.

✓ 1966 *The Late Bourgeois World* is published, but it is banned until 1976.

Verwoerd is assassinated and B. J. Vorster becomes prime minister.

1968   Steve Biko founds black South African Students Organization (SASO), which promoted the black consciousness movement.

1969   Gordimer is granted South Africa's Thomas Pringle Award and is a visiting professor at Harvard and Northwestern Universities.

1970   *A Guest of Honour* is published.

Bantu Homeland Citizenship Act tries to enforce a homeland citizenship on every African in South Africa. Cosmos Desmond's *The Discarded People* reveals horrors of resettlement villages for blacks.

1971   *Livingston's Companions* is published.

Desmond banned, rendering his book unquotable. Transkei becomes "self-governing" territory.

1972   Gordimer is awarded England's James Tait Memorial Prize.

Ciskei, Zululand, Bophuthatswana, and Lebowa, become "self-governing" territories.

1973   Gordimer publishes *The Black Interpreters: Notes on African Writing* with David Goldblatt.

Black consciousness movement grows in early 1970s.

1974   *The Conservationist* (joint winner of the Booker Prize) is published. Gordimer is also awarded South Africa's CNA Prize.

1975   *Selected Stories* is published. Gordimer is awarded France's Grand Aigle d'Or Prize and the CNA Prize.

Black People's Convention (BPC) is founded with Biko as president.

1976   *Some Monday for Sure* is published.

The Soweto Revolt takes place after 15,000 schoolchildren protest the compulsory use of Afrikaans as medium of instruction, and police open fire, killing two. Violence erupts nationwide; by 1977 the official count puts 575 dead and thousands injured.

1977   Biko is arrested in August and dies from brutal treatment after 26 days in police custody.

1978   *No Place Like: Selected Stories* is published.

       P. W. Botha becomes prime minister.

1979   *Burger's Daughter* is published, banned in July, and reinstated in August.

       The ANC, in exile, is flooded with new recruits after the Soweto Revolt. It redoubles its onslaught on the military and pushes for international isolation through sanctions, embargoes, and boycotts through the 1980s.

1980   Gordimer publishes "What Happened to *Burger's Daughter.*" She is awarded the CNA prize for *Burger's Daughter.*

1981   *July's People* is published. Gordimer is awarded Scottish Neil M. Gunn Fellowship; USA's Common Wealth Award; and the CNA prize. She receives an honorary doctorate from University of Leuven, Belgium.

1982   Gordimer is granted the Modern Language Association (MLA) Award.

1983   In August, 1,000 delegates of all races representing 575 organizations found the United Democratic Front (UDF) to coordinate internal opposition to apartheid.

1984   *Something Out There* is published. Gordimer receives an honorary doctorate from University of the Witwatersrand, Johannesburg.

       A new constitution provides participation for Coloureds and Asians, but elections are marked by widespread violence and boycotts. An unprecedented number of strikes, 58 incidents of sabotage against the state, and 26 attacks on police occur.

1985   Gordimer is awarded Italy's Premio Malaparte Prize.

       School and bus boycotts, worker stayaways, and attacks on black police and councillors increase. Insurgency attacks rise to 136, deaths by political violence to 879, and strikes to 390, involving 240,000 workers.

1986   Gordimer is awarded West Germany's Nellie Sachs Prize. She is awarded honorary doctorates from Harvard, Yale, and Cape Town Universities. She assists in organizing the Anti-Censorship Action Group (ACAG). She is also elected vice president of the International Association of Poets, Playwrights, Editors, Essayists and Novelists (PEN).

Pressure from the international community is increasing. South African forces attack alleged ANC bases in Zimbabwe, Botswana, and Zambia. Indefinite, nationwide state of emergency is declared.

1987 *A Sport of Nature* is published. She is elected patron and regional representative of Congress of South African Writers (COSAW).

Officials estimate that 13,000 people—many of them children—were detained and tortured under state of emergency. National Union of Mineworkers strike for three weeks—500,000 people participate.

1988 *The Essential Gesture: Writing, Politics and Places* is published.

South Africa signs an accord with Cuba and Angola for phased withdrawal of troops.

1989 P. W. Botha is forced out by ministerial rebellion and replaced by F. W. de Klerk.

1990 *My Son's Story* is published.

Mandela is unconditionally released, and the ANC and other outlawed organizations are unbanned.

1991 *Jump and Other Stories* is published. Gordimer is awarded Nobel Prize for Literature. She is elected Publicity Secretary of COSAW.

Conflict between Inkatha (Zulu chief Buthelezi's group) and alliance of the ANC and Congress of South African Trade Unions now reaches endemic proportions.

1992 Gordimer is elected COSAW vice president. She takes part in Mayibuye Community Arts Academy concerning the role of the arts in the transformation of South Africa. She participates in Grahamstown Winter School lectures. She is awarded honorary doctorates from

Cambridge University and University of Durban-Westville.

De Klerk calls whites-only referendum to obtain a new mandate for political reforms. Codessa (Convention for a Democratic South Africa), a multiparty forum, negotiates a new constitution.

1993   Gordimer is elected member of the Board of Trustees responsible for a proposed Foundation for Arts and Culture concerned with the process of transformation and cultural reconstruction in South Africa, under the ANC's Department of Arts and Culture.

De Klerk and Mandela receive Nobel Peace Prize.

1994   *None to Accompany Me* is published.

The ANC is elected with 62 percent of the vote in the first free and fair elections in South Africa's history. On May 9, Mandela is elected president of the Republic of South Africa.

1995   Truth and Reconciliation Commission is appointed under Bishop Desmond Tutu's chairmanship.

1998   *The House Gun* is published.

Chapter One

The Rise of a Writer:
"Falling, Falling through the Surface"

Nadine Gordimer's acclaim, culminating in the Nobel Prize for Literature awarded to her in 1991, has established her in the international literary world as South Africa's leading voice depicting the realities of life under apartheid. Firmly anchored in the specifics of South African politics and history, Gordimer's work grants us an unflinching look at white South Africa's neuroses as it struggles to know and belong in Africa. Recognizing the limitations that apartheid society imposed on writers, Gordimer has said that she is fully aware that her consciousness has the same tint as her face.[1]

Apartheid has long been the starting point for understanding Gordimer's work, and its demise in 1994 raises new questions about how her work will be evaluated in the future. Any reader of Gordimer's work should understand that under apartheid, South African society was rigorously segregated to maintain and promote white economic and social privilege. It was a society where class and race coincided by design, by law, and by the coercive power of the state. As Stephen Clingman has said of South African apartheid society, "To be born black is not only to be deprived of the vote, but virtually to be committed to the role of the worker, whether in industry, mining, or agriculture, at generally extortionate rates of pay. To be born white, on the contrary, is to enjoy a position of privilege, most obviously in terms of the vote but also socially and economically, even at the lower echelons of white society."[2] Through the keen observation of the lives of those within her ruptured society, Gordimer grants us a unique sense of her nation's unfolding history.

Though her position as spokesperson has been questioned by some South African academics, critical interest in Gordimer has never been stronger. Between 1985 and 1995, eight major texts on Gordimer's work were published, with many of the authors drawing on aspects of her life to assist their readings of her fiction. While Gordimer has warned against straining the boundaries of what she calls the "I spy" game in

1

the critics' search for meaning, the perversity of South African society under apartheid and the psychological aberrations it produced make it particularly important to understand where her journey began and, therefore, how remarkable the transformation of her consciousness has been.

On November 20, 1923, in the small gold-mining town of Springs, 30 miles east of Johannesburg, Nadine Gordimer was born into a family that bore the wounds of its immigrant status. Like the majority of Jewish people in South Africa, her father, Isidore Gordimer, came from Lithuania. A victim of the *pogroms*, he was poor, uneducated, and unable to speak a word of English. He struggled to make his living as a watchmaker; by the time he married, he owned a small jeweler's shop. Nadine's mother, Nan Meyers, was a socially ambitious Anglo-Jewish woman whose aspirations to join the gentile bourgeoisie were hampered by her Yiddish-speaking husband's passivity and foreign difference.

Nadine grew up in the 1930s in a home environment devoid of political consciousness when segregation and racism were strong (though before the formal institution of apartheid in 1948). In an interview in *Conversations with Nadine Gordimer,* she claims that her father's attitude toward blacks was simply that "they were beyond the human pale," his struggles in life producing "merely the desire to get what you can and just hang on to a cosy life."[3] Her mother, the dominant partner in an unhappy marriage, "did good works. . . . she was always uneasy and angry if she saw black people being treated badly, but it was always as a form of charity. She didn't connect it with the law . . . with the fact that they didn't have rights as white people had" (*CNG,* 307).

It was in this atmosphere that Gordimer, the younger and more spoiled of the family's two daughters, was nurtured. Her childhood passion was dancing, though as early as age nine she evinced an interest in writing: She wrote a patriotic ditty about the Boer Republic president, Paul Kruger, for a school assignment. When she was 10, however, a family doctor diagnosed a rapid heartbeat, a common malady at puberty, and her protective mother overreacted by stopping her dancing. A year later, her mother even withdrew Gordimer from the private convent school she attended and engaged a tutor. Gordimer describes this period from age 11 to 16 as "such incredible loneliness . . . a terrible thing to do to a child" (*CNG,* 133). She turned inward and read omnivorously; the local whites-only library became her lifeline. She nurtured her imagination on a variety of texts, from Pepys's *Diary* and *The Anatomy of Melancholy* to *War and Peace* and *Gone with the Wind.* Closeted in the company of her mother's generation, carted to tea parties and dinner parties where women talked of household matters and men talked of golf, Nadine became a jester for grown-ups. At 15 and 16 she would mimic people they knew, developing a keen ear for dialogue as well as irony, since those entertained today would be mimicked tomorrow.

Critic Stephen Clingman notes that Gordimer began publishing stories of "notable poise and sensibility" in South African journals when she was only 14, stories—Gordimer now says—that are full of "the respectable bourgeois sentiment one might expect" (21). But, outside her readings, Gordimer had not yet met people who lived in a world of ideas that challenged the conventional and stunted existence of her home environment (21). Thus the paucity of political awareness in Gordimer's earliest work can be traced to the isolation, self-focus, and dependency her mother fostered in her as a young person. Still living at home and supported by her father at 23, Gordimer today speaks with shame of the "outward life of sybaritic meagreness" she led. In 1963 she wrote, "No conditioning can excuse the absence of the simple act of courage that would resist it. . . . I cannot understand why I did not free myself in the most obvious way, leave home and small town and get a job somewhere" (*EG,* 24).

Gordimer's early reading of Upton Sinclair's *The Jungle* prompted a shocking analogy in her mind between exploited meatpackers in America and exploited mineworkers in South Africa. But it was thanks to her one year at Johannesburg's University of the Witwatersrand when she was 22, and to her friendships through the early 1950s with black and white activists, artists, musicians, and writers that her political consciousness was truly roused. She lacked the politicized background of some of the young people from the liberal families she met in Johannesburg, but through the multiracial friendships forged with blacks from the racially mixed and vibrant Sophiatown ghetto crowd and through mutual interests in art and literature, she awakened to the "shameful enormity of the colour bar." As she put it, it was not the "problems" of her country that set her to writing; rather, it was learning to write that sent her "falling, falling through the surface of the South African way of life" (*EG,* 26).

Gordimer married Dr. Gerald Gavron in 1949, the year her first volume, *Face to Face: Short Stories,* was published. A few years later, shortly after their daughter, Oriane, was born, she republished many of these in a second volume, *The Soft Voice of the Serpent and Other Stories.* Her stories reveal an observational skill and psychological insight of searing preci-

sion, honed, no doubt, during those adolescent years spent at tea parties. These skills have served her well in the broader, more historical topics of her novels. Her first published novel (two unfinished, unpublished
manuscripts are extant), *The Lying Days* (1953), appeared after her
divorce from Gavron. In 1954 she married Reinhold Cassirer, an art
dealer originally from Heidelberg, Germany; their son, Hugo, was born
the next year.

A talent for capturing nuance in behavior is not enough to make a
great writer, however, and in Gordimer's early novels, unforgettable for
the intensity of relationships afflicted by politics, we see her working for
greater narrative muscle and a more mature political vision. *The Lying
Days* (1953), *A World of Strangers* (1958), and *Occasion for Loving* (1963)
capture her unwavering scrutiny of white South African society through
an essentially liberal lens. Her talent for imbuing seemingly minor incidents with political intensity dramatizes her early fiction, making it
powerful and compelling. The development of her characters charts her
budding political consciousness as it was spurred by her need to establish an identity and a sense of belonging as a white person in South
Africa, achievable—it first seemed—through the practice of "decent,"
humane liberal values. But in the 1950s, the failure of these liberal values to overcome the militancy of apartheid drove her to reject individual
humanism as a route to political change and to explore more consciously
the complexities and contradictions of nationhood in the South African
context.

In her middle period Gordimer wrote what I believe are her most
enduring novels: *The Late Bourgeois World* (1966), *A Guest of Honour*
(1970), *The Conservationist* (1974), *Burger's Daughter* (1979), and *July's
People* (1981). She strengthened her narrative strategy, and her political
consciousness embraced the need for radical commitment and action. In
the 1960s, the tightening of government controls and laws through
bannings and brutal detentions resulted in her marked politicization. In
the 1970s, the black consciousness movement's rejection and alienation
of politicized whites challenged her to a greater radicalism. The South
African regime's pursuit of separate development—black "independent"
homelands created by the state—as a means to maintain white
supremacy and white Afrikaner nationalism came at a time when many
African countries were struggling with their recent independence from
Europe. The issue of independence alerted Gordimer to the significance
of nation building, and we witness her deliberate engagement with the
idea and the difficulties of the process. Combined with her exceptional

artistic sensibility, these novels achieve a balance and power rarely matched in her later work. During this middle period her international renown grew, and the pressure to act, speak, and write for the cause of black liberation increased. Gordimer began to take on a clear political affiliation that, as a writer, she had earlier resisted, formally joining the African National Congress (ANC) party when it was unbanned in 1990.

After *July's People,* the novels *A Sport of Nature* (1987) and *My Son's Story* (1990)—though still powerfully compelling—became increasingly ideologically prescriptive. The impending change in power in the late 1980s focused her attention on the creation of a new nation and its future. Her work took on greater symbolic and prophetic significance. These novels take on a literary and political self-consciousness that distances the reader from a narrative and characters ideologically weighted. Though Gordimer holds that her community involvement—"another part of my life where I put my life on the line for what I believe in"— apparently frees her to write "as if one were already dead, afraid of no one's reactions, answerable to no one's views" (*CNG,* 311), her talent for seamlessly unfolding the intricacies of human interaction seems strained in these later novels. Her 1994 novel, *None to Accompany Me,* straddles the transition to the new future. It steps back from prophecy and prescription to reflect more tranquilly on the process by which the private and political past has finally brought the long-awaited future to the present. The novel stands between eras—after Nelson Mandela's release but before free elections, an interregnum of a new kind. Mindful of the pitfalls of entrenched patterns, it nevertheless reaches beyond its present to probe the imaginative possibilities of a new form, a new structure, and unique relationships that could embody a nation of greater equity and harmony than we presently know.

In 1998 Gordimer published her first truly postapartheid novel, *The House Gun.* Though still haunted by the climate of violence generated by a callous and brutal past, this novel embraces the inevitable mingling of cultures that begins to take place in a society now founded on principles of equity and dignity. Ever conscious that nothing can prevent random horror and disaster, it demonstrates that a system based on a constitution of freedom and justice, such as the new government of the ANC, can certainly ameliorate the consequences of such misfortune.

Gordimer has continued to write and publish prolifically, and she has steadily gained a wider international audience. In addition to her 12 novels, she has published over 150 short stories and about 200 nonfictional essays and reviews to date. She has also granted over 100 interviews. A glance at the titles of South African and international news articles by and about her since the early 1950s shows her consistent involvement in the art and politics of her country. She has been the recipient of the major literary awards of many countries: South Africa's Thomas Pringle and CNA prizes; the United States' Ford Foundation Fellowship, the Modern Language Association Award, and the Common Wealth Award for Distinguished Service in Literature; Britain's James Tait Black Memorial and Booker prizes; Scotland's Arts Council Neil M. Gunn Fellowship; France's Grand Aigle d'Or prize; Germany's Nellie Sachs Prize; and Italy's Premio Malaparte Prize, all culminating in the Nobel Prize for Literature in 1991. She has been a visiting lecturer at many major universities and has received honorary doctorates from three South African universities, seven U.S. universities (including Harvard and Yale), Cambridge and York universities in Britain, and the University of Leuven in Belgium. Gordimer cofounded the Congress of South African Writers (COSAW) in 1987, where she works concertedly to assist young black writers, and she has served for a number of years as vice president of PEN International. She has traveled widely in Africa over the years and has been increasingly committed to the development of African and South African literary culture. The formal innovations of her novels and her exploration of what makes a novel or a writer African have broadened the debate about African and postcolonial literature as well as about nationality, ethnicity, gender, and race. Much of her fiction has been translated into other languages, and she continues to be sought after for appearances and commentary on a variety of issues.

The enormous body of criticism on Gordimer's work—too vast to include in this study—is well documented in an excellent 1994 bibliography compiled by Driver, Dry, MacKenzie, and Read. Any reader of Gordimer's work, however, will want to be aware of the following significant studies. Abdul JanMohamed's *Manichean Aesthetics: The Politics of Literature in Colonial Africa* (1983) examines Gordimer's work in the context of colonialist society's Manichean structure and ultimately redeems her from the label of "colonial" writer. Stephen Clingman, author of *The Novels of Nadine Gordimer: History from the Inside* (1986) and editor of Gordimer's nonfictional work published in *Essential Gesture: Writing, Politics and Places* (1988), shows how Gordimer's work is caught up in the major literary and ideological movements of South Africa. He examines Gordimer's acute apprehension of how she as writer acts upon history, while at the same time history is acting or shaping her consciousness as well. He calls his study of her work "a history from the

inside" and notes how Gordimer's development—political and formal—
can be traced in her writing. Clingman remains the leading critic of the
historical and political dimensions of her work, while other critics focus
on other conditioning factors. An earlier study by John Cooke, *The Novels of Nadine Gordimer* (1985), holds that Gordimer's private world, particularly her relationship with her mother, informs the public themes of
her novels. Cooke asserts that the liberation of children from unusually
possessive mothers is her main private theme, and that attaining such
liberation depends upon successfully challenging the dominant political
order. He argues that the private and the political in her novels unite
through the "gradual accretion of public resonances around her private
themes."[4] Judie Newman's fine monograph *Nadine Gordimer* (1988)
examines the way gender complicates the intersecting themes of race,
sex, and colonialism in the novels. Her poststructuralist approach
extends Clingman's interrogation of Gordimer's use of narrative realism
as the way to "know" white South Africa, and it traces Gordimer's own
deconstruction of her narrative style as a new route to cultural and political decolonization.

Two critics who have written on South African literature with a
strong focus on Gordimer's work are David Ward and Michael Wade.
Both further the debate about her narrative strategy and its clinically
detached style. In *Chronicles of Darkness* (1989), Ward revises Cooke's
term *voyeurism* to acknowledge the texts' concern with distance between
observer and observed,[5] but he notes also an alienation of the observer
due to the often ambivalent records that cast doubt on the validity of
the observer's creation of the "other." Ward sees this doubled distancing
as an aspect of Gordimer's artistic ability designed to subvert conventional expectations of form, shaking any secure sense that our experience
of the world can be other than flawed, fractured, and contradictory. He
holds, too, that Gordimer's fiction follows a steady movement away
from chronicle to prophecy in an "attempt to capture and direct a
future" (134). In a more recent study, *White on Black in South Africa*
(1993), Michael Wade examines English-speaking white South African
writers' inscriptions of black South Africans. While in his earlier work he
documented how Gordimer represses the theme of Jewishness in her fiction, in this new study Wade notes the white English-speaking community's tendency to define its identity through "the other"—African or
Afrikaner. The English South African literary tradition assumed a cultural unity with metropolitan England when, in fact, England was for
them also an encounter with "the other." Through their tradition of dis-

sent, the South African English writers exhibited deeply defensive patterns of stereotypes and rituals when inscribing black South Africans. With its "own perceptual system, its own constellation of myths"[6] and burdened by its contradictions of privilege and dependency, this English-speaking group manifested an intense level of emotionality—often unconscious—about blacks. Wade claims that Gordimer's work both reflects and charts a shift in her perceptual patterns, and he argues that over a 30-year period, her inscriptions mark a major change in the group's psychic functioning, demonstrating its growth toward a clearer understanding of its own identity through a more accurate understanding of its internal and external environment.

Kathrin Wagner's *Rereading Nadine Gordimer* (1994) picks up on the repressions and evasions that epitomize white English-speaking South African culture; she indicts Gordimer's consciousness—and therefore her fiction—as irredeemably tainted and unreliable. She provocatively challenges Gordimer's perceived status as spokesperson for white South Africa, citing the South African academic community's critical response as "often overwhelmingly dissatisfied with a number of aspects of her work,"[7] and she questions Gordimer's status as a political writer through an unearthing of "the subtextual survival and prevalence of cultural and ethnic stereotypes in her novels" (Wagner, iv). While Wagner's criticism may offer some fruitful analysis by studying the slippage between intentional and subconscious renderings in Gordimer's novels, her reliance on "implication" and "suggestion" to uncover so-called subconscious racist tendencies undermines her critique. Written as a doctoral dissertation for a segment of the South African academy critical of Gordimer's international acclaim, this text's determination to prove its thesis ultimately raises more questions about its own subconscious thrust than it does about the quality of Gordimer's fiction. In an arena as politically charged as South Africa and its arts, passion and partisanship may be expected.[8] One South African reviewer critical of Wagner's text wrote that while it provides a field for review and response, it unfortunately "continues a tradition of hostile reception reserved by some local literary sectors for Gordimer, without making any significant contribution to the scholarship on a leading author."[9] Two collections of essays—Rowland Smith's *Critical Essays on Nadine Gordimer* (1990), which reprints noteworthy essays published between 1953 and 1988, and Bruce King's *The Later Fiction of Nadine Gordimer* (1993), whose focus is "the changing face" of Gordimer's later fiction—provide a variety of challenging readings of Gordimer's novels and short fiction.

Gordimer's own comments on her work—and on writing and politics in general—add yet another perspective to the reading of her fiction. Clingman's edition of her nonfictional writing, *The Essential Gesture: Writing Politics and Places* (1988); Topping Bazin and Dallman Seymour's edition of interviews, *Conversations with Nadine Gordimer* (1990); and Gordimer's own *Writing and Being* (1995) are sources critics often use to interpret her fiction. Commenting on these critics' use of her prolific body of non-fiction in the search for "truth," Gordimer has cautioned the reader that

> nothing . . . will be as true as my fiction, and I believe that with all my heart and mind. I write non-fiction only for political reasons, because I believe there's perhaps something I have a little wrinkle on that you don't get in the newspaper; but I always feel that the writing is self-conscious, somehow tailored by some other force in me. . . . it is never as true as what I imagine. (*CNG,* 260)

Yet Gordimer's nonfictional writings and interviews do sometimes highlight the connections between her "real" world and the fiction, and they also mark ideological shifts in her political consciousness as her world enacts change upon her, even as she engages with history in assessing and shaping its forces. A glance at Gordimer's early nonfictional writing provides insight into some of the major concerns that continue to surface in her fiction. Publishing locally and internationally, her articles address issues about the ambiguity of the position of whites in South Africa, the dilemmas of the development of the English novel in South Africa and Africa, and the impact of increasing government repression and bannings in the country. She has also written about her childhood, as well as her travels in Africa. Most of these topics appear in one way or another in all her published novels.

Gordimer's vast body of work spans almost 50 years; it covers the entire National Party government's apartheid era from its inception in 1948 to its reluctant, but remarkable, relinquishing of power in the April 1994 election. Clingman writes, "To many she has, through her fiction, become the *interpreter* of South Africa as, over the years, her country has marched down its doom-ridden slope of apartheid" (*EG,* 1). During the apartheid years until the liberating independence of South Africa in 1994, Gordimer's *raison d'être* was clear to readers across the world, but critics must now ask what the relevance of her work will be in the postapartheid era. Now that South Africa has joined the ranks of independent nations, the present volume revisits Gordimer's work to consider its relevance and endurance beyond historical documentation of a brutal regime.

Gordimer's work remains relevant most especially because of its power of insight into human behavior beneath its outward manifestation. Her expression in art of "what really exists beneath the surface" is part of the transformation of her society.[10] Her accident of birth as a white South African has granted her challenges most writers never face, and—from her fractured and alienated world—her interrogation of the meaning of home has relevance for all of us in a diverse and displaced world. Trapped in the extreme political climate of apartheid, her quest becomes a coherent political and artistic identity in a new South Africa, a quest that explores the individual's relationship to self, family, and society; the meaning and construction of "nation"; and the role of nationalism. Highlighting the fictive quality of the idea of nation and claiming for art a transformative power in society, she seeks new structures that fracture old patterns of authority embedded even in the smallest social unit, the family. She envisions a national culture and consciousness that enshrines the values of nonracialism with economic, political, and cultural equity for each and for all.

Gordimer's admirers and critics widely acknowledge her importance as a political writer driven by antipathy to the racist ideology of apartheid. Yet in an interview as late as 1995, Gordimer herself rejected the political situation in South Africa as incentive for her writing: "I wouldn't agree that my novels have arisen from the political context. I happen to have lived in a politically charged atmosphere and milieu all my life; but I was writing long before I was aware of what politics was, so I don't really write out of motivation of politics."[11] She has admitted, however, that politics has turned out to play a very important role in her work. Acknowledging writers to be "lucky" if—like the Russians in the nineteenth century—they have the challenge of great themes, she believes nevertheless that it is good writing that makes great literature: "If you are a writer, you can make the death of a canary stand for the whole mystery of death . . . it's all a matter of the quality of the writing." A writer before politics impinged on her consciousness, her struggle has been, she says, "not to lose the acute sensibility . . . the acuteness of catching nuance in behaviour . . . and to marry it successfully to a narrative gift" (*CNG*, 141).

So while political themes connect her work like vertebrae, it is this acute sensibility—her extraordinary ability to register subtle shifts

between people, to capture the excruciating significance of private
details as they reverberate, ripple, into the ever-widening public and
political world—that is the marrow of her work. This quality, when
combined with a maturing political consciousness and a strong narrative
strategy, keeps readers coming back to her work. Through an exquisite
rendering of relationships that speaks clearly to readers across cultures
and time, despite their anchor in the specifics of South African politics
and history, Gordimer's novels expose the perversity of power when
focused so single-mindedly on racial discrimination as its main structural component of a nation. Her fiction over the years, responding
inevitably to the shifts and changes in the society around her even as it
probed new directions, provides not only the stories of individual consciousnesses mired in—or struggling to break free from—racist confines
but provides also a meticulous record of a society's descent into brutality
and inhumanity due to blind prejudice and abuse of power. But it is
essentially the power of her craft, her keen ear and unwavering eye for
the layered (political) significance of intimate detail, that has propelled
Gordimer to international recognition.

Chapter Two

Where Do Whites Fit In?
The Lying Days, A World of Strangers, and *Occasion for Loving*

The Lying Days

Like many first published novels, *The Lying Days* contains autobiographical elements drawn largely from Gordimer's childhood in the mining town of Springs and from her intense relationship with her mother. The novel is essentially one of personal exploration in which the young protagonist, ordinary Helen Shaw, struggles to break free of conventional white attitudes as her awareness of the racial and social injustice in the country is nudged into life.

This first novel is significant because it establishes the concerns that Gordimer pursues throughout her writing career, exploring, shifting, and refining her views over time. First, it engages quite deliberately with its historical time, documenting the pre- and post-1948 ascension to power of the National Party's apartheid government. Second, through Helen's interaction with her society, the novel establishes one of Gordimer's abiding themes—the inextricability of the political and personal worlds—and initiates the increasingly sophisticated historical consciousness of her work. Third, seeking to find a place for whites in South Africa, the novel explores the conventional theme of the ambiguity of the European in Africa through the colonial life-style of the white mining community. It quite deliberately takes a topic and setting specifically South African and establishes Gordimer's commitment to such a story and setting for a novel and the validity of her choice. Helen's complaint that she had never "read a book in which I was recognizable" is effectively solved for future generations.[1] Fourth, the novel experiments with form and narrative strategy by subtly subverting the traditional form of bildungsroman, which usually chronicles a young man's adventures on the road to manhood. The form of the novel asserts instead the significance of a young woman's voice and the story of her personal, sexual, and social development as it collides with the political world and, typically, turns inward. The fractured experience that marks the female *bildung* is mimicked in the episodic structure, and the metaphorical and structural use of space reinforces themes of control and transgression. Also initiated as recurring themes in Gordimer's work are the assertion of the body as a contested site and sensuality as a powerful formative force that permeates every aspect of life and nature.

In *The Lying Days,* narrator/protagonist Helen tells of her cloying childhood in the white mining community of Atherton, where a strict patriarchal social hierarchy matched one's position on the mine to the street and size of one's house. Helen's potential growth is measured by the extent to which her curiosity and intelligence lead her to break away from the stifling conformity of home. The novel is divided into three parts: The Mine, The Sea, and The City. The story follows chronologically her white middle-class upbringing in the mining community, whose racial fear and prejudice blinds her to social injustices. It follows her self-absorbed and politically oblivious first love and sexual awakening, as well as her struggle for independence and adulthood as she wrestles with an emerging social awareness and its consequent alienation and guilt.

In the first section, Gordimer establishes the parameters of the white world that shape young Helen's consciousness. Gordimer's acute sensibility captures the claustrophobic presence of a manipulative and controlling mother in the cramped, dark sitting room with its "willow pattern tea things out. Embroidered cloth and tea cozy in the shape of a china doll in a wool crocheted crinoline, crumpets polished with yellow butter, the whole covered with a square of green net weighted with beads" (*LD,* 18). Mrs. Shaw's weeks are "pegged out to street collections and galas and dances and cake sales and meetings of this committee and that" (*LD,* 21) as part of the war effort, and she regards the old African gardener who has worked for her two Saturdays a month since she was married as "one of the old kind . . . A good old thing" whom she rewards with "a big dish of tea and some meat between thick bread" and a chat on the lawn about "bringing up children" (*LD,* 24). Obsessive motherhood fosters female dependence and manifests itself in her complete absorption with preparations for Helen's first dance: sewing and fitting the girl's first long dress late into the night, then talking about hairdos and drinking tea at the kitchen table. Mrs. Shaw's identification with all things English as the standard of civilization determinedly shuts out all of Africa except for the "old kind"—domestic servant Anna and Paul the gardener—who minister to her needs. Helen is cocooned in this world. Despite her bold and transgressive escapade to the unknown, noisy black world of the mineworkers' concession stores one after-noon—an area replete with smells of stale urine and cooking entrails, African medicine shops crowded with "dusty lions' tails . . . flaking gray roots and strange teeth," and the dark brown faces of sauntering mine boys (*LD,* 11)—Helen flees back to the security of the Saturday after-noon tennis and tea, an event to which she had refused to accompany her parents earlier in the day. Staring into the stores, she feels "for the first time something of the tingling fascination of the gingerbread house before Hansel and Gretel" (*LD,* 13), but the powerful sensuousness of that foreign black world overwhelms her curiosity, and she finds herself back at the colonial tennis courts where she becomes, as the more mature narrator Helen puts it, "quite one of them" (*LD,* 16).

This first section establishes the ingrained racist attitudes bred by families and communities into young white South Africans like Helen. It also establishes the critical distance between narrator-Helen, and young character–Helen, laying the foundation with which to measure the shifts in consciousness that the older Helen undergoes in the third section of the novel. Commentary on the young Helen's unconscious acceptance of an overt racism is made through the more politically mature eye of the narrator-Helen, who documents the bigotry of charac-ters like her father and a young neighbor, Raymond. The ragged black children who pester them to earn pennies by watching her father's car on the family's Saturday morning shopping outing draw comments from the father, comments that are typical of the racist attitudes of middle-class whites: "Something should be done about it . . . little loafers and thieves, they should chase them off the streets" (*LD,* 20). Given the stage of political awakening that Helen has reached by the time she turns narrator, however, we grasp her implied criticism of what was an accepted expression of the white community. She also obliquely critiques Raymond's report of the effects of the mine strike on the compound manager's lawn: "Man, there's a whole lota niggers round Ockerts', all over the garden and in the street and everywhere. Just a lot of munts from the Compound" (*LD,* 26).

While narrator-Helen intends a critique of attitudes like Raymond's and her father's, her own comments unwittingly reveal the limits of her political growth and, by extension, expose Gordimer's time-trapped consciousness. With no authorial irony evident, the narrator refers to the gardener, Paul, as "one old boy" (*LD*, 24) and uses expressions like "our native girl Anna" (*LD*, 18) and, even at the end of the novel, "native children" (*LD*, 376) as opposed to the more acceptable "African." Gordimer's authorial blind spot is more evident later in the novel, when Helen derides her parents' fear of an "Afrikaans or—heaven help them—a Jewish son-in-law" (*LD*, 248). But, as Clingman notes, there is no mention of the possibility of a black son-in-law, suggesting such a thought to be not only outside the mental parameters of Helen and the mine but outside the parameters of the novel itself. He points out, too, that the mine strike that Raymond describes bears no relation to the real strike that took place during the historical period covered by *The Lying Days*. Clingman describes the strike as "the largest single stoppage in South African history up to that time, involving 50,000 men, closing down nine mines and partially paralyzing twelve others" (29–30). Gordimer admits she would have known little of the real strike at that early stage of her political development.

The difficulty of breaking out of the mind-set of white society is portrayed in the second section of the novel when 17-year-old Helen escapes the claustrophobic mine life for the equally closeted south coast vacation home of her mother's friend Mrs. Koch and her son, Ludi. The novel turns inward, losing any connection with the outside world as it explores Helen's Lawrentian sexual awakening and self-absorbed infatuation with the older Ludi. Scornful of doing well or "getting on," Ludi longs to make permanent his reclusive life free of societal obligations and expectations, to live peacefully in nature with his mother while perhaps raising a few chickens, a path the novel disallows, for, ironically, he is trapped into military service and only temporarily on leave. Despite Helen's shifting values, she fails to see that Ludi's disdain for the mining community's lifestyle is undercut by his inability to keep himself out of the military, a system even more perniciously repressive and racist than the mine's; it is only after her return to Atherton and her enrollment in a university that Helen's values are challenged. First she is harassed by her parents because of her developing relationship with Joel, the son of a Jewish storekeeper. She must defend her friendship against the deep anti-Jewish prejudice of her mother, who reveals a double prejudice when she describes Joel as "someone brought up among the dirt and the kaffirs" (*LD*, 192). Next, shocked by the difficult study conditions in the black township endured by a black classmate, Mary Seswayo, Helen befriends and tries to help her. Helen's sincere attempt to break free of her ideological conditioning by befriending Mary, however, is complicated by guilt, and it results in overcompensation and awkwardness. Helen's naïve conviction that she can overcome the ills of apartheid by the simple act of moving Mary into her home in "the cooler"—a place symbolically "neither inside the house nor out" (*LD*, 186)—despite her mother's resistance, ends in embarrassment and failure. Mary points out to her, "If I am good enough, I'm good enough not to go where I'm not wanted" (*LD*, 202).

The final section, The City, is the most politically aware part of the novel, very conscious of its setting in the pre-and post-1948 period when the National Party's apartheid government came to power. It explores the rising untenability of the views of well-intentioned white liberals who become increasingly alienated and irrelevant as apartheid intensifies. This section also examines the difficulty of an intimate sexual relationship in a patriarchal culture, and it traces alliances that, across the political and gendered landscapes, further complicate and threaten meaningful change. Helen's effort to become more politically aware and responsible, to find her place in South African society, means breaking away from the racial and sexual stereotypes of her conventional life in Atherton and moving to Johannesburg. She lives for a time with her friends the Marcuses. While they facilitate her relationship with her handsome lover Paul, a young man from Natal, they effectively assume the parenting role, calling Helen a "good girl" (*LD*, 310).

Infatuated with her new group of young armchair intellectual friends who pride themselves on their progressive racial attitudes and bohemian Hillbrow lifestyle, Helen moves into a flat with Paul. An anthropologist, fluent in Sotho and Zulu, Paul works as a welfare officer for the Native Affairs Department. Using his government job to help the blacks on the one hand, and collaborating with the progressively radical black nationalists on the other, Paul teeters precariously between two worlds, establishing the bankruptcy of such a position as the novel progresses. What he is able to do is "pitifully little and pitifully inadequate" (*LD*, 265). Helen leaves the university; she works for a while as a typist, and then, finding herself increasingly alienated and shunted into irrelevancy by her inability to find a focus in her life outside of Paul, she simply stays at home doing nothing except watching life from the flat's balcony. Because they are unable to act meaningfully, their personal lives disintegrate. Helen comments on the slow, corrosive effect of the change after the National Party comes to power:

> The people I knew were "politically conscious" and as liberals or left-wing sympathizers they knew more thoroughly and perhaps felt more

deeply than the United Party conservatives the reactionary shade into which the country had passed simply by the fact of the Fascist Nationalists coming to power . . . it was only very slowly, as the months and then the years went by, that the moral climate of guilt and fear and oppression chilled through to the bone, almost as if the real climate of the elements had changed, the sun had turned away from South Africa, bringing about actual personality changes that affected even the most intimate conduct of their lives. (*LD*, 258)

The novel uses Helen and Paul's relationship, intense and fervent in the beginning, to demonstrate one of its major tenets: the unavoidable impact of broad political shifts on the most intimate aspects of our personal lives. In an exchange that exemplifies Gordimer's extraordinary literary ability to imbue behavior with nuance, Helen and Paul return one night from a township debate he had arranged. After bemoaning the timidity with which black speakers challenge whites now that bright radical youth like the activist Sipho are boycotting these events, Paul irritably cuts Helen's consolation short. She realizes: "It was somehow impossible for us to go on talking of Sipho because we sensed it would not really be talking of Sipho, but a dragging up and examination of what we had settled to live by: Paul in the job he did every day, I in the symbol I had made of him for myself" (*LD*, 271).

But political irrelevance is not the only thing that paralyzes Helen. Critic Judie Newman examines the crushing weight of the patriarchy on Helen's development through the displacement of female aspiration by controlling males. Newman compares Helen's tentativeness in the earlier sections of the novel with the confidence of the unnamed young white boy who moved through the African concession stores "with the ease of finding his way around his own house" (*LD*, 12), and the "ludicrously phallic" (*LD*, 18) figure of Ludi Koch, who had temporarily squelched any ambition Helen might have to attend university by mocking her: "Getting on, the bright ambitious daughter of the Mine Secretary" (*LD*, 85). In the last section of the novel, the pressure is more insidious. Even among a group ostensibly "enlightened," gender attitudes that devalue women still prevail. Paul patronizes Helen when she struggles with an essay on George Eliot—"What's addling your little brain?" (*LD*, 242)—but happily uses her labor to type his thesis. He complains when his meal is late, "Hell, Helen, you're becoming a rotten wife" (*LD*, 290), and aligns himself with the black male in denigrating the female when they laugh "like two men in a pub" about the ugliness of the black man's wife (*LD*, 243). When Helen tries to tell the horrify-

ing story of the township riot she has witnessed from the car, their friend
Laurie, who was with her at the time, appropriates the telling, while
Paul trivializes it as "Helen's adventure at the barricades" (LD, 334).

Paralyzed by the disintegration of her relationship and by the irrelevance of her place in the increasingly radicalized society, Helen
decides—like her Jewish friend Joel—to leave South Africa. Joel exudes
a fatherly wisdom that Helen admires, and his character has thus far
been endorsed as the moral authority in the novel. When Helen and
Joel meet in Durban before their boats depart, they frankly analyze why
their relationship remained unfulfilled. Joel explains to Helen that their
"difference in nationality" was a taboo, at least for their parents, against
anything but friendship: "emotional contact reaches back into the family. It's very old, very deep, very senseless; and harder than you think to
overcome . . . the unreasoning ties of blood" (LD, 368). Joel's commitment to ethnicity both personally and politically is disturbing in the
South African context (he is going to Israel), yet neither Helen nor the
novel itself appears to contest the power of ethnic prejudice to keep
them apart. Subscribing instead to what Clingman finds a disturbing
and naïve "ethic of acceptance," this deeply socially aware novel "does
not consider . . . that a thoroughgoing principle of 'acceptance' (embrac-
ing all contradictions and paradoxes) must ultimately fall subject to the
governing terms of an apartheid environment; for this in the end decrees
the social reality to be 'accepted' " (42–43). Moral ambivalence plagues
the end of this novel. Though Joel's moral authority is endorsed by this
ethic of acceptance, Helen's unexpected decision to return to claim
South Africa as home seems to undermine Joel's decision to emigrate.
Her return suggests, however, no way out of the paralysis she seeks to
escape. When she hears "some little native minstrels, singing as they
padded along in the rain" (LD, 376) and suddenly knows she is returning to South Africa, her epiphany seems triumphant. But, as Newman
points out, the "small sad voices" are singing "Paper Doll" (LD, 376), an
"appropriate image of the arrested quality of both female and black
development."[2]

Central to The Lying Days, then, is the charting—all the way to its
somewhat muddled end—of the progress of the essentially liberal consciousness of Helen, as well as of Gordimer herself. Through the personal voice of a young white woman in a racist and patriarchal society,
Gordimer's novel wrestles to escape the confines of the white South
African mentality and, through its awareness of its sociopolitical context, move toward an African identity. The integration of Gordimer's

form, vision, and narrative buckles, however, at the end of the novel, as characters and situations become plagued with ambiguity, with significance they are not ready to carry. The novel's power remains the evocatively drawn relationships between Helen and the other characters.

A World of Strangers

A World of Strangers, like The Lying Days, seeks through the principled engagement of its white characters in South Africa to justify their presence in Africa. In what way and to what extent they engage is determined by the historical space of the two novels, though as history intensifies in South Africa, we witness the acknowledged need for a more politicized and militant engagement. A World of Strangers is a novel more fully socialized than its predecessor, generated out of the political, social, and cultural circumstances of the 1950s that Gordimer experienced. Her experience becomes the transformational medium between the history of the era and the novel. A World of Strangers endorses a multiracialism and a social way of life espoused by the Congress Alliance of the 1950s, itself a movement grown out of the liberal traditions of nonviolence, parliamentary democracy, and interracial cooperation. The Congress Alliance subscribes to the purest liberal tenet of "the brotherhood of man."

A World of Strangers takes a different narrative structure than The Lying Days. Instead of a young, white South African woman narrating the interior journey of her growth, Gordimer uses an outsider, an Englishman—newly arrived in South Africa as literary agent for his family's publishing company—to relate his adventures in the split world of the black ghettos and the leisured, high-living, white suburban set. Traditionally the male narrator is considered more suitable for the type of adventures this outsider must encounter in South Africa, and the narrative strategy endorses the psychological detachment that seems typical of the narrator character. Divided into five parts, the novel traces Toby Hood's escape to Africa from his well-to-do family's preoccupation with "just causes." He is determined not to be trapped into being what he sees as "a *voyeur* of the world's ills and social perversions."[3] The novel's prologue sets him among a group of English travelers on an Italian liner to South Africa where—lolling in the ocean at his first port of call in Mombasa—he feels that "the last jagged crystal in my English blood melted away" (WS, 15). Toby insistently expresses his attitude to life in South Africa:

I want to live! I want to see people who interest me and amuse me, black, white, or any colour. I want to take care of my own relationships with men and women who come into my life, and let the abstractions of race and politics go hang. I want to live! And to hell with you all! (*WS,* 36)

Part 1 of the novel documents Toby's arrival in Johannesburg and establishes the amoral, aesthetic creed by which he judges any and all. European literary and artistic references and images abound in the book, and the indulgent lifestyle of the wealthy whites he encounters overlays the struggles and chaotic poverty of the black townships. The veneer of luxury, of cheap European imitation, masks a cruder, uglier existence. In his office building, for example, "the Gorgonzola stairway gave way, after the first floor, to narrow cement steps; the inner corridors, with their plumbing system running exposed along the greenish walls, were like the intestines of some cold-blooded animal" (*WS,* 40). In this first section, Toby meets the two worlds—strangers to each other—between which he moves throughout the novel.

Once in Johannesburg, he meets the world of the wealthy white socialites. He contacts gold-mining magnate Hamish Alexander and his wife, Marion, who live in the High House in the posh suburb of Illovo. He chooses them from his list of contacts because his mother had hesitated over their name: They lacked the politically left credentials of her other friends. Predictably, he is inducted into a superficial lifestyle where women have "short, bright fashionable hair . . . sunburned necks and brilliant finger-nails, the high actressy voices and oddly inarticulate vocabulary—vogue words, smart clichés, innuendo, and slang—of young upper-class Englishwomen" (*WS,* 50). At one of the Alexanders' many lunches, overflowing with wines and liqueurs and an endless stream of visitors, he meets the "very attractive; knowing, greedy, unsentimental" (*WS,* 76) Cecil Rowe—a name that barely disguises its parallel to empire builder Cecil Rhodes—with whom he develops a superficial and predatory relationship. Her face, "so pretty above the hollow collar-bones," occurs to him, significantly, as "the face of another species" (*WS,* 82).

Toby is content in this luxurious lifestyle that awakens in him "a great respect for the life lived in the exquisite orderliness of wealth" (*WS,* 58), but he unexpectedly encounters the underbelly of Johannesburg high society when he meets Anna Louw, an attorney from the Legal Aid Bureau committed to the cause of political justice for Africans in South Africa. She asks him to grant his African office worker leave to testify in a case. Anna introduces Toby to the other world: the interracial and politically liberal group with whom she socializes. It is at one of their parties that he meets Steven Sitole, a charming, feckless young man who does not "want to be bothered with black men's troubles." Drunk in a she-been late one night after a party, Steven and Toby discover a bond. They want the same thing: "a private life." Narrator Toby writes, "There it was, the truth. The drowned, battered out, howled down, disgraced truth . . . this young man and I, two strangers, had just cornered it in a small hour of the night like an animal almost believed to be exterminated entirely. . . . It was ours, a mouse of truth, alive" (WS, 102).

Toby's determined pursuit of self-indulgent pleasure is matched by Cecil Rowe on the one hand and Steven Sitole on the other: "both . . . were people who had not found commitment" (WS, 168). It is in part 2 of the novel that Toby realizes he cannot introduce Cecil to Steven or even discuss with her his friendship with Steven. She would not understand. Cecil and Steven's common aim of personal pleasure can never bridge the gulf of racist fear and prejudice Cecil harbors against black South Africa. Toby admits, "I knew that if I told Cecil that my closest friends in Johannesburg were black men, and that I ate with them and slept in their houses, I would lose her. That was the fact of the matter. And I was damned if I was going to lose her" (WS, 163–64). Toby cynically determines to keep his two worlds apart, since he is loath to give up the pleasure he derives from each. He claims: "I had come to feel curiously at home, a stranger among people who were strangers to each other" (WS, 168).

Parts 2 and 3 of the novel develop Gordimer's major concerns. The exploitative side of Toby's pleasure-seeking lifestyle is exposed when—plumbing deeper into the implications of an irresponsible life under apartheid—the complications and contradictions become apparent. Toby confesses, "I was gratuitously dipping into the pleasures of a life for which I had to take no responsibility, pleasures for which I would not have to settle, even with myself" (WS, 142). But his continued contact with Anna Louw and Steven's black jazz musician friend, Sam Mofokenzazi, whose inner eye is "fixed quietly and steadily on his and his people's destiny as decent bourgeois" (WS, 161), provides a standard of political commitment against which to measure the profligacy of his life with Cecil and Steven. Crucial incidents in this central section alert the reader to the bankrupt and untenable nature of Toby's way of life. His secretary's sullen, racist response to an office visit from Steven and his gambling friend, Lucky Chaputra, upsets Toby unexpectedly:

How was I, how was anyone to know it was like this? This evil embarrassment, a thing like a spell, like the moment in a dream when you wish urgently to speak and nothing comes out of your open mouth, that had suddenly sucked all the normality out of a room in which I sat between two men and a drab girl whose maximum assertion in life would not exceed the making of a crocheted tea-cosy. (*WS*, 148–49)

A second racist incident, when Toby's landlady viciously reacts to having "kaffirs" in her building while Steven and other African friends are visiting, leaves Toby in an ugly mood, unable to sleep well, waking himself "like an uneasy animal that is on guard, even in its sleep" (*WS*, 219). Not even the festive Christmas party at the High House brings the ease that Toby, as well as Cecil, seeks. When she and Toby return to her flat, Cecil's jangled and fearful response to the unnerving howling despair of a Zulu flat cleaner, high on marijuana, belies the strange freedom they seek to inhabit, "the freedom of the loose end" (*WS*, 168).

In contrast to the profligacy of Toby, Cecil, and Steven's shebeen friends is Anna Louw. Her marriage to a South African Indian and subsequent divorce, her trade union work for Africans, and her steady commitment to change in South Africa place her in a no-man's-land, "the black-and-white society between white and black" (*WS*, 175). Toby says of her, "Anna was a real frontiersman who had left the known world behind and set up her camp in the wilderness; the skirmishes of that new place were part of the condition of life, for her" (*WS*, 175). He notes that "the boundaries she had left, and probably could never re-enter . . . gave her the face of burned boats, blown bridges" (*WS*, 184). Before Toby—driven by fear rather than desire—makes love to Anna in her garden cottage late one rainy night, she warns him that he won't be able to sustain his detachment from the society: "You think you'll keep free, with one foot here and another there, and a look in somewhere else, but even you, even a stranger like you, Toby—you won't keep it up" (*WS*, 184). Anna's warning foreshadows Toby's shock of realization when Steven dies suddenly at the end of the novel.

Part 4 describes Toby's bird-hunting trip with the male group from the High House social set, a description that foreshadows Steven's death. Like overgrown Boy Scouts, the group of businessmen camp out for a few days to shoot guinea fowl, talking "the talk of good children occupied in a game . . . [they] rushed about like boys who have come back to an old hide-out" (*WS*, 227–28). But Gordimer's description belies the apparent innocence of their game. Patterson, a senior official in Hamish Alexander's mining group, emerges from a shoot in the bush with his trophies: a "cluster of dark bodies hung from the hooks on his belt, bumping against his hip as he walked . . . a feather, stuck in the band of the shark-skin cap" (*WS*, 236), while Hughie's perverse refrain echoes: "Let's go out and murder the bastards" (*WS*, 241). The mindless destructive power of the technologically advantaged white patriarchy reverberates with their gunshots and results in the boot of the car being "piled with the thick, soft bodies of birds" (*WS*, 246). With three African manservants in tow to minister to their every need, the white men are free to revel in their blindly racist assumption of superiority. They attend more humanely and affectionately to John's obedient old setter bitch, ironically named Grace, whose stomach tumor leaves her lifeless in the back of the car after her strenuous participation in the hunt.

The last section of the novel tells of Toby's return to town after the hunt, when he learns—shockingly—of Steven's senseless death in a car chase accident after an attempted getaway from police at a late-night shebeen. Stunned, unable to find Sam, Toby seeks out Cecil and, in some immediate way, reaffirms life through urgent sex. Neither able nor willing "to take her in and make life real for her" (*WS*, 254), Toby nevertheless shelters in the superficiality of his relationship with Cecil. But faced squarely now with the waste of Steven's life, Toby is forced to reevaluate his own lifestyle. He finds he can no longer visit the Alexanders, for he realizes that he has not been "consciously aware of the enormous strain of such a way of life, where one set of loyalties and interests made claims in direct conflict with another set, equally strong" (*WS*, 258). Shrewd enough to sense Toby's exploitation of her and his unwillingness to protect her from herself, Cecil decides to marry wealthy Guy Patterson. Now alone, Toby comments that "in her greed and fear of life, surely and fatefully, her hand had closed on [Guy]" (*WS*, 261). Though Toby finds it easy to give up the High House set in favor of the warm and comforting friendship of Sam and his wife, Ella, he nevertheless fears his genuine connection with them—deeper than ever since Steven's death. He fears it has engendered in him a commitment from which his life will never again be free. His indefinite extension of his stay in South Africa; his visit to Anna Louw, out on bail after being arrested on a treason charge for her work with an organization of African women; and Sam and Ella's choice of him as godfather of their expected baby seem to confirm his commitment to a more politicized existence.

The end of the novel, however, raises a question about the endurance of Toby's commitment. At the Johannesburg train station, Toby's insistent assurances of his imminent return from business in Cape Town before the christening of Sam's baby are muted by Sam's caution. Their warm good-byes are interrupted when they're pushed apart in Forster-ian fashion by the crowd on the platform, with Sam shouting, "Who knows with you people, Toby, man? Maybe you won't come back at all. Something will keep you away. Something will prevent you, and we won't—" (*WS*, 266). The rest is drowned out, but unlike *A Passage to India* where Aziz and Fielding cannot reconnect, this novel offers some hope: at the bottom of the steps where the train is waiting, Toby and Sam meet once more in a warm and bonded embrace: "and we held each other by the arms, too short of breath to speak, and laughing too much to catch our breath, while a young policeman with an innocent face, on which suspicion was like the serious frown wrinkling the brow of a puppy, watched us" (*WS*, 266). So despite Sam's ambivalence about Toby's long-term commitment, the novel—through its recognition of the complex difficulties of interracialism—nevertheless suggests a deeper, more cognizant resolution of commitment than *The Lying Days.*

The social world of *A World of Strangers* draws its inspiration from what Lewis Nkosi has called the "fabulous decade" of the 1950s (Cling-man, 49). Home to many of the writers and artists featured in *Drum* magazine, mouthpiece of the cultural renaissance in jazz, art, and fic-tion, Sophiatown became a vital symbol of interracialism. Social contact between whites and blacks in this township represented a form of rebel-lion that took on a heady resistance against a regime that legislated against such contact. Nkosi recalls that even one drink with a white per-son represented a blow against apartheid. Gordimer was part of the white liberal set that frequented parties in Sophiatown, and she describes being politicized by her African friends as well as by Bettie du Toit, a banned Afrikaans trade unionist on whom the character of Anna Louw is modeled. Some characters and events correspond to real people and events, and Toby Hood's name is drawn from Toby Street, the road that divided Sophiatown from the white area surrounding it. Toby Street represents the place inhabited by Toby Hood in the novel, the place between two worlds (Clingman, 71).

Military references and metaphors describe the embattled social land-scape, from the early mention of Toby's grandfather's role at Jagers-fontein in the Boer War to Anna's Boer grandfather, who may have killed the old man there. In his generation, Toby inhabits "the space of a few rooms between the black encampment and the white" (*WS*, 168), while Anna Louw is the "real frontiersman" (*WS*, 175). The novel's delineation of boundaries emphasizes a nation divided. It insists, in fact, on two nations—divided socially, economically, politically, and racially. Only a precarious strip of gray exists where contact can take place.

The contact area of black and white—this no-man's-land, this wilderness—is where Gordimer pursues her interrogation of the legitimacy of Europe in Africa, a concern established in *The Lying Days*. She chooses a symbolic space, complicating what appears at first to be a simple realistic mode. Her choice of a sexist, educated, upper-class English narrator from a Eurocentric and patriarchal world who blunders into a deeply complex and divided society grants her room to explore patterns of race, nationality, gender, and the imagination as they intersect in the collision of cultures. Michael Wade points out that Englishman Toby provides one pole against whom the white South Africans read their "civilized" selves, "the extremely suprahuman component, the imagined, the half-internalized, half-reified, ideology of the metropolis [England]," while the other measure of self-definition is achieved by contrast with other inhabitants: blacks, Coloureds,[4] Indians, and Afrikaans-speaking whites (Wade, 84). Toby's outsider status frees his relationship with Steven of the disabilities that would encumber a white South African's friendship with a black South African (Wade, 94).

Freed of a South African's disabilities Toby may be, but Gordimer takes care to ensure that the reader understands that his perceptions have been formed by his own cultural heritage. A literary man imbued with the aesthetic values of the 1950s, which placed art beyond politics, Toby reads his experience through the lens of European literary myths, his imagination shaped by the multitude of literary and artistic reference points in the text: Lawrence, Forster, Dickens, Modigliani, and Barrie, to name a few. Being male presents him with little problem in Africa it seems, though he experiences his whiteness as a certain loss, a nostalgia for a spontaneity long past. His mission is a personal one: to pursue that African warmth, and, like "Alice plunging after the White Rabbit" (*WS*, 129), he follows Steven into the township shebeens. Watching the Africans dancing at a party one evening, Toby reflects on the "strange innocence of their dancing," which makes him feel as if he were "maimed in that press of dancing people" (*WS*, 128). He feels an attraction for their capacity for joy, "as one might look upon someone performing a beautiful physical skill which one has lost, or perhaps never had. Lopped off, gone, generations ago; drained off with the pigment fading out of our skin." He understands, for the first time, "the fear, the sense of loss there can be under a white skin" (*WS*, 129). Wary of racial stereotyping in "colonial" fiction, some critics like Kathrin Wagner warn that Gordimer falls prey to certain stereotypical myths and anxieties of a white consciousness that—despite her anti-apartheid thrust—she implicitly valorizes. But Gordimer *is* cognizant of the danger. She defines cultural identity as "nothing more nor less than the mean between selfhood and otherwise" and admits that "the dilemma of a literature in a multiracial society, where the law effectively prevents any real identification of the writer with his society as a whole, so that ultimately he can identify only with his colour, distorts this meaning irreparably" (Wagner, 46). Gordimer acknowledges the stereotypes as an embedded facet of the white mind-set, asserting not Toby, but Anna Louw as the moral authority in the novel. Toby's superficiality is framed by the clear and serious consciousness of South African Anna, whose efforts to live a meaningful life beyond stereotypes have already entailed the difficulties of a multiracial marriage and divorce and will soon include detention and imprisonment.

Anna's remarkable shift in consciousness away from her narrow and bigoted Afrikaner family in rural Neksburg begins, ironically, as a "revolt of taste" (*WS,* 181). Her family's pursuit of sham metropolitan culture through radiograms and artificially tinted photographs that made girls blonder shame her into recognizing the value of the rural life her family lived, but despised: the enduring old pepper trees and the humanity of the fellow "carrying a goat tied on his back while he rode a bicycle" (*WS,* 181). Despite their gutsy (though bigoted) Voortrekker predecessors, fear and hate for everything and everyone now dominates her family's lives, and she comments that "there's very little dignity left in them" (*WS,* 182). As Toby notes, it is Anna who has made the trek this generation.

But the reader must question Toby's relationship with Anna and, indeed, his relationship with women in general. The inadequacy of the male who has, as Toby owns, "an Eastern equation of women with pleasure" (*WS,* 150), who "liked to see them, in a flash, now and again, as some charming creature in a tank or a cage" (*WS,* 82), is sharply critiqued by Gordimer. Anna's refusal to be objectified confuses Toby. He admits that he doesn't really want to see Anna, yet "once I was in her company, I was always glad of it, and couldn't understand my reluctance" (*WS,* 174). Talking with her late one night he feels suddenly afraid of her. "I put out my hand and touched, with the touch of fear, the thing I fled from. I had no desire for her but I kissed her. The rain had stopped as if to listen; the whole night was very still. She did not shut her eyes for an instant; every time I opened mine, she was looking at me, as if she were waiting for something to be over, to have done" (*WS*, 184). Incapable of a relationship of any responsibility or commitment with a woman, Toby flees back to the pretty face of Cecil, "the face of another species than myself" (*WS*, 82). Even after she tells him she's marrying Guy, he admits, "For me, the exoticism of women still lay in beauty and self-absorbed femininity, I would choose an houri rather than a companion." Then with a Lawrentian echo, he adds, "No doubt what I had seen in the nasty woodshed of childhood was a serious-minded intellectual woman" (*WS*, 261). At the end of the novel, Toby has two clippings in his pocket, one announcing Anna's arrest on a treason charge, the other a charity ball photo of Cecil and Guy Patterson. Curiously at peace with the polarity in his wallet, the image conjures a struggle he glimpses is still to come.

Significantly, it is Toby's progress that the novel places at its center, and Gordimer chooses the landscape, the natural world, as the site of learning and symbolic truth in the novel. Gordimer's complication of her novel's form by shifting from a realistic to a symbolic mode receives instructive attention from Clingman (63–66). He shows the objective or realist status of the outside narrator deliberately undermined by the humanistic tenet of liberalism that holds that detachment cannot remain if observation is good. All humans change if we observe accurately. While a stranger's view (that of the outsider Toby) is often unwittingly more revealing, Clingman argues that realism in this novel is extended to contest social reality rather than to merely reinforce or represent a prestructured way of seeing the world. Toby's description of the false naturalism of the mining landscape, where cyanide mine dumps masquerading as hills seem to emanate from the subconscious of those who create them, challenges the veneer of reality. But it is in the bird-hunting episode of part 4 when realism gives way fully to the symbolic mode, that the deepest truths emerge at the subconscious level. Only in the bush, stripped naked in the hunt, is the horror of brute power and inhumanity laid bare. Landscape, the site of symbolism, reveals the social offense as an offense against human nature, and against nature itself. Only through the police hunt that kills Steven at the end of the novel, can Toby, also a hunter, learn the deepest truth about his culpability for Steven's death. Once realized, he must now prove himself in the outside world, moving toward a rehabilitative social commitment through a redemptive relationship with Sam. Toby's lesson is that a private life is impossible without social integration, that to be disconnected is illusory and culpable.

Critics Wade and Clingman both find that the romanticism innate in the notion of the essential unity of man, society, and nature de-emphasizes a more political resolution of the novel. Wade holds that Gordimer's immersion in the aesthetic values of the 1950s, which depoliticized art; her depoliticization and emasculation of Steven (perhaps to render him harmless and therefore more acceptable to her reading audience); and her view of the struggle presented through the eyes of a white "double outsider" suggest a dissonance between her and the more militant historic trends in the country with which she was soon to ally herself (Wade, 97). Clingman, on the other hand, finds the novel more in line with the opposition methods of the Congress Alliance, for example, challenging the apartheid structure through passive civil disobedience for the extension of rights rather than seeking a complete change of the system; he, therefore, finds Gordimer less at odds with unfolding history than Wade suggests. Like Anna, says Clingman, the novel occupies a frontier; like the jazz that Sam loves and plays, it bridges two worlds. But by creating a "moral" class that transcends economic and social distinctions, the novel ignores the economic realities of the characters' worlds. Ultimately, it crosses no borders, and though the political structure may have been challenged or shaken by a stronger, deeper liberalism, the humanist framework remains the same (67–68). As Judie Newman points out, the novel is unable to suggest a political or formal remedy (26).

Though critics question the political shift of the novel in historical terms, none questions the power of Gordimer's acute sensitivity, which catches the nuance in the behavior of her characters, subtly lifting the edge of the seemingly unremarkable to expose glimpses into the emptiness and devastation that lie beneath the superficial clatter of South Africa's everyday life. Her unerring gift for penetrating the surface with a throwaway line or the wave of a hand reveals in that instant an unflinchingly clear recognition of a common truth. One such moment takes place at a multiracial party when a pretty young university girl chatting in a group with Steven asks for a cigarette. Steven, the only person with just one cigarette left, deliberately, and without comment, lights, then slowly smokes the cigarette she assumes with outstretched hand, like the rest of the crowd, he is about to offer her.

The silent rebuff resounds like a slap in the face. Gordimer captures the looming significance of such a minor detail, and reads it unsparingly for what it implies:

No one said, "Hey, what's the idea? What about the cigarette?" No one laughed. No one acknowledged, made of the incident a moment's absentmindedness on the part of a man who had a lot to drink. We exempted him, and so gave away what he and all black men must always suspect of the company of white men: he was not like us, after all; after all, he was black. (*WS*, 173)

It is this brutal honesty, this willingness to peel back the layers and hold the gaze that gives Gordimer much of her power. The craft of her extraordinary descriptive talent—exemplified in this passage on Sophiatown jazz—explains much of the compelling power of her work.

There was a little breeze of notes on the saxophone; it died down. A clarinet gave a brief howl. Somewhere behind the press of people, the big bass began to pant. Music grew in the room like a new form of life unfolding, like the atmosphere changing in a rising wind. Musical instruments appeared from underfoot; people who had been talking took to another tongue through the object they plucked or blew. Feet moved, heads swayed; there was no audience, no performers—everyone breathed music as they breathed air. Sam was clinched with the piano in some joyous struggle both knew. A yellow youth in a black beret charmed his saxophone like a snake, with its own weaving voice. The bass thumped along for dear life under the enchanted hand of a man with the bearded, black delicate face of an Assyrian king. A fat boy with a pock-marked face jumped with rubber knees into a little clearing; girls began to swing this way and that from their partners' hands, like springs coiling and uncoiling. (*WS*, 127–28)

It is the resonance of such descriptive power that prepares Gordimer for her place among the enduring writers of literature. As she engages more radically with the politics of South Africa, Gordimer crafts these talents into increasingly complex novel forms. She seeks those narrative strategies and structures better able to express the depths and contradictions of her ruptured African society.

Occasion for Loving

In *Occasion for Loving*, Gordimer moves further away from the Forsterian humanist concept of art that she began to question in *A World of Strangers*. She debunks particularly the Eurocentric psychological novel that emphasizes the primacy of personal relationships rather than facts of cultural and social difference (Newman 29). This third novel also acknowledges unequivocally the failure of liberalism as an ideology to resist the force of apartheid's racial politics. With the hardening stance of the apartheid government, the rise in repression and brutality, the determined resistance of the African people, and her travels in Africa, Gordimer has become much more aware of political currents in South Africa and the African continent, and her consciousness has become much more historical. *Occasion for Loving* is understandably far more politically engaged than the first two novels.

The inclusion of contemporary political history makes the novel evidence of the times. Clingman notes that the novel's interracial love affair between Ann Davis and Gideon Shibalo bears close resemblance to Lewis Nkosi's description of an affair *Drum* writer Can Themba experienced during the Sophiatown years (76); the novel also incorporates current discussion of the relative merits of the ANC and its anti-Marxist/white breakaway party, the Pan-African Congress (PAC). The novel also mentions the 1958 All African People's Conference in Accra, the 1959 Extension of University Education Act (limiting access to black students), and the 30,000-strong march on Cape Town city center led by Philip Kgosana. When the multiracialism of Sophiatown of the 1950s foundered as the dominant ideology of opposition to apartheid, white liberals had to face the failure of humanism; isolated, irrelevant, and alienated, they sank into apathy. On the other hand, the apartheid state was very active. It introduced the Native Laws Amendment and Group Areas Act (1957) designed to cut off multiracial contact; its police opened fire on PAC protesters in the infamous Sharpeville incident, which killed 67, most shot in the back as they fled the attack; it outlawed the ANC and the PAC whose military wings, Umkhonto we Sizwe and Poqo, as well as the predominantly white African Resistance Movement (ARM), began sabotage against the state; and it drove the *Drum* writers into exile.

Occasion for Loving acknowledges the utter defeat of humanism in the face of such political extremes, epitomized in a comment protagonist Jessie Stilwell makes to her husband about Gideon Shibalo. Because he is black, the government refuses Gideon a passport, which would allow him to accept a scholarship in Italy; later, in love with a white woman, he must leave South Africa if he wishes to maintain the relationship without breaking the law. Jessie remarks, "First he couldn't get out [of the country] on his scholarship because he's black, now he can't stay because she's white. What's the good of us to him? What's the good of our friendship or her love?"[5]

The novel opens with Jessie Stilwell, who, while watering her garden, is revisited by a sense that she has "never left her mother's house"(*OL*, 3). This sense is symptomatic of Jessie's inner struggle to unravel the meaning that her psychologically convoluted past has for her present, and it introduces one of the main themes of the novel: the questionable relevance of the pursuit of personal history. Her mother's oppressive love had catapulted Jessie into early marriage and child; widowed after a few years, she grieved, not for the young, dead husband but for the lost years of her youth. Blaming her mother for her losses and unable to relieve the awkward detachment she feels for her adolescent son, Morgan, Jessie seeks shelter in an intimate conviction that she practices in her marriage to Tom, that "to celebrate love, you must do no work, see no friends, ignore obligations" (*OL*, 5). She wants to "live in secret," a way to resist her relationship being fixed rigid by public scrutiny, becoming "like a dance that acts out some great ceremony whose meaning the dancers have long forgotten" (*OL*, 6). Jessie's private quest to unravel the implications of her stifling childhood is distracted—yet, ironically, also facilitated—by the arrival from England of her professor husband's friend, musicologist Boaz Davis, and his young wife, Ann, who are to stay with the Stilwells until Boaz finishes his field research. Jessie, the deeper and more dominant consciousness of the novel, watches as vivacious, good-looking Ann becomes embroiled in a complicated and ultimately disastrous affair with African artist Gideon Shibalo. The intensity of the illegal interracial relationship proves too shattering for Ann, who, unable to see it through, flees back to England with Boaz. By witnessing the insidious power of apartheid to infect the relationship of the interracial couple and the lives around them, Jessie ultimately understands that her personal quest for understanding is utterly inadequate in the face of overwhelming political intrusion.

The first of the novel's four parts is devoted to Jessie's scrutiny of her past. It tells of tears of rage when she realized that her mother's confining love had cheated her of a normal youth. It examines the oedipal overtones of young Jessie's feelings for her stepfather, Bruno Fuecht (who turns out to be her real father), and for the man she believes to be her real father, known only through the photograph beside her bed. It also sets up the political dimension of the novel—to establish the irrelevance of white liberals to the anti-apartheid struggle. Jessie's husband, Tom, who is writing a book on African history from what Jessie calls the "black perspective," has been at a meeting to protest the closing of the universities to nonwhite students. An African acquaintance comments to him as he turns to say goodnight: "Fight them over this business if you want to, man, but don't think that anything you do really matters. Some of you make laws, and some of you try to change them. And you don't ask us" (*OL,* 63).

Part two explores the developing relationship of Ann and Gideon as, in the flush of reckless passion and bravado, they hurtle toward inevitable disaster. Ann meets Gideon through Jessie's friend Len Mofolo and socializes with his black friends. For the blacks, Ann is a "white, top-class beauty, young; young and beautiful enough for the richest and most privileged white man" (*OL,* 92). And she, born and raised as a child in Rhodesia, enjoys showing "other men, simply by a companionable silence with Shibalo over a cup of coffee, that she could ignore them for a black man" (*OL,* 102). Soon a recognizable pair, Ann and Gideon lunch regularly at the multiracial Lucky Star restaurant, picnic carelessly by the side of the road, and even try to get Gideon into a whites-only nightclub. The novel notes that "there are certain human alliances that belong more to the world than to the two people who are amusing themselves by making them; this diversion taken up by Shibalo and Ann was one" (*OL,* 101). We learn of Gideon's history: the lost scholarship to Italy; an affair with Scottish rationalist Callie Stow, who warns him that the passport issue shows that "the only thing that means anything if you're African, is politics" (*OL,* 123); a self-serving relationship with black Ida, who "did the things—like taking his washing away for him—that a casual bed-companion does not do, but that a woman does for her man" (*OL,* 132); and an unwelcome reminder of an estranged wife and child. Gideon's troubling history with women makes his attraction to Ann questionable. His racial stereotyping, which contrasts Ann's ankles and build to those of black women (*OL,* 151), indicates the way apartheid has permeated and perverted his imagination. It is her whiteness, her difference, that captures him: "The *idea* of her possessed his imagination entirely" (*OL,* 177). Gideon, like Toby in *A World of Strangers,* is guilty of objectifying women, but he is also guilty of conflating class with color and physical type. Nevertheless, Gideon and Ann are intoxicated with each other, and Ann finally informs Boaz of the relationship. Unsure how to respond to the affair, he socializes tolerantly with Gideon at the Stilwells' home, because—as Tom puts it— "Boaz cannot kick a black man in the backside" (*OL,* 160). Jessie explains that Boaz is "so afraid of taking advantage of Gideon's skin that he ends up taking advantage of it anyway by refusing to treat him like any other man" (*OL,* 278). Just as no one challenged Steven's snub of the white girl who asked him for the cigarette in *A World of Strangers,* so Gideon's affair with another man's wife goes unchallenged.

Part 3 finds the couple in flight. Haggard from emotional strain, Ann and Gideon crisscross the country desperately in her little black car for a week in an attempt to hold on to each other. The narrator notes that "fear of the vacuum it leaves is as common a reason for prolonging a love affair as continuance of passion" (*OL,* 227). Masquerading as madam and boy in public, and dodging dangerous racial situations everywhere they go, they eventually turn up, exhausted, at Jessie's family's beach cottage, where Jessie and her two girls are staying for a holiday. At first resentful of being drawn away from her personal meditations, Jessie soon recognizes the affair is more serious than she and Tom first assumed. She learns what a harrowing experience the interracial couple has been through, and she admits to Tom in a letter that unlike before, when she tolerated them for Tom and Boaz's sake, she is no longer "putting up with them for anybody" (*OL,* 247). Surrounded by a hostile, racist white community at the beach, Jessie witnesses their relationship as it is reduced to a battle of social deception—exhausting, demeaning, and painful. Jessie recognizes that "what Boaz felt for Ann; what Gideon felt for Ann; what Ann felt about Boaz; what she felt for Gideon—all this that was real and rooted in life was void before the clumsy words that reduced the delicacy and towering complexity of living to a race theory" (*OL,* 219). In this context, stripped bare of the protection granted them by the liberal environment of their Johannesburg milieu, Ann is brought face to face with the enormous responsibility of an interracial relationship. It is in this context, too, that Jessie must acknowledge the bankruptcy of the pursuit of the personal in South Africa.

The last part of the novel chronicles Ann's failure of nerve to see the relationship through. After the journey back to Johannesburg, their plans to leave South Africa together for Tanganyika or Italy are jettisoned by Ann, who, when faced with choosing a life with Gideon, ultimately lacks the courage to be claimed by his people and history, by the "men and women and children outcast for three hundred years" (*OL,* 276). By virtue of her whiteness, Ann is always seen—despite her black friendships—in the context of the white city, "to which, after all, she belonged and to which she could return whenever she chose" (*OL,* 102). Without any warning, Ann slips away with Boaz, who announces their imminent departure at the last minute to Tom and Jessie. Stunned by Ann's turnaround, Jessie searches for Gideon, learning only that he has given up his job and is drinking heavily. Talking later with Tom about their role in the affair, Jessie uncovers the flaws, previously unrecognized, in their liberal, color-blind attitude toward race in South Africa: "We don't see black and white and so we all think we behave as decently to one colour face as another. But how can that ever be, so long as there's the possibility that you can escape back into your filthy damn whiteness? How do you know you'll always play fair?" (*OL,* 278). Gideon avoids the Stilwell household, but months later at a party, Jessie sees him very drunk and slumped on a sofa. Filled with "a deep, uncomplicated affection" for him, she tries to talk to him, but "his gaze recognized something, though perhaps it was not her. He mumbled, 'White bitch—get away' " (*OL,* 296). This encounter forces Jessie—who has worked all her life to rid herself of racist stereotypes and who sees blacks as people and friends—to acknowledge, as Wade puts it, that "the process of perception is not a white monopoly" (*OL,* 98). The reader, who has come to know and care about Gideon as much as Jessie has, also feels the profound rebuff of the unexpected perceptual shift. Jessie's personal quest ends, according to Newman, not in the psychic integration of an individual, but in shocked realization that she is merely a "type" to Gideon, a flat character, one white who can be substituted for another (Newman, 32). This powerful scene exemplifies Gordimer's destabilization and politicization of identity through perception and is an example of her evolving narrative power and politics. When Gideon and Jessie meet later, Gideon is quite friendly; he clearly has no recollection of the party. But as Gordimer writes, "so long as Gideon did not remember, Jessie could not forget" (*OL,* 297). In South Africa, until there are significant political changes, the "occasion for loving" cannot arise.

Critics have remarked on the interracial love affair as an obsessive theme of South African fiction, a theme that in some ways moves South African fiction away from the traditional European novel.[6] Clingman points out that Gordimer uses the theme differently from her South African predecessors, such as Plomer, Millin, and Paton. Instead of their framework of sin or abnormality, Gordimer normalizes the love affair: "The illusory beast of 'sex across the colour line' is tamed and demystified by being named with dispassion, and also with beauty" (Clingman, 81). By presenting interracial love as humanly normal, the novel makes the legal restrictions that damn such love appear all the more preposterous. The ability to create an interracial love affair in the oppressive context of South Africa—and make the passion unremarkably natural—

illustrates Gordimer's astonishing craft, most powerful in the description of Ann and Gideon asleep after making love at the beach cottage:

> [Jessie] opened the door into Ann's room to look for a vanished pair of scissors. She was barefoot, from the beach, and the house was silent; the two lying there did not wake up as she gazed at them. She felt neither the guilty recoil of one who sees suddenly, as a spectator, a part of life where one is never a spectator and only a protagonist, nor did she feel the shame of the voyeur. She looked with calm a moment at the ancient grouping of the two bodies, the faces flung away from each other, the arms lax where they had held; all that had been centred, rolled apart in sleep. Ann's one brown-tipped breast was pressed out of shape, like her cheek, by the angle at which she lay on her side, with the whole of the lower part of her body swung across as if she were lying face-down. And he lay on his belly with his head over the outstretched arm whose curved fingers, no longer within reach of her head, still conformed to the shape of it. his dark body had a shine going down the curve that followed the groove of the spine to the short, gleaming roundness of the buttocks. Their faces were sweaty. A fly rose and settled indifferently on either. Clothes dangled from the bed and lay sunk upon the floor; round the edges of the curtains, a frill of fire ran where the midday sun was held out. Jessie slowly closed the door and went away. (OL, 254)

In addition to breaking from tradition by being normalized, the love affair is shifted from the central focus of the story; instead, it is used tangentially, to facilitate and question Jessie's exploration of her private past. Jessie's past bears striking resemblance to Gordimer's childhood—both suffered a heart ailment and possessive, unhappily married mothers. Newman asserts that Gordimer transforms her own personal trauma to political metaphor in the novel in order to investigate the relation of love to power (26). Jessie, caught up in the tangle of her mother's controlling love for her as a child, admits that power is not something restricted to politics, but that it operates also within the tension of attraction and love. She calls it "a ghastly thing to resist taking hold of, anywhere." Afraid of it, she admits nevertheless she "is always fondling it, like a dirty habit" (OL, 146). Jessie's private meditation on love and family relations is forced—through the intrusion of Ann and Gideon's affair, which demonstrates that even between lovers blackness counts—to abandon more Freudian explanations and recognize instead the social and political forces that permeate and misshape South African consciousnesses. While external politics—the line in the statute book forbidding miscegenation—accounts in part for the failure of Ann and

Gideon's relationship, it is rather the silent internalization—the effects (as Clingman calls the process)—of apartheid's social sanctions that erode it. Once dismissive of the society's restrictions, Ann has now absorbed the poison of apartheid and is gripped by its fears and obsessions. The deeply ingrained patterns of irresponsibility and indifference sanctioned by the system provide white Ann with a way out when she cannot cope with the reality of loving a black man: "There was no recess of being, no emotion so private that white privilege did not single you out there; it was a silver spoon clamped between your jaws and you might choke on it for all the chance there was of dislodging it" (*OL,* 286).

Those same internalized patterns, however, only guarantee black Gideon the "position of a passive object, either as the beneficiary of white goodwill or as its victim" (Clingman, 82) and leave him devastated and broken at the end of his relationship with Ann. Through her closeness with Ann and Gideon, Jessie grows gradually aware of the deeply corrosive power of racism embedded within all South Africans. Now able to see the inescapable inscription of apartheid's sanctions in her own psyche, Jessie recognizes the source of her childhood fear of her stepfather, Fuecht, coming upon her in the bathroom not as the Freudian taboo of the European father, but as the racist taboo of "the black man that I must never be left alone with in the house . . . the man of the sex fantasies" (*OL,* 253). Newman confirms that "her [Jessie's] admission historicizes her trauma, now comprehensible not as the individualist product of bourgeois repressions within a nuclear family, but as stemming from political and social conditions" (31). So, however distorted her consciousness may be, the novel insists that Jessie has been constructed not by Europe and its psychological theories, but by an African past tainted by the politics of Europe.

Gordimer consciously raises her concern with the Africanization of the novel and the development of an indigenous artistic culture. *Occasion for Loving* highlights, and then subtly undermines, an assumption of a Christian European cultural uniformity. On the one hand, scenes like the family discussion about Christmas gifts when Boaz's Jewishness is overlooked and the picnic where Ann assumes Gideon will have the same romantic notion about landscape as she does suggest a misplaced sense of uniformity. On the other hand, Boaz's collection of traditional African instruments, debated as being mere fossils; the lively communal performance of mine-dancing, however commercialized; and the references to the history of Chaka, the Zulu king—all suggest an African

Heritage
+ Change

heritage upon which South African artists can draw and depend. The
novel deliberately promotes the view that culture is not static, that the
past is a source and connection that can direct and adapt to the present.
Culture is also politicized. Through the political machinations of the
apartheid state, Gideon loses his scholarship to Italy, notably the traditional center of European art. This event signals a rejection of the European conception of the transcendence of art over politics; by blocking
Gideon from acquiring and conforming to European aesthetic traditions, the novel insists that a more culturally and politically appropriate
form must be found.

imp
act

With the world of art of the 1960s circumscribed by politics, *Occasion
for Loving* moves toward politicized posthumanist forms, more suited to
the literature of Africa and more in line with writers like Ngugi Wa
'Thiongo, Chinua Achebe, and Wole Soyinka, all of whom assert quite
overtly the political dimension of their work. Gordimer had been traveling in Africa when the colonies were demanding independence, and she
was aware of how irrelevant white history had become, its significance
appropriately reduced to a mere subset of African history as a whole.
Wade points out that until the independence movements of the late
1950s and 1960s blacks had been seen as victims, but after that the
struggle was no longer defined by the intellectual tools of the liberal
establishment. Like Gideon's "white bitch" remark, a shift has been signaled, from accessibility to nonaccessibility (Wade, 98).

Polit.
Shift

trapped
+ danger

As in *A World of Strangers,* space and landscape are politicized in this
novel. No landscape is beyond the control of racial legislation. Reminiscent of Helen trapped in the car during the township riot in *The Lying
Days,* Ann and Gideon are trapped in the car on their trip; any venture
outside of that space—the fields where Ann meets a farmer who warns
her of "drunk boys," the beach where self-righteous beach-house owners
campaign against blacks on the beaches—results in dangerous encounters. After hearing complaints about blacks from the beach community,
Jessie looks out at the "wild, innocent landscape; the rain-calmed sea,
the slashed heads of the strelitzia above the bush almost translucent
with sap," but realizes "there was nothing innocent. . . . there was no
corner of the country that was without ugliness" (*OL,* 264). Gordimer
undercuts the power of white control and possession of land, however,
with a deeper, older kinship to the earth. Driving back to Johannesburg
from the beach with Ann, Gideon, and the children, Jessie sees kraals,
the huddled huts grouped at intervals all along the way, and marvels at
the continuity of African presence on the land: "In this hold that lay so

lightly, not with the weight of cement and tarmac and steel, but the
sinew of the earth's sinew, authority of a legendary past, she had no
share" (*OL*, 275).

Occasion for Loving also moves from the realistic mode to a symbolic
mode when the true horror of apartheid's pervasiveness is realized, signaling a deep shift in consciousness. Just as an undefined wilderness
space was used for the hunting episode in *A World of Strangers* to evoke
the perceptual shift Toby undergoes, so Gordimer uses the ocean to signal deep levels of consciousness that power Jessie's perceptual shift.
Even Ann, rarely able or willing to see beyond the surface of things,
feels emotions of which she is not entirely conscious. Anxious about
Gideon, who has wandered off too long on a walk, Ann mouths the half
wish, half fear: "he wouldn't just walk out into the sea . . . ?" Inadequate
before the complex and painful situation she and Gideon have created,
she reveals in this comment to Jessie "the unconscious desire to have the
course of this love affair decided by something drastic, arbitrary, out of
her power" (*OL*, 266). Critic David Ward has described Gordimer's con-
juring of this attraction of a death by water as the attraction between
Thanatos and Eros—as a desirably simple deflection from the struggle
of humanity (119).

Occasion for Loving's chronological narrative is deliberately destabilized
by shifts in the narrative perspective, as well as by individual perceptual
changes during the course of the novel. Ann and Gideon are presented
as all too human: they are shortsighted, indulgent, and self-absorbed.
Ann lacks reflection; she reads the Stilwells' life as merely "a set of circumstances—children, the queer elder kid from the other marriage,
ugly old house, not enough money . . . She did not think of it as something that had begun somewhere different and might be becoming
something different. The present was the only dimension of time she
knew; she awoke every day to *her* freedom of it" (*OL*, 91). But Ann's
perceptions are forced to change, and the reader witnesses, for example,
the contamination of Ann's view of Gideon, when she tells Jessie about
the role-playing she and Gideon were forced to perform in front of the
white man at the garage. She remarks to Jessie that "when the man in
the garage looked at Gid, and I stood next to him seeing Gid at the
same time, it wasn't the same person we saw" (*OL*, 277). Gideon, on the
other hand, is plagued by the ambiguities of living a split existence and
loses himself in the confusion generated by the relationship. His perception of Ann is faulty, for "like many people he confused spirit with brav-
ery, and he saw her old thoughtlessness and recklessness as courage"

(*OL,* 274). He admits with disbelief that since his involvement with Ann his sustaining political priorities have become cloudy and receding, yet he is too weak to act. Jessie, the dominant consciousness of the novel, provides the detachment by which to judge Ann's unreflective and irresponsible living, but Jessie's observer status, however much critical distance it may grant, is also flawed and shifting. Her antisocial exploration of her own personal history is shown to be empty when she realizes—through her involvement in the affair of Ann and Gideon—that her (and Tom's) belief in the "integrity of personal relations" (*OL,* 286) is, in fact, a failure: "The Stillwells' code of behaviour toward people was definitive, like their marriage; they could not change it. But they saw that it was a failure, in danger of humbug. Tom began to think there would be more sense in blowing up a power station; but it would be Jessie who would help someone do it, perhaps, in time" (*OL,* 287).

Ironically, instead of working toward a resolution, *Occasion for Loving* reaches a paralyzing impasse. All the characters are incapacitated in the face of the failure of liberal humanism; there seems no way into the future. It is only in the hint, almost melodramatic, that Jessie would perhaps assist in blowing up a power station, that we can anticipate the radicalization that will mark a profound shift in Gordimer's ideological philosophy; for Clingman, *Occasion for Loving* stands "as a distinct moment of transition for the South African liberal novel in general" (89).

Read sequentially, Gordimer's first three published novels trace her gradual recognition that liberal humanism could not resist the intransigent racist system of apartheid that so deeply scarred the psyches of all South Africans. Her hopes for the triumph of liberal values in *The Lying Days* faced disillusionment in *A World of Strangers* and culminated in her rejection of liberalism in *Occasion for Loving,* thus establishing the failure of liberalism as one of her most insistent themes. The novels chart the ineffectualness of liberal white South Africans who—their hopes dashed by the failure of integration—feel helpless and alienated from both black and white South Africans. Blacks, radicalized by incidents like the Sharpeville shootings in 1960, reorganized their resistance without white liberals; most whites, fearful and defensive, hunkered down behind the government's increasingly repressive laws and brutal actions, leaving liberal dissenters adrift.

The early novels also document Gordimer's determination to explore through art a legitimate place for white South Africans in their country of birth. We witness her efforts to assert through narrative structure, landscape, and culture a heritage fixed in modern South Africa.

Through the commitment of characters like Helen, who opts to return to South Africa; like Anna Louw, who dedicates her life to the struggle against discrimination and segregation; and like Jessie Stilwell, whose search for answers to a personal quest unveils the bankruptcy of liberal resistance, Gordimer establishes a foothold for committed whites in a future new nation of South Africans. This foothold is contingent upon her premise that racism and its empowerment by colonial history are utterly wrong. Recognizing that by virtue of colonial history and its legacy the private is inextricably linked to the political, Gordimer's novels begin to align themselves with the more politicized work of other African novelists of her time. She develops in her next novels—both politically and formally—a more rigorous and less naïve resistance to a systemic evil.

Chapter Three

The Novel and the Nation:
The Late Bourgeois World, A Guest of Honour, and *The Conservationist*

The Late Bourgeois World

After tracing in her first three novels the disillusionment with liberalism as a meaningful mode of resistance and change, Gordimer turned her attention to finding new ways to overcome the political impasse that faced dissenting white South Africans since the collapse of liberal hopes and the failure of revolutionary sabotage efforts. She took stock particularly of the shattered resistance of the revolutionary groups of the early 1960s. The protagonist of her next novel explores more deliberately and less naïvely the paralyzing irony that ends *Occasion for Loving* when Jessie Stilwell gains deeper political understanding but is unable to act. Gordimer sets *The Late Bourgeois World* (1966) in the mid-1960s— beyond the time of blowing up of power stations that Jessie had imagined—after such revolutionary sabotage attempts had already been tried and ruthlessly crushed by an ever-vigilant government. In this short novel, the ruminative interiority of the first-person narrative is increasingly appropriate to her subject of political and personal paralysis, for, as she claimed in 1983, "style and content must be married completely or the approach to a piece of writing does not work" (*CNG,* 225).

The Late Bourgeois World is more explicitly intertwined with the actual political events of its time than any of its predecessors. The increasing repression in the 1950s had triggered more intensive resistance, and violence erupted in both rural and urban areas across the nation. Afrikaner nationalist ideology slammed headlong into African liberation ideology, and the government responded with a state of emergency and massive arrests. It outlawed the ANC and the PAC, and targeted writers and journalists as well (the paperback edition of *A World of Strangers* was banned in 1962). Britain was moving toward granting independence to her African colonies, and Africa's independence movement had set 1963 as the date for their total liberation from the colonial powers; the South African struggle, by contrast, was driven underground. Banned movements adopted tactics of strategic violence in a new historical phase of resistance in South Africa, and three groups in particular—the ANC's Umkhonto we Sizwe ("Spear of the Nation"), the PAC's Poqo ("alone" or "pure"), and the largely white African Resistance Movement (ARM)—initiated campaigns of sabotage. But by the mid-1960s these groups had been thoroughly crushed: Nelson Mandela, head of Umkhonto, was captured and arrested in 1962, by 1964 several arrested leaders of PAC and ANC had been sentenced to life imprisonment and ARM was fractured and scattered by the police. Clingman notes the government's efficiency in smashing the fledgling revolution by pointing out that in the first six months of 1964 there were 203 cases of sabotage, while in 1965 there were none. Powers of detention without trial were raised from 12 days in 1962 to 180 days by 1965; detainees were dying in prison; and 531 banning orders had been served by 1966 (94). Clingman maintains that Gordimer's fourth novel "can properly be understood only in the context of this aftermath" (91). "The novel," he says, "exists in a stunned world, down on the ground after having been knocked off its feet. It is a post-war novel attempting to find ways to restart the war" (Clingman, 95).

Taking this world as her subject matter, Gordimer faced the challenge of finding a narrative strategy that could transmit the shock, ennui, and cynicism that had overwhelmed the small group of white dissenters who found themselves alone on the margins of both black and white society. She used the ironic juxtaposition of two relationships experienced by her narrator and protagonist, Liz Van Den Sandt—her past with ex-husband, Max, and her present with lawyer lover, Graham Mill—to examine the revolutionary crisis of the early 1960s and assess its implications for future action.

The novel opens one sunny Saturday morning at breakfast at home with Graham when Liz receives a telegram informing her that Max has committed suicide. Max, once a member of a revolutionary group very reminiscent of ARM, had recently failed in his sabotage effort to set off a bomb. Arrested, he turned state witness at his trial, and—shortly upon release—he drove his car over a cliff into the sea below. The occasion of his suicide becomes the center from which the novel explores the deepening ironies that liberal whites were facing in their need to find a way to resist apartheid's tightening grip. Though the story of *The Late Bour-*

Time of LBW only 24 hrs.

geois World is confined to a time period of less than 24 hours, the female narrator's consciousness carries us through her perceptions of the historical and personal past, to awaken—at the end of the novel—to possibilities of resistance in the current choked political climate. No formal chapter divisions disrupt the reflective mood of Liz's narrative flow, though spatial divisions signal chronological shifts.

Form

Liz fumes at Max's intrusion—even in death—in her life yet again, and, refusing Graham's offer to tell her son, Bobo, of his father's death because "Graham tries to move in on responsibility for the child as a means of creating some sort of surety for his relationship with [her],"[1] Liz drives out to Bobo's boarding school. Bobo has not seen Max for over a year, but divorced Liz has never judged the lack of a traditional family structure as a loss because "the code of decent family life, kindness to dogs and neighbors, handouts to grateful servants" had failed to provide anything except bewilderment for her generation. She sees such a code as inadequate to cope with the deficiencies of the South African system, and she wishes rather to ensure that Bobo gains "his kind of security elsewhere than in the white suburbs" (*LBW,* 12). She tells the happy, stable youngster that his father at least "went after the right things, even if it was perhaps in the wrong way," acknowledging that Max was not really equal to the tasks he took on. She explains that it is "as if you insisted on playing in the first team when you were only good enough—strong enough for third" (*LBW,* 18). Bobo responds that politics has brought them a lot of trouble, and later—exhibiting his developing sense of racial responsibility and social alienation—he tells his mother he is no longer friends with a schoolmate who makes thoughtless racist comments. He adds wistfully, "Sometimes I wish we were like other people. . . . They don't care" (*LBW,* 20).

white male inadequate

imp book

Gordimer devotes over three-quarters of the novel to the paucity of the larger white South African community's life and relationships, examining the political crisis in the light of their ineffectualness and culpability. On the way back from the school, Liz sees a woman at a shopping center who reminds her of Max's mother, Mrs. Van Den Sandt: charming and pleasant, "pink-and-white as good diet and cosmetics could make her" (*LBW,* 22). Gordimer uses this opportunity to establish a type of white South African family, an affluent but emotionally deprived amalgam of the Anglo and Afrikaner, that borders on caricature. From a wealthy and powerful family of old Cape Dutch origins and married to an English South African industrialist, Mrs. Van Den Sandt always entertained lavishly. Liz recalls being patronized at her parties by her showy and effusive greeting of "the children," though after "we'd shouldered our way in among the behinds in black cocktail dresses and the paunches in pinstripe, and had been introduced to a few people here and there . . . we were forgotten" (*LBW,* 23). Max's father paid for Max's defense when he was arrested for sabotage, but he never once came to court. His mother came several times, carefully made up and perfumed, ignoring all. When faced unexpectedly with Liz, her concern was for herself: "What have we done to deserve this!" (*LBW,* 24).

Max's personal investment in being a revolutionary savior, his egocentric idealism, must be read in the light of his background. Clingman sees Max as a symptom of the world that produced him; he "dies of the personality and historical situation he rejects but cannot transform" (97). Max's need to assert himself is so desperate he makes a fool of himself time and again: an embarrassing speech at his sister's wedding about the "moral sclerosis" of the white community, his self-inflating determination to formulate the methodology of African socialism (perhaps in the form of Platonic dialogues), and making love to "big arse Sunbun" (an unattractive American political groupie) because he needed admiration so much. Yet Liz's final judgment on Max—while unyielding—is compassionate: "In his attempts to love he lost even his self-respect, in betrayal. He risked everything for them and lost everything. He gave his life in every way there is; and going down to the bed of the sea is the last" (*LBW,* 55).

Graham, a different portrait of liberal white manhood, is utterly dependable and practical. He defends people on political charges and, like Liz, who analyzes stools and blood at the Medical Research Institute, he is scrupulously careful not to make any money out of cheap labor nor to "perform a service confined to people of a particular colour" (*LBW,* 37). Liz admits that Graham "lives white." He questions the point of the gesture of living any other way. "He will survive his own convictions, he will do what he sets out to do, he will keep whatever promises he makes," and when talking politics or history she feels the "magnetic pull of his mind to the truth" (*LBW,* 37). But, unlike her experience with Max, who was "wonderful in bed because there was destruction in him" (*LBW,* 49), and despite Graham's "majestic erection" (*LBW,* 37), Liz feels with Graham as though she is the one who has "drawn him up . . . the one who has him, helpless . . . holding him as if strangled: warm, thick, dead, inside" (*LBW,* 38). She describes the inadequacy of the relationship as "a power failure" between them, a failure that Clingman ascribes to Graham's neutral legalistic sense of truth that

ultimately upholds the status quo. Clingman holds that any idea of the
purity of truth is a deception, for truth is always historically involved
and requires a principle of partisanship. The novel seeks a new code of
action that must historically transform truth through responsibility,
advocacy, and commitment (Clingman, 103). So, despite his political
scruples, Graham's sense of neutral truth is delusional and his laws work
counter to meaningful change.

It is Liz's visit to her grandmother on her eighty-seventh birthday at
the home for the elderly that provides, ironically, the path (of which
Graham would disapprove) that could lead to a new code of action. It
also provides yet another perspective of white South African existence.
Liz, who has power of attorney over her grandmother's bank accounts,
provides the old lady with the last recognizable base in a life of self-
indulgent trivialities. Delusional and frightened, the old lady at once
inhabits the 1928 world of Noel Coward and recalls a jarringly lucid
contemporary visit from her grandson, Bobo. She is interested only in
the fashion colors of the season (black and white, the colors of death and
race), and her comfortable but unmemorable life (supported by dividends from her father's association with imperialists Rhodes and Beit) is
now just a jumble of disconnected flashbacks. Liz is unable to explain
that only death awaits her and that—despite her privileges—nothing
can make death more bearable for her.

Back at her flat, Liz prepares dinner for an expected visitor, Luke
Fokase. She has lied to Graham that she is going out to dinner and,
when caught in the midst of dinner preparations by Graham, both she
and he tactfully ignore her lie and instead discuss the news report of the
American space-walk that day. Introduced to Liz by an old PAC contact
of Max's, Luke has asked to see Liz and she—despite knowing this
means he wants something—invites him to dinner because "she missed
their black faces" (*LBW*, 70). Aware that "friendship for its own sake is
something only whites can afford" (*LBW*, 71), she settles down to await
Luke's arrival and certain request. Luke is the only black presence in the
novel besides the black delivery worker Liz smiles at on the back of the
truck when she is returning from Bobo's school. But the delivery
worker, joking with black women in the street, ignores Liz completely:
"When he caught my smile he looked right through me as though I
wasn't there at all" (*LBW*, 21). Both this incident and Luke's visit show
the disintegration of relationships between black and white now dis-
tanced from the idealistic friendships of the 1950s and underscore the
irrelevance of whites except for the most utilitarian of purposes.

At dinner Liz plays Luke's flirtatious game, enjoying his easy, smiling presence, all the while alert for the real reason for his visit to emerge. This interaction between them is stripped of the naïve delusions of a Jessie Stilwell; it is a much more knowing and cynical awareness of the realities that govern relationships between the races, and Luke finally asks Liz if she knows of a possible bank account that the PAC can use to launder money from overseas. Expecting only a request for a small loan of some sort, Liz is unexpectedly trapped, caught out, "like that game we used to play as children, when the one who was 'he' would drop a handkerchief behind your back and you would suddenly find yourself 'on' " (*LBW*, 85). The game continues with Luke barring Liz's escape despite her denials. As they talk and he wheedles, she remembers her grandmother's account with some dividends coming in from overseas, and the thought of using that account for Luke's purposes grows like "sexual tumescence" in her. Afraid that Luke can divine this possibility, she quickly agrees to look around and let him know if she learns of something. He leaves with the promising and intimate air of an imminent return with the possibility for lovemaking, while Liz is left behind like "pale Eurydice" to contemplate the events of the evening. Liz understands that

> a sympathetic white woman hasn't got anything to offer him—except the footing she keeps in the good old white Reserve of banks and privileges . . . and it's quite possible he'll make love to me . . . that's part of the bargain. It's honest, too, . . . it's all he's got to offer me . . . You can't do more than give what you have. (*LBW*, 94)

At the end of the novel Liz—stripped of the delusionary relationships of Max, Graham, and her grandmother—awakens during the night to an acute lucidity. The irony of using her grandmother's account for political purposes—that is, of using the capitalistic system to undermine itself—heightens and revitalizes her sensuality, and the beats of her heart repeat like a clock; "afraid, alive, afraid, alive" (*LBW*, 95).

It is through Liz that the historical consciousness of the novel unfolds, and Clingman lauds this work for its ingenious "working out of a principle of transformation . . . that shows how the terms of the 'late bourgeois world' can be entirely reconstituted through altered historical usage" (104): private property is seized for social purposes and personal love becomes politicized in the exchange of sex and the bank account. He finds that the novel's historical consciousness has three primary fea-

tures. First is the stunned mood of the time after the revolutionary
groups were crushed. Their consequent alienation—laced with desperation—prompts the second feature, a radical utilitarianism (channeling
money to the PAC) that abandons ideological differences as a luxury
when up against the indiscriminate brutality of the government. The
third feature—contested by other critics—is a "massive romanticism"
that Clingman reads in the metaphor of the godlike astronauts who, like
Liz, are transcending boundaries of the past. This romanticism, which
connects the transcendence of Liz and the astronauts, is troubling to
Clingman, who notes that Liz sees the impulse to go beyond barriers as
emanating from the old mythic, archetypal, or religious sources of the
search for immortality: Liz muses that "what's going on overhead is perhaps the spiritual expression of our age" (*LBW,* 92). Clingman contends
that the novel creates an equation in which "everything that applies to
the astronauts in this doctrine of transcendence by implication applies to
[Liz]" and holds that "both in form and content the novel's historical
realism is counterposed by a sudden and vast mythology. Gordimer is
seeking security on strange and extraordinary heights" (Clingman, 109).
Reading this romanticism as an extreme response that matches the
extremes of the time, the novel—Clingman says—ultimately fails to
supersede its period, a failure he traces to the desperation to act in an
overwhelming moment of crisis (110).

Newman on LBW

   Newman's reading of *The Late Bourgeois World* finds Liz guilty of no
such romanticism at the end of the novel. Newman, who explores the
intertextuality of the novel with Marxist Ernst Fisher's *The Necessity of
Art,* finds that Liz's initial attraction for the yearning for immortality
represented by the astronauts is brought up short by Luke's suggestion
of channeling money to the PAC. Liz nods off thinking of the astronauts
but is jolted awake to clear thoughts of Luke's plan: "I must have
dropped off for a moment; I return with the swoop of a swing towards
the ground from the limit of its half-arc" (*LBW,* 93). Newman argues
that "this Eurydice will follow her Orpheus into the future without
looking back," that the fetal position aligning Liz with the astronauts
should be read as "the possibility of rebirth into a world of historical
rather than metaphysical meaning," and that the thought of the bank
account growing like sexual tumescence "indicates the reawakening of
Liz's deadened emotions" (39).

   Critic David Ward, however, does not see this Eurydice as necessarily
able to escape her "life-insured shades" (*LBW,* 89), but sees her rather as
self-consciously trapped in her late bourgeois world. He invokes

through the consciousness of Liz the consciousness of the artist as well who, he believes, is raising a question about the validity of the artistic gesture in the climate of such extreme paralysis (Ward, 121). Michael Wade concurs with Ward that Liz's isolation mirrors Gordimer's own position in the artistic world of the time. By tracing Liz's view of Luke, Wade demonstrates that Liz has undergone a whole perceptual shift that strips away the comforting illusion of the white community's stereotyping of blacks, leaving Liz (and Gordimer) alone on the very edge of their white group, yet unable to make a perceptual connection with the other. Over dinner, Liz repeatedly notes the difficulty of connecting with Luke: "He looked straight at me for a moment with calm, oval eyes from which all communication seemed to slide wide away" (LBW, 84). Wade claims that it is at this point that "a revolution in consciousness takes place. Elizabeth becomes 'pale Eurydice'; she gains a level of self-perception that shows her own inadequacy, not only as an individual but as a possessor of a particular version of the mythology of her group" (Wade, 100).

However one chooses to read the subtle shifts of the developing consciousness in the novel, the most compelling section is this visit from Luke at the end. Here Gordimer's facility with nuance in behavior is most evident. Here readers also see her evolving and integrating that skill into the developing ironic consciousnesses of her characters and the concerns of the novel. When Luke walks into Liz's home for dinner, he teases her about a gray hair. She counters playfully that it is a new fashion at the hairdresser, thinking all the while "it was a game; he gave me a little appraising lift, with the heel of his hand, on the outer sides of my breasts, as one says, 'There!' " (LBW, 75–76). In previous novels, the interaction between black and white has been governed by a naïve or delusional quality that could only lead to a growth in consciousness in her white characters through the shock of some unexpected and unforeseeable encounter (Gideon rebuffing the white girl who wanted the cigarette or Jessie's "white bitch" experience). Here, the entire interaction between Luke and Liz is premised on their recognition of the dance, the deadly serious game they are playing. Despite being shocked by Luke's request for a bank account the PAC can use, Liz reads the nuance of his behavior dispassionately and accurately:

> He laughed with me, at last, but beneath it, I saw his purpose remain;
> the laughter was an aside. . . . We kept up the talk on a purely practical
> level, and it was a game that both of us understood—like the holding

and the flirting. The flirting is even part of this other game; there was a
sexual undertone to his wheedling, cajoling, challenging confrontation of
me, that's alright, that's honest enough. (*LBW*, 86)

In *The Late Bourgeois World*, Gordimer raises the question of authenticity. The nuanced behavior of the characters is much more conscious,
more deliberate. Liz and Luke both know this is a game with a purpose
beyond their own individual lives. It is a novel in which behavior cannot
be innocent anymore, where nuance is noted and readily interpreted by
the other, and an ironic consciousness abounds. It is consciousness
matured, no longer masked by blinding and wishful ideals, a political
consciousness with a transparency that cuts through the cushioning context of dinners and games. Graham's and Max's codes are shown as *made quite white male*
inauthentic; their consciousnesses lack ironic self-reflection. They are too
steeped in past paradigms of control and ego, and they ooze their bourgeois origins. Liz, although trapped in her white world, is saved by her *white is black or*
sense of irony. She learns through Max's death and Graham's liberalism
of the need to follow Luke's lead; she learns that relinquishment and
submission are the road to authenticity. She retains a wry awareness that
disallows any self-inflation or sense of self-importance while remaining
aware that Luke offers her, both politically and sexually, an extremely
dangerous way to exercise her power and commitment.

Newman believes that the Orpheus myth, which shows Luke leading
the way out of a deadened impasse, suggests the need for both political
and aesthetic leadership by black Africa (36). The relationship of African
politics and art, central to Gordimer's concern about the Africanization
of the novel, is raised by Marxist thinking, which inspired not only
visions of African socialism but asserted a role for art as well. In *The Late
Bourgeois World* Max has read and admires Nyerere, and we find Liz and
Gordimer groping toward a new definition of art. To be anything except
an opiate (as the Chagall floating lovers hanging in Graham's bedroom
appears to be), should art not be connected to social transformation?
Newman notes that Gordimer approved of Ernst Fisher's arguments
that art represents the freedom of the spirit and is therefore automatically on the side of the oppressed. Fisher, from whose work the title of
the novel is drawn, holds that art has and always should have a social
utilitarian function; socialist art should envision reuniting the individual
with communal existence. Art must have a vision for the future and
show the world as changeable, ultimately recognizing the historical condition as transformative. This is where late bourgeois art fails for Fisher;

he believes that "mystification and myth-making in the late bourgeois world offer a way of evading social decisions" (Newman, 36). Liz and Graham discuss the morality of art through their perceptions of the relative beauty of sunsets, wondering whether, if their beauty is produced by nuclear fallout, they nonetheless remain beautiful. Graham claims no moral basis for art, but Liz contradicts the Keatsian claim insisting that "truth is *not* beauty" (*LBW*, 65).

But even the grave considerations of the role of art are treated with a certain irony in the novel. After Luke leaves, Liz rather dramatically buries her face in the bouquet Graham had sent her that morning; yet, intelligent and aware, she deflates the drama of the act through her ironic reference of the Greek myth—"my Orpheus in his too-fashionable jacket . . . pale Eurydice and her musty secrets"—and recognizes as "half-theatrical" her gesture of putting her face in among the ether-cool snow-drops (*LBW*, 89). Evoking the paralysis of T. S. Eliot's etherized sunset, the self-mockery of both protagonist and artist questions the relevance of art. Ironically, however, in a shift from the realist to the symbolic mode it is Max's death by water that echoes through the novel, drawing Liz out of her cynical lethargy and proving the source of her political (and artistic) resurrection. Dozing on the divan covered by Bobo's rug in the afternoon, Liz envisions Max's drowning:

> Down, down, to where the weeds must, at last, have their beginning . . .
> He had succeeded in dying. . . . The flowers had stirred and opened while
> I slept and the warm room was full of scent. I lay quite still and felt
> myself alive, there in the room as their scent was.
>   Max's death is a postscript. A postscript can be something trivial,
> scarcely pertinent, or it can be important and finally relevant. (*LBW*, 39)

If Liz acts on the PAC's behalf and grants access to her grandmother's account, Max's death must be judged as finally relevant, given its role in bringing to life the possibility of meaningful action that so persistently evaded Max: *"There are possibilities for me, but under what stone do they lie?"* (*LBW*, 45). The path for Liz and for the artist seems clear, and it appears they will have the courage to follow it.

Liz's connection with Luke, political and sexual, signals the symbolic shift from the colonial pattern of white men's alliance and possession of white women (threatened but retained by Boaz with Ann in *Occasion for Loving*) to the more subversive pattern of white women's alliance with the black male. This novel is crucial in establishing this power shift from the white male to the black male. In *Occasion for Loving,* Gideon—for all *[handwritten: Book]* *[handwritten: SHIFT White ♂ to black ♂]*

the assumptions of friendship and equality—remains a victim of the
exploiting white world. Luke, on the other hand, is in control of his
world: "Luke knows what he wants, and he knows who it is he must get
it from" (*LBW*, 94). He is a figure alive with the power of the future,
whose potency we will see developed in the African leadership portrayed
in Gordimer's next novel, which displays her familiarity with African
thinkers and theorists, and African politics. *[handwritten: Black = future]*

Notably, Liz, the female narrator of *The Late Bourgeois World,* follows
in a line of strong, intelligent, insightful women: Helen Shaw in *The
Lying Days,* Anna Louw in *A World of Strangers,* and Jessie Stilwell in
Occasion for Loving. Liz has the intelligence and power without Max's
debilitating ego or Graham's blinders of faith in the neutrality of law.
Clingman remarks that in this novel "a matter of sexual politics with
special reference to South Africa seems to be emerging. In a white-male-
dominated culture, which has abrogated to itself a fiction of romantic
bravado . . . it has very frequently been women (both black and white)
who have been amongst the most courageous opponents of apartheid"
(105). *[handwritten: more often oppose apartheid Take risks; Anna Jessie Liz]*

A Guest of Honour

A Guest of Honour, Gordimer's longest and possibly most complex novel,
won her the prestigious James Tait Black Memorial Prize. One of her
most integrated and balanced novels, her descriptive power and nuance
of behavior carry without strain multiple levels of meaning: personal,
ironic, symbolic, psychological, theoretical, and ideological. It is one of
her most beautifully crafted novels, and she succeeds in her self-
appointed task to "write a political novel treating the political theme as
personally as a love story. . . . to put flesh on what has come to be
known as the dry bones of political life" (*CNG,* 57). South African critic
Stephen Gray called the novel "a very powerful *tour de force* . . . a landmark in our [South Africa's] fictional affairs." He claims that "Gordimer
comes out with a new kind of muscle and authority," that "the story is
an archetype of so much recent African history that it is not only rivet-
ing as a documentary in its own right, but hugely informative and relevant" (*CNG,* 67–68).

A Guest of Honour tells the story of an unspecified, newly independent
African nation's troubled genesis as seen through the eyes of a former
colonial official, Evelyn James Bray, who was expelled by the colonial
government for his sympathies toward African independence. Divided

into six parts, which unfold chronologically, the novel opens with Bray taking leave of his wife, Olivia, at their country home in Wiltshire, England. He returns to Africa as a guest of honor for the independence celebrations of the country he helped to free. Instead of returning home he succumbs under pressure from his long-time political confidante and friend, the new President Adamson Mweta, to the temptation of accepting the newly created post of special education advisor in the northern district of Gala, where he and his wife had been stationed previously. In Africa, Bray is reacquainted with the white community he left 10 years before: those who welcome independence from British colonial rule like Roly Dando (now attorney general), the Wentzes (proprietors of the Silver Rhino hotel and pub), and the Bayleys (Neil is principal of the university), as well as those cruder, racist whites who opposed decolonization and had engineered Bray's expulsion 10 years earlier. He meets Mr. Joosab of the Indian community again, a man who shields himself and his community from danger "by bowing in all directions at once";[2] and he settles in to work on his education project with Mr. Aleke, the new provincial officer, and Mr. Sampson Malemba, the education officer. In Gala Bray begins an unanticipated but passionate and intense affair with Rebecca Edwards, mother of four and secretary to Aleke (her adventurer husband, Gordon, is in the Congo somewhere). The thread of this affair weaves the personal dimension inextricably through the unfolding political narrative. Bray's daily encounters, his visits with friends, and his relationship with Rebecca unravel in a seamlessly natural way the complexities, contradictions, and absurdities that interlace the political and private worlds. That the everyday behavior of her characters carries quite invisibly some of the weightiest political issues and concepts of the contemporary world is one of Gordimer's major achievements in the novel, and it grants the novel the narrative muscle to which Gray alludes.

Bray soon learns that his old friends and political partners, Edward Shinza and Mweta, with whom he had worked so closely to bring about independence, are now ideologically split. Shinza, whose power lies with the workers and the unions, accuses Mweta of abandoning the workers to pursue a neocolonialist path with foreign investors and big business, while Mweta accuses Shinza of being an inflexible troublemaker intent on disrupting the new regime and whose plotting must be checked. Disturbed by the split but hesitant about his right to interfere, Bray tries to focus exclusively on his education report. But after discovering the illegal detention and torture of a dissident youth, after various discussions with Mweta and Shinza, and after the People's Independence Party Congress where a power struggle between Shinza and Mweta ends in Shinza's defeat, Bray feels bound by principle to support Shinza's socialist vision, the original vision he believes they all shared but from which Mweta has now strayed. Faced with the sweeping powers of Mweta's new Preventive Detention Bill and mounting violent unrest, Bray agrees to assist Shinza's forces by secretly going abroad to raise support for Shinza's cause. Rebecca, whose children are now in South African schools, accompanies Bray on his journey (he is also transferring her money to safety in a Swiss bank), but they are ambushed en route to the capital—ironically—by Shinza's forces, who mistake Bray for one of the white mercenaries who have been assisting Mweta. Bray is brutally beaten to death while Rebecca cowers in a roadside ditch. At this point, 32 pages from the end of the long novel, the third-person narrative switches to Rebecca's viewpoint. Bereft, she escapes to Mozambique with a corrupt African business associate of her husband's and from there flies to Switzerland. After collecting the money that Bray had secretly transferred before his death, she moves to England where— unable ever to live with Gordon again after knowing Bray—she plans to send for her children. Mweta meanwhile brings British troops into the country to restore order, and, with Shinza in exile and others in detention, he ironically co-opts Bray's memory as faithful friend and conciliator and "publishes a blueprint for the country's new education scheme, the Bray report" (*GH*, 525).

Published at a time when South African independence seemed further away than ever, *A Guest of Honour* appears to turn away from South African events to explore more general African concerns, yet the novel nevertheless probes a number of the questions raised in Gordimer's previous novel, *The Late Bourgeois World*. The issue of black African solidarity and leadership—suggested previously through the figure of Luke Fokase—is examined here through the escalating clash of Mweta and his political partner and mentor Edward Shinza. The paradoxes and pitfalls of African leadership are revealed through an interrogation of the growing practice of neocolonialism in newly independent countries. The novel also pursues—through the figure of Bray—the possibility of political commitment for a white man in Africa without the ego investment of a Max Van Den Sandt. It also confirms Gordimer's Marxist leanings, broached in the previous novel through the engagement with Ernst Fisher's ideas.

Gordimer's interest in the African continent—political, social, and environmental—was stimulated in the early 1950s when she began vis-

NG's travels

iting Rhodesia, Zambia, and Botswana (*CNG,* 70). She visited Egypt in 1954 and 1958, and she traveled up the Congo River across the Ruwenzori Mountains and into East Africa just before the Belgian Congo gained independence. In 1969 she visited Madagascar, and in 1970—the year *A Guest of Honour* was published—she went to the Botswana desert (*EG,* 147). Her writing about these trips shows that her sensual receptiveness to the landscape remains informed by keen political and social concerns, and the influence of these travels finds its way into her novel and asserts the reality of the unnamed country she describes. In 1973 Gordimer said that in *A Guest of Honour* she returns to her feeling that the context one lives in is *Africa,* and though there are differences, there are also tremendous similarities in the countries that comprise it: "It's the superstructures that are different, but the underpinnings, the earth is the same" (*CNG,* 60).

Clingman notes that Gordimer uses these similarities to construct a fictional African country at the level of the typical, its social particulars symptomatic of widespread patterns (113). Gordimer calls it a "nonexistent, composite, central African country. Imagine a place somewhere between Kenya, Tanzania, Zambia, Rhodesia, and Angola—you know, just make a hole in the middle of Africa and push it in" (*CNG,* 53). This construction of an abstract model where social and individual forces could be explored results not only from her broader interest in African events but also from South Africa's historical situation at this time, when all past oppositional paths seemed totally shut down. By the late 1960s, South Africa's underground organizations were crippled and, while exiled organizations were trying to patch themselves together, state control had never been stronger. White Rhodesia was celebrating its Unilateral Declaration of Independence from Britain, and Angola and Mozambique were still securely in the hands of the Portuguese colonial government. With all expectations of a power change indefinitely postponed, this novel provided Gordimer time to reappraise the situation with "clarity and disillusion," her method being "meditational and theoretical" (Clingman, 115). Her unnamed representative country has an all-inclusiveness that predicts neocolonialism to be a most persistent and problematic condition, a condition seemingly not applicable to South Africa because independent nationhood seemed more remote than ever. But Clingman argues otherwise, claiming a definite South African resonance in the novel. He notes that South Africa took up the neocolonial attitude of détente during the late 1960s, when Prime Minister Balthazar John Vorster offered to send troops anywhere in Africa on request, set up a special relationship with Malawi, and sent South African police to Rhodesia. Also, apartheid was undergoing a cynical ideological renewal. Influx control laws facilitated forced removals and resettlements of communities under the guise of "homeland independence" and "multinationalism," a facade of political autonomy designed to hide the continued exploitation of the African. *A Guest of Honour* gave Gordimer the opportunity to explore the concept of "nation" and nationalism in Africa, integrating in a much more sophisticated way the issue of the white South African's place in Africa.

Historically speaking, in Africa and elsewhere the nineteenth-century European concept of nation has been used very significantly as a site of resistance against imperialism, its abstract construction of a community of common goals and identity proving an irresistible force against the very Europe of its genesis. But the role of nation building in postcolonial countries needs closer scrutiny. Gordimer explores Benedict Anderson's view that nations are abstract constructs with "imagined communities" that depend for their existence on an apparatus of cultural fictions, in which imaginative literature plays a decisive role.[3] Obviously aware of the coterminous rise of European nationalism and the novel of the nineteenth century, Gordimer cautiously probes the role that fiction can play in creating a nation. The story of a nation and the narrative form of the modern novel inform each other in complex and reflexive ways, and their relationship has implications for the place and role of Gordimer's work in South African culture. The "nation" is what Foucault has called a "discursive formation," a gestative political structure the third world artist is consciously building or suffering the lack of (Brennan, 170). Unlike black South African writers, who have the weight of African national culture endorsing their endeavors, Gordimer has rejected racist white South African culture, and, alienated, a minority within a minority, she must envision a South African culture with a place for herself and the few whites like her if she is to belong to the country of her birth. Gordimer recognizes the challenges facing new nations in Africa, and— noting the racial bond among blacks that the legacy of colonialism has ensured—she has stated that "for a long time to come any white South African must expect to find any black man, from any African territory, considered by the black South African as more of a brother than the white South African himself . . . it is a nationalism of the heart that has been brought about by suffering" (*EG* 33). The national borders of African countries, which were drawn arbitrarily by Europe's leaders, and, later, South Africa's "homeland" borders drawn by the apartheid regime (Kwa Zulu, for example), have created complexities and problems that demand African solutions. But African nationalism, like its Euro-American counterpart, maintains its own form of patriarchy. It is at odds with the gendered aspect of reality and, along with class and race, it continues to destabilize the unity of the nation. Nation building is clearly a precarious business to be approached with the utmost caution and care.

Gordimer's considerations of the theoretical notions of nationhood are subtly embedded in the novel and are made manifest through their impact on the lives of the characters. The exquisite social observation that distinguishes Gordimer's work here reaches new heights for, while the usual white characters—the Mrs. Pilcheys, and the Gordon Edwardses—are all exquisitely rendered, they are now seen in the light of the Dandos, the Shinzas, the Mwetas, and the Bayleys, whose characterizations include a sophisticated understanding of and interest in the issues of decolonization and government. The novel's consciousness displays Gordimer's engagement with Marxist debate, as well as her more recent familiarity with radical thinkers on issues of nationalism like Fanon, Nkrumah, Cabral, among others. The policy of neocolonialism also comes under close scrutiny. Alliances with foreign interests are scrutinized in the novel through the examples of the fishing and the mining industry. While the Belgian-British fishing company has transferred 20 percent of its stock to the new government, the workers have seen no improvement in their wages or prospects; though the foreign-owned mines now employ more African workers in higher positions, these workers' efforts still only ensure greater profits for overseas shareholders who siphon off the country's wealth. Gordimer also highlights the fracturing effect of class stratification. It pits the most destitute (the nonunionized fishdryers who scratch out a diseased existence in hovels at the fishing plant) against regular union workers, who, in turn, are pitted against the labor elite. These elite control the unions by neocolonial policies that align state and foreign capital against the workers. Such a system promotes a local elite—often with government links—that exists at the expense of the poor (Clingman, 120).

Clingman holds that Gordimer's nationalist conception of neocolonial relations expands in this novel to a domain of class analysis, thus taking a clear socialist standpoint. The novel damns the priority of personal relations by proving the power of the personality as suspect. Mweta, who throughout the novel is associated with the warmth and ease of friendship (Rebecca tells Bray, "You love that man, that's the

trouble" [*GH*, 262]), proves politically treacherous (he introduces the
Preventive Detention bill, which is not unlike the apartheid government's detention bills), while the more aloof Shinza holds to his socialist
ideological course. The political question is at last solved for Gordimer:
neocolonial methods involve social betrayal; therefore, some form of
socialism is the only way to go (Clingman, 119–20). *influ. of* *Fanon*

The controlling political thinker invoked in the novel is Frantz Fanon
who, though not essentially a Marxist, approaches Marxism in his belief
that it is the masses, not the leaders or systems, who ultimately make
and determine history. Fanon's theories on colonialism and nationalism
are linked intertextually through Shinza and Bray's references to his
work, references that indicate that their ideology has been powerfully
directed by Fanon's ideas (Bray brought Fanon's *The Wretched of the Earth*
back to Africa with him). Fanon was one of the first theorists to warn of
the danger of a national consciousness being co-opted after independence by a rising national bourgeoisie to perpetuate and feed their own
hegemonic status. In the novel, Shinza quotes for Bray a snippet of
Fanon's theory from *The Wretched of the Earth* that complicates the issue
of independence; the Fanon section from which the snippet is drawn
encapsulates one of Gordimer's central concerns in *A Guest of Honour.*
Fanon writes:

> The militant who faces the colonialist war machine with the bare mini-
> mum of arms realizes that while he is breaking down colonial oppression
> he is building up automatically yet another system of exploitation. This
> discovery is unpleasant, bitter, and sickening: and yet everything seemed
> to be so simple before: the bad people were on one side, and the good on
> the other. The clear, unreal, idyllic light of the beginning is followed by a
> semi-darkness that bewilders the senses. The people find out that the
> iniquitous fact of exploitation can wear a black face, or an Arab one; and
> they raise the cry of "Treason!" But the cry is mistaken; and the mistake
> must be corrected. The treason is not national, it is social. The people
> must be taught to cry "Stop thief!" In their weary road toward rational
> knowledge the people must give up their too-simple conception of their
> overlords. The species is breaking up under their very eyes. As they look
> around them, they notice that certain settlers do not join in the general
> guilty hysteria; there are differences in the same species. Such men, who
> before were included without distinction and indiscriminately in the
> monolithic mass of the foreigner's presence, actually go so far as to con-
> demn the colonial war. The scandal explodes when the prototypes of this
> division of the species go over to the enemy, become Negroes and Arabs,
> and accept suffering, torture, and death.[4]

yet killed for their color

The last sentence pinpoints Gordimer's concern about how the outsider in Africa becomes the insider and about how the European Bray—by becoming politically involved (he goes "over to the enemy")—makes Africa his place. Overcoming issues of racial and national identity, Bray—despite his white skin and British background—becomes an African, claimed by the country, ironically, in death. His commitment to Africa shifts the novel's concern about African identity to one that is neither racial nor national, but rather social and cultural.

In previous novels we have seen Gordimer wrestle with the question of what being a white African means. In *A Guest of Honour* she answers that question unequivocally. Political commitment is the way to become a white African, and through its critique of neocolonialism and narrow nationalism, as well as its references to radical thinkers on African affairs, the novel affirms a socialist path particularly suited to Africa. The identity and role of the artist in Africa, particularly the writer, is also of central significance to Gordimer, as she seeks to establish herself as an African artist. Defining African writing as "writing done in any language by Africans themselves and by others of whatever skin colour who share with Africans the experience of having been shaped, mentally and spiritually, by Africa rather than anywhere else in the world,"[5] Gordimer draws a distinction between the European novel, which has exhausted its social reality and turned to more experimental forms, and the African novel, where—due to its historical context—content must take priority over form. Realism and external reality assert themselves over experimentation and introspection, and *A Guest of Honour* is "in the best tradition of Lukács's 'critical realism', which Gordimer claims . . . represents the most important genre in African writing." Clingman asserts that this novel "represents an achievement in the forefront of African literature at the time, and even now [1985] the novel is probably unparalleled in its specific fusion of complex political theory and discourse with more conventional narrative forms." Unlike Joseph Conrad's colonial novel *Heart of Darkness,* the mysterious "unspeakable horror" of the dark continent is "broken down into questions of historical struggle" and demystified by a clear examination of the African political and social realities (Clingman, 126–28).

But Gordimer's consciousness is not entirely historical. As witnessed in earlier novels there is always a space where historical and political existence fuse with the natural and psychological world, where the rational and concrete interface with the irrational and intuitive. Gordimer's vehicle for this linkage is often through the realm of sexuality, which also introduces the complex world of gender politics and allows her to explore the role of women in political transformation as well. In *A Guest of Honour* Bray's relationship with Rebecca is the primary mechanism used to probe this ambiguous and intangible sphere; and from Bray's first significant encounter with her in Gala, Rebecca is linked—both in name (Edwards) and essence—with the potent and irresistible political and sexual power of Shinza, who, despite middle age, has recently fathered a son with his new young wife. Once home from visiting Shinza in his village on the northern border, where he has learned of the torture and detention of the young political dissenter, Bray lies on the couch with a throbbing headache; he is interrupted by Rebecca returning his car keys. Half-awake, he draws her to the couch and "they began to make love to each other fiercely and while his body raced away from him—extraordinarily, he was thinking of Shinza. Shinza's confident smile, Shinza's strong bare feet, Shinza smoking cigars in the room that smelled of baby, Shinza. Shinza" (*GH*, 152). This linking of Rebecca and Shinza deliberately suggests a new political and sexual vigor for Bray, and prompts the oppositional pairing of his wife, Olivia, with Mweta, the two waning influences in his life. His attachments to his life in Wiltshire wither; they belong to a world with a different life (his daughter has given birth to his grandchild), which Bray now relinquishes. This separation from spouse and space is signaled from the beginning of the novel when Bray takes leave of Olivia to return to the African country he had helped to free. The parting is deeply significant because Olivia—whose life is emotionally rooted in England—senses Bray's need to be back in Africa. Her "hidden, pressed-down, banked-over desire to know whether this house, this life in Wiltshire, this life—at last—seemed to him the definitive one, in the end" is answered by her premonition that "in middle age you could find you had lost everything in a moment: husband-lover, friend, children, it was as if they had never happened, or you had wandered off from them without knowing, and now stood stock-still with the discovery" (*GH*, 11). Bray's response when he thinks of Wiltshire while driving back from his first visit with Shinza confirms Olivia's fears: "The house in Wiltshire with all its comfortable beauty and order, its incenses of fresh flowers and good cooking, its libations of carefully discussed and chosen wine came to Bray in all the calm detail of an interesting death cult; to wake up there again would be to find oneself acquiescently buried alive" (*GH*, 138).

   The images of birth, death, and rebirth in the novel reinforce what Bray is learning about the shifting and contradictory nature of what it means to be truly alive. In bed with Rebecca, unable to sleep, he worries about politics; yet "all the hours of these nights when he was in turmoil he was also in the greatest peace. He was aware of holding these two contradictions in balance. There was once an old crony of his mother's who used to say gleefully of anyone who found himself suddenly subjected to extraordinary demands—Now he knows he's alive" (*GH,* 310). Bray comes to accept that contradiction and doubt are what we live by, and only change is assured. He learns that commitment must be made in principle to assure the triumph of the cause; it must be made without expectation in the full knowledge that the individual may not succeed. On the road to the capital shortly before the ambush, Bray considers his secret mission abroad for Shinza:

> It was not that he had no doubts about what he was doing, going to do; it seemed to him he had come to understand that one could never hope to be free of doubt, of contradictions within, that this was the state in which one lived—the state of life itself—and no action could be free of it. There was no finality, while one lived, and when one died it would always be, in a sense, an interruption. (*GH,* 487)

Through Bray, Gordimer confronts the reader with the fact that a principled commitment to social change risks the culpability of waste, confusion, and violent death. Bray admits that

> the means, as always, would be dubious. He had no others to offer with any hope of achieving the end, and as he accepted the necessity of the end, he had no choice. The instincts in himself that he had unconsciously regarded as the most civilized, unwilling to risk—as a fatal contradiction in terms—his own skin or that of others for the values of civilization, were outraged. He was aware . . . of going against his own nature . . . But he had put aside this "own nature." It was either a tragic mistake or his salvation. (*GH,* 488)

Bray's acceptance of the doubt, paradoxes, and contradictions makes him able to accept the secondary and supportive role history now appoints for whites; it allows him to work for the long term, to filter his ego out of the scenario and commit on both the historical and existential level at once. It enables the reader to reject his death—however distressing and ironic—as a failure of his life's work, and it links the historical consciousness of the novel with existence and nature. History becomes naturalized in a Foucaultian ebb and flow of power in an unpredictable variety of combinations and contradictions guaranteeing that change will come.

While acknowledging the political and historical achievements of the text, Newman focuses more on the ambiguities that gender and language introduce into the novel. She questions the clear political narrative of Bray's journey to active commitment when it is his sexual relationship that becomes a symbolic endorsement of his new life. Rather, through a focus on gender relations and psycholinguistics, Newman uncovers the instability of the central political narrative, which is jostled for prominence by the subjectivity of the personal narrative of Bray and Rebecca's relationship. Newman believes this strategy raises crucial issues about social and political transformation that neither Bray, Mweta, nor Shinza address consciously in their struggle for change. Newman notes the text's reference to Wilhelm Reich, whose Freudian-Marxist ideas were popular in the 1960s. Reich believed that all revolutions based only on the political and the economic would automatically fail if they did not conquer the repressive morality—established through an authoritarian patriarchy—that is endemic to family life as well. Acknowledging that Bray's affair with Rebecca appears to be a rejection of the repressive institution of marriage as a capitalist prop, Newman nevertheless challenges Bray's relationship with Rebecca as a symbol of renewal and vigor. Rebecca and Bray's relationship is not yet the liberated "rearrangement of intimacy" that could undo authoritarianism; that role seems to be Shinza's, who with his new young wife has a baby boy, for Bray and Rebecca—despite taking no precautions—do not reproduce. Both Bray and Rebecca are still mired in the repressive past: Though estranged, both are still married to partners rooted firmly in the past, and both fall back in their new relationship into past patterns of patriarchy. Bray uses his influence and position to secure Rebecca's money overseas, thus protecting her property and belying Shinza's quote from Nyerere: "The development of a country is brought about by people, not by money" (GH, 362). Rebecca is emotionally dependent on Bray. She is self-admittedly "an ass at politics" (GH, 237) and she sends her children to South Africa for their education ostensibly because "they say the schools are good" (GH, 249).

Breaking free of old patriarchal patterns is portrayed as difficult, and we see Bray slip back, in the crisis of the riots, into the role of authority: "He was deafened to noise and chaos by the bellow of his own voice, brutally commanding, hard and ringing, a voice dredged up from his racial past, disowning him in the name of sea-captains and slavers between whose legs his genes had been hatched" (*GH,* 466). But—unlike sea captains of yesteryear—Bray is speaking Gala to the rioters, and through the lens of language acquisition Gordimer probes further the relationship between psychology and ideology. Fanon states that "to speak means to be in a position to use a certain syntax, to grasp the morphology of this or that language, but it means above all to assume a culture, to support the weight of a civilization."[6] Newman notes that Gordimer draws on George Steiner, who held that "patterns of thought echo systematizations of language, which carry culturally ordained values" (Newman, 47). She notes, too, the particular selectivity of language in literature. But selectivity implies omission, and Gordimer is careful to alert us to the gaps, the silences in the text, to the stories not told. Bray speaks fluent Gala, but Rebecca speaks none, and it is Bray who now tries to draw her more fully into the culture by teaching her the language in which she struggles to find the right words. Her stilted conversation with Bray reveals her lack of readiness; she inadvertently reveals her husband's impending visit, her marriage to a man who "wanted only to 'make his pile and get out' " (*GH,* 519). Bray's impersonal commitment to his ideological principles are compromised by his personal caretaking of Rebecca, while her attachment is to Bray, the personal. It is no surprise that Africa claims Bray from her in death, no surprise that Rebecca ends up alone in England, for she is not ready for the impersonal political commitment Gordimer valorizes. But Rebecca does at least recognize that although what had happened to Bray was "pure faceless horror to her . . . he would have known why it had happened to him" (*GH,* 520). Unable to decipher his last message, she is left to find her own way. Anticipating Hillela in *A Sport of Nature,* she is described early on "like one of those hitch-hikers who let the world carry them, at home with anybody in having no home, secure in having no luggage, companionable in having no particular attachment" (*GH,* 242). Her attachment to Bray and the growth she begins to undergo suggest a potential evolution of gender relations beyond the bounds of this novel.

Critics who berate Gordimer for her nonfeminist stance should note her implicit criticism of women's complicity with, and their oppression by, the patriarchy in this novel. Olivia opts for living in the old privileged system: a comfortable retirement and collecting antiques. Even Rebecca—unconventionality not withstanding—marries an adventurer husband, takes advantage of the privileged white South African schools, and ends up dependent on Bray and the European banking system. Gordimer notes too the dangers of African patriarchal attitudes: women are excluded from the Party Congress, Aleke and Mweta's family structures perpetuate an authoritarian mode, and African wives at the banquet are "dumped like tea cosies" (GH, 208). Gordimer makes the Foucaultian point that unless there is a genuine restructuring of intimate relationships, no lasting systemic change can be made. She suggests that women carry part of the responsibility for that change.

To his credit, Bray has shed much of his patriarchal heritage, prepared comfortably to play a secondary and supportive role in Shinza's struggle. His alignment with Shinza is prompted not by his attraction for Shinza's magnetic masculinity as critic Elaine Fido suggests,[7] but rather by Shinza's support for the weak, the masses, whose stories cannot be heard. These submerged stories, the silences, the indecipherabilities, are all elements that destabilize the primary narrative, exerting a pressure that undermines and fragments it. Shinza, for example, is most potently threatening when mysteriously absent in his northern territory, and weakest, ironically, when he rationally argues at the Party Congress his ideological stance in opposition to Mweta. At Congress the power of silence becomes Mweta's: He says nothing, relying on his authority as president to bind the delegates psychologically to his path. Irrationally, they reject Shinza's cause.

The strength of *A Guest of Honour* comes ultimately from its ability to capture a tenuous but authentic role for the individual within the tremendous complexity and confusion of politically and personally entangled worlds. Though perceptions fail us, situations shift, and language falters (Bray cannot communicate with Olivia's world anymore, neither can he find the Gala words to stop the attackers who kill him), Gordimer does not succumb to an existential despair. She holds determinedly through the character of Bray to a principled plan of action in which the individual cannot expect to know or see the final outcome. Acting, rather, with humility on behalf of the collective, he or she must keep—despite doubts, ambiguities, and contradictions—the original idea of what independence should mean. As Bray tells Mweta, Shinza's job within the party is "to oppose that idea all the time against a government's acceptance of what is expedient, consistent with power. The dialectic, in fact" (GH, 175). It is from this dialectic within the national debate that a healthy national consciousness is born. And as Fanon remarked, "national consciousness, which is not nationalism, is the only thing which will give us an international dimension . . . It is at the heart of national culture that international consciousness lives and grows. And this two-fold emerging is ultimately only the source of all culture"

(Fanon 1963, 247–48). In her next novel, Gordimer searches for the heart of national culture in South Africa, for the source from which healing and unity must come to the nation.

The Conservationist

The Conservationist, Gordimer's sixth novel, can be considered her most remarkable novelistic achievement. Decidedly anticolonial, the novel resonates with the literary history of white South Africa. In obvious contrast to Olive Schreiner's famous late-nineteenth-century colonial novel, *The Story of an African Farm,* it spans the evolution of the relationship of white South African writing with the African landscape from Schreiner to Gordimer's present determination to be regarded as an African writer. The novel spans cultures and languages as well, an effect achieved by interspersing the narrative with Zulu quotations drawn from Henry Calloway's 1878 work, *The Religious System of the Amazulu,* as well as by depicting cultural interaction among the South African urban and rural black and white characters. The novel achieves this profoundly resonant span through a subjective narrative of the interior life of the white industrialist protagonist, Mehring, whose voice is alternately melded with that of a real narrator in a stylistically innovative mode. Predominantly Joycean stream-of-consciousness, the narrative incorporates a spectrum of white South Africans cleverly characterized in the interior dialogues in Mehring's head that are triggered by personal associations. Gordimer's most extraordinary literary feat is how, through this highly personal story of the inner devolution of one man, she delivers a devastating political critique of two supposedly benign attitudes of white South Africans: the liberal, whom she castigates for fraudulent inefficacy, and the capitalist, for cynical exploitation. She extends her theme of nation building through commitment, explored in *A Guest of Honour,* beyond consideration of the structure and ideology of systemic organization to a deeper, more profound level of a people's psychospiritual connection with and responsibility to a particular place as home.

Gordimer's political focus shifts from *A Guest of Honour*'s pan-African concerns of nationhood and neocolonialism to a more regional focus on South Africa and its neighboring states at a time of significant impending change. In the early 1970s, white South Africa saw itself as increasingly vulnerable when its front-line states, which had provided a buffer from black independent Africa, showed signs of crumbling under the pressure from revolutionary forces. Resistance fighters had begun to attack farms in Rhodesia, Mozambique's colonial government was engaged in a bitter struggle in its war against Frelimo, and South Africa's claim to Namibia was in dispute. The apartheid government's détente initiatives had delivered nothing. Seeing themselves as the last outpost, fearful English, Afrikaans, and neighboring whites put aside their petty differences and drew together in alliance against the impending black force. A rise in Afrikaner fortunes, facilitated by the apartheid regime through government contracts and contacts, had created a new class of pragmatic Afrikaners now well established in the business and industrial sectors, and often linked to English families through marriage and business interests. More flexible than their government, they became an insidious force wearing a benign face, socially progressive only as long as their privilege to exploit economically was not disrupted. Their alignment with other South African and international industrialists made them part of a growing international class focused only on profit and power, with little or no interest in genuine nation building. But the tenuous white unity was faltering, shaken by black labor strikes in Namibia and later in Natal. The black consciousness movement led by Steve Biko had spread to black university campuses and would erupt into the Soweto uprising in 1976.

Mehring, the central character of *The Conservationist,* is drawn from this wealthy industrialist set. He is English-speaking but has an Afrikaans surname, and owns a 400-acre farm outside Johannesburg. He initially saw it as a good place to bring women, but now he seeks respite there from the world of stocks and shares. Though owner of the farm, he is not a farmer; he made his fortune selling pig iron to the Japanese (who the government declared "honorary whites" due to their economic power). He uses his farming activities as a sentimental site of connection to the African earth, and, cynically, as an income tax write-off. Divorced, with an ex-wife in America and a probably gay son, Mehring's materialism extends beyond the ownership of things. It includes his objectifying attitude toward women, which is explored largely via his defunct affair with Antonia, a socially pretentious liberal whose dabbling in racial politics precipitated her flight from the country. It also includes his exploitation of his black farmworkers and his implied complicity with the law enforcement apparatus of the apartheid regime. He sees a use for everything. But his ambiguous relationship to the land (to which all other forms of exploitation are linked) is the main focus of the novel. Mehring's cynical, self-interested, and schizophrenic need to both exploit and conserve the land drives him to a state of frenzied collapse, his accumulation of guilt and alienation compounded by the discovery—early in the novel—of an anonymous, murdered black body in the third pasture of his farm. After a crude burial by police too lazy to remove the body, Mehring remains haunted by its presence on his farm. Near the end of the novel, a freak cyclonic storm blows in from the Mozambique channel, grotesquely raising the body out of the mud to create a nightmare vision that shatters Mehring's last tenuous grip on reality. He flees from the farm in a delusory state. His final fate, however, is deliberately muddled by the impressionistic style of the narrative. He appears to end up among the wasteland of the mine dumps, symbols of his wealth, in a compromising position—possibly a setup—with some poor white or "coloured" tart. He is watched by a white police/thug type from whom he either escapes or by whom he is attacked. Reflecting his instability, the narrative breaks down completely as Mehring's grip on reality disintegrates. On the farm, meanwhile, the body—despite its anonymity—is at last claimed in brotherhood and harmony by the black workers on the farm. Fusing Christian and African rites, they give it an appropriate ceremonial burial, symbolically reclaiming the earth, or Africa, for the Africans.

Linked to *A Guest of Honour* through its concerns about capitalism and international exploitation, *The Conservationist* relinquishes the conventional realism of the preceding novel for a highly symbolic structure. The psychological disintegration of Mehring signals the demise of white power, and the resurrection of the black body suggests the rising force of a black South Africa's agenda—an agenda familiar to Gordimer through her knowledge of black consciousness doctrine and African culture. Gordimer's clear sense of the undercurrent of power shifting from white to black in the region—suggested in the novel by the massive storm from Mozambique—was endorsed uncannily by ensuing political events in the region. Gordimer could not have known that there would be a coup in 1974 by the Portuguese army fighting Frelimo that would bring down the Caetano government and result in Mozambique's independence—her manuscript was already at the publisher. The freedom of Mozambique from the Portuguese colonialists boosted the morale of all southern African resistance movements and marked the beginning of the end of white domination in the region.

The characters of Mehring, representative of the powerful capitalist world, and his ex-lover, Antonia, a sentimental liberal, elucidate the complicity of the two ideologies through their relationship. Mehring subscribes to the modernization theory of economic development: Progress means that black South Africans have greater material opportunity than before. He counters Antonia's earlier criticism about capitalist developers:

> The people are all better off today than they ever were. They have work and they eat. They wear shoes. A uranium deposit . . . can raise the gross national product to a level where development—viability—becomes a reality, not a dream that depends on justice, wherever you're expecting to find that.[8]

Antonia, on the other hand, promotes the supposed humanism of liberalism by defining herself against capitalist values. She attacks Mehring's values with sarcasm:

> "Development"—one great big wonderful all-purpose god of a machine, eh, Superjuggernaut that's going to make it *all right,* put everything right if we just get the finance for it. The money and the know-how machine. Isn't that it with you? The politics are of no concern. The ideology doesn't matter a damn. The poor fellows don't know what's good for them, anyway. That's how you justify what you condone—that's what lets you off the hook, isn't it—The Great Impartial. Development. No dirty hands or compromised minds. Neither racist nor kaffir-boetie. Neither dirty Commie nor Capitalist pig. It's all going to be decided by computer—look, no hands! Change is something programmed, not aspired to. No struggle between human beings. That'd be too smelly and too close. Let them eat cake, by all means—if production allows for it, and dividends are not affected, in time. (*Cons,* 82)

The seriousness of Antonia's (and by extension, the liberal community's) criticism is undercut by her hypocrisy. Guilty of using the privileges of the affluent white community for her own pleasure or protection, her protests ring hollow. Mehring notes that when her self-righteous dabbling in interracial politics drew police attention, she called him for a "respectable, shrewd company lawyer. . . . not so free and bold when answering questions about your poor bloody black friends at John Vorster Square" (*Cons,* 79). Her political hypocrisy extends to their sex life. Just as liberalism is at the calling of big business, Antonia is his disdainful mistress: "After making love it was always necessary to her ego to establish the difference, the vast gap between herself and a man like him, that might seemed to have bridged itself in pleasure. And at the same time she was offering flattery: no ordinary pig-iron dealer, then?"

(*Cons,* 106). Gordimer's caustic criticism of the liberal position pierces Antonia's coy confession to Mehring: "I want to change the world but keep bits of it the way I like it for myself" (*Cons,* 71). Clingman aptly defines this kind of liberalism as "the flourish of conscience whose possibility is created materially and licensed morally within and by capitalist society" (145).

But despite Mehring's exploitation, the novel grants him some credence for his realistic attitude. He sees through Antonia's pretentious sentimentality about race relations, and knows from historical precedents that his good life cannot last: "How long can we go on getting away scot free? When the aristocrats were caught up in the Terror, did they recognize: it's come to us. Did the Jews of Germany think: it's our turn. Soon, in this generation or the next, it must be our turn to starve and suffer. Why not?" (*Cons,* 46–47). What damns both Antonia and Mehring, however, is bad faith. Their differences are regarded not as a site from which to struggle and grow, but as a combative game that heightens the tension and desire of their sexual encounters, a game that must be read as the tacit and secret collusion between liberalism and capitalism. Antonia is aroused by Mehring's brazen dismissal when he tells her that he never thinks about the emotional complexity of sex for which she argues. She retorts:

—No, you just do it.—
—That's right.— With a particular smile that she took eagerly as evidence against him but that roused her to him in spite—or because?—of this. (*Cons,* 102)

The dysfunctional sexuality in the novel is both a function of the warped society and an analogue for political attitudes. It thinly veils its inherent aggression and abusiveness (and indicts women for a certain collusion), depicted most graphically in the incident on an airplane when Mehring detachedly "fingers" a probably underage Portuguese girl traveling with her family. His view that "there's a special pleasure in having a woman you paid" (*Cons,* 77), and his discovery that, rather than his female friend, it is her daughter "whom he wanted to meet and undress in a hotel room" (*Cons,* 30), convey the brazen mercantilism and utter cynicism accommodated in his moral world. It is no surprise to find women and animals intertwined in his consciousness, benignly sensual on the one hand—"breath from the mouth of a cow, or the mouth of a warm sleepy woman turned to in the morning" (*Cons,* 10)—and viciously aggressive on the other: "My God, what a state of heat, over that bitch"

(*Cons*, 43). His creed of possession and control extends to the landscape as well. Mehring reads the Namibian landscape he sees from the plane in sexually possessive terms:

> The dunes of the desert lie alongside the road between Swakopmund and Walvis Bay. Golden reclining nudes. Torso upon torso, hip sweeping from waist, smooth beyond smoothness, suggesting to the tactile imagining only the comparison, in relation to the hand, of the tongue when some substance evanesces on it. (*Cons*, 103–4)

His possessive attitude is summed up by Antonia's reminder in a discussion about Namibia that "you don't own a country by signing a bit of paper the way you bought yourself the title deed to that farm" (*Cons*, 101).

Mehring's relationship with the land is plagued by contradictions. His sensitivity to the beauty and moods of the countryside is palpable; it remains the one redeeming quality about him, and its evocation is a tribute to Gordimer's craft:

> Oh my God. The field dips away before it rises again towards the river. It has drifted into flower since the sun rose two hours ago—yesterday afternoon it was still green, with only a hint of sage to show the bloom was coming. Just touching, floating over its contours, is a nap of blue that brushes across the grain to mauve. There is no wind but the air itself is a constant welling. It is the element of this lush summer. He has plunged down past the pump-house where a big pipe makes a hidden foot-bridge buried in bowed grasses and bulrushes over an irrigation furrow. His shoes and the pale gray pants are wiped by wet muzzles of grasses, his hands, that he lets hang by his sides, are trailed over by the tips of a million delicate tongues. Look at the willows. The height of the grass. Look at the reeds. Everything bends, blends, folds. Everything is continually swaying, flowing rippling waving surging streaming fingering. He is standing there with his damn shoes all wet with the dew and he feels he himself is swaying, the pulsation of his blood is moving him on his own axis (that's the sensation) as it seems to do to accommodate the human body to the movement of a ship. A high earth running beneath his feet. All this softness of grasses is the susurration of a slight dizziness, hissing in the head. (*Cons*, 183)

Mehring's sensitivity is corrupted, however, by a central paradox. It is his exploitation of the land—extraction of pig iron—and the people with indisputable claim to it, that affords him the luxury of conserving his 400 acres; unconsciously his sense of oneness with the land slips into the inescapable shadow side of his guilt and conjures the presence of the black body. Still admiring the land, his mind wanders: "No wound to be seen; and simply shovelled under. He looks out over this domain almost with fascination, to think that, somewhere, that particular spot exists, overgrown. No one'll remember where you are buried" (*Cons,* 184).

Mehring's determination to conserve his land means that his workers are viewed primarily as a method to further his conservation policy, and, except for a few moments of delusory sentimental bonding or fear, he is largely indifferent to them. They are—like most things in his life—a means to an end. Watching his farm manager, Jacobus, at work, Mehring assesses his worth:

> He certainly has a sense of attachment to the place; one could do a lot worse, although it's business-lunch exaggeration to say (he sometimes hears himself) his old boy does better than any white manager. What this really means is that they're more honest than any white you're likely to get on a menial yet responsible position. He may filch a bag of mealie-meal for perks but why the hell not, who wouldn't—but he hasn't the craft to crook you. There is laughter when—frankly confidential—there comes the observation that you can always trust a man who can't write not to keep a double set of books. (*Cons,* 145)

Jacobus's attachment to the farmland is real, and the novel depicts the relationship of the black farmworkers and their families with the land as natural and unselfconscious. During Mehring's absences they run the farm effectively, from maintaining the machinery to gathering wild spinach from the veld. Even Mehring acknowledges their sense of belonging: "They were squatting God knows how long before he bought the place and they'll expect to have their grandchildren squatting long after he's gone" (*Cons,* 202). Their organic connection to the land is reinforced by events on the farm like the worker Phineas's wife's induction as a diviner. After Mehring and his son Terry have visited and then left, the Africans—to whom the white men mean nothing except employment—participate in the ceremony:

> All the farm was dark except for where they gathered the life of the place together for themselves. He and his son with woman's hair came and went away, leaving nothing, taking nothing; the farmhouse was empty. Stamping slowly, swaying from one foot to another, dancing conferred a balance of its own that drunkenness could not fell. . . . The sleeping cat-

tle, the barn, the sheds, the fanged and clawed machines the colour of
football jerseys and smelling of oil, the pick-up and the caterpillar trac-
tor, the water obediently flowing forever down there in the reeds—all—
all might have been theirs. (*Cons,* 172)

Clingman warns, however, that the black Africans' natural affinity with
the land does not mean that they can assume real control, for the system
is rigged to ensure white supremacy. It demands loyalties to a system
that divides the people, who must then exploit each other to survive: It
ties them to their white bosses, who are part of the system that
oppresses them, instead of to each other. They cannot take on Mehring's
power (156). It is only through a complete revolution, a complete shift
in power, that real change will come about.

The novel achieves this broader vision of white power shifting to
black power primarily through its formal structure—the insertion of
Zulu quotations. The disruption of the narrative with quotations from
Zulu mythology evokes—like the black body in the pasture—the sense
of a deep but pressing African presence. While the story is ostensibly
that of Mehring and his white world, Newman holds that the quotations—each introducing or reinforcing an event in the novel—steadily
uncover the real story as that of the blacks. The quotations are "the
organizing points for a subtext which slowly comes into the foreground"
(Newman, 39). Each quotation more overtly than the last asserts the
African connection to and possession of the land, collectively suggesting
what Newman calls "a buried logic of fictional events, which may be
expressed in the rhetoric of myth" (56). The early quotations are predictable expressions of concern during the terrible drought described in
this section of the novel: prayers for corn (*Cons,* 39) and for children and
the continuation of life (*Cons,* 61); an African presence at this point of
the novel is unremarkable. Newman notes, however, a strengthening
connection with Zulu mythology in the rest of the quotations:

A further series of quotations (83, 93, 113) is taken from a dream by one
of Calloway's informants, in which he dreams he is awoken and ordered
to go down to the river with his brother, there to grapple with a spirit
ancestor. This precedes the episode in the novel in which Solomon is
awakened in the night, by mysterious figures, supposedly at the behest of
his brother, and attacked. Later quotations introduce the image of the
"Amatongo," the ancestors who are beneath the earth (163, 193) (linked
to the dead man buried in the third pasture), the question of material
possession of Africa (213), and the bringing of rain and floods by a rain-

maker (231) which precedes torrential rain and floods in modern South Africa. (Newman, 56)

The sense of African belonging to the land is consolidated for Newman in the last quotation (*Cons* 247) which she believes "widens the historical perspective to suggest the enduring occupation of the land by the blacks" (Newman, 56).

The novel brilliantly integrates Zulu myth with the real events experienced by the blacks in the novel. The dead body found "on a nest of reeds it has flattened" relates specifically to the Zulu myth of origins relayed in Calloway's book. Newman explains that reeds are metaphors for the ancestors; a father—the ancestor, or *uthlanga*, of his children—is like a reed because they broke off from him. When the farmworkers disown the dead black body they therefore deny the ancestors; this denial triggers a response. Solomon, who found the body, is chosen to awaken them to their cultural duty. He is beaten up (apparently for debts owed) near the place where the body lies buried, an experience that approximates the dream myth of a fellow being called to the river to wrestle with an ancestor spirit. Solomon, reports say, was "attacked in the night by a spirit" (*Cons,* 92). The veld fire, which ravaged the third pasture and burned through the compound where the workers and their families live, also has mythological significance. Newman explains that in Zulu mythology rainmakers burn the earth around their homes so the god will know from the blackened area that the rainmaker is seeking rain. The sacrifice of colorful birds to bring about rain (taking color from the earth, as does drought) is invoked in the novel through the description of the storm as a "monstrous cosmic peacock" that shed "gross paillettes of hail" (*Cons,* 232). Newman asserts that "drought, the dead black fire and images of the rainbird are carefully organized into a coherent pattern of Zulu belief" (Newman, 58). Also significant is the feast celebrating the initiation of Phineas's wife as a diviner. Possessed by the spirit of the ancestor, she conjures up images of destruction and mayhem: "In her sleep there were also elephants and hyenas and lions and full rivers, all coming near to kill her" (*Cons,* 166). She is tormented by the ancestors, and only after the storm and the proper burial of the body at the end of the novel is there resolution for her. At the burial "Phineas' wife's face was at peace, there was no burden of spirits on her shoulders" (*Cons,* 267). Gordimer's use of myth solves the central dilemma of the novel. Confident that a shift to black history is imminent, but unable to see how this new reality will come about, her use of Zulu mythology to appropriate the surface narrative, and the symbolic use of the dead body to claim the land, evades the need for a specific answer, yet nevertheless gathers an irresistible force of change. The novel effects a shift to African culture whose reality has survived (or has been conserved) beneath the surface reality of the dominant white culture. It now rises, still connected not only to its mythological past but to its language as well.

Zulu is but one of many languages spoken in South Africa, though only the two European-based languages of English and Afrikaans were recognized as official under the apartheid regime. Language, therefore, is politicized, and it is presented in the novel as one of the boundaries that limits communication. Mehring, we note, opportunistically speaks Afrikaans to the police. Once off the telephone he curses their incompetence in English, but—typical of white South Africans—he speaks no African language. Gordimer's introduction of an African language asserts a certain cultural claim and builds on her use of Gala in *A Guest of Honour*. Separated from black Africans by language, and therefore by culture, Mehring—unlike Bray—exists in a closed system ranging "from the flat to the car to the office, from tables to beds, from airports to hotels, from city to country" (*Cons,* 75) and in a limited consciousness locked in its assumptions of cultural superiority. In this novel it is the Africans who move with ease across cultural boundaries, mixing the languages, a "jaunty greeting, one word in Afrikaans and one in their language: More, Nkos' " (*Cons,* 181), while the whites and Indians (represented by Bismillah and his family) remain isolated in their huddled laagers of fear and arrogance. Bismillah's family lives and operates their general store in what has been designated a white area, and to stave off government removal they must bribe the authorities and stay out of trouble. Culturally exclusive, they deliberately use language to isolate themselves: "In a full shop, the privacy of this talk in Gujerati was as secure to the family as if the shop were empty. The language reached nobody else's understanding" (*Cons,* 120). Their communication with their black customers is curt: "Demand. Response. Counter-demand. Statement. No word was given away. Communication, narrowed down its closest immediate confines, was complete" (*Cons,* 119–20). The 10-foot fence that encloses the Indians' property becomes symbolic of their guarded mind-set. It went

> right round the partly bricked-in yard, taking in the tin hovels supported
> by the yard wall down where the blacks lived. The fence was shored up
> here and there with sheets of corrugated iron and even an old bedstead—

the blacks had built it for their employers, to keep blacks out. The two
great dogs—cross-breeds of the white men's favorite watch-dogs, Alsa-
tion and Dobermann Pinscher—who were chained to runners along the
fence had worn a shallow ditch inside the length of it, bounding, racing
and snarling at everything that passed within their hearing or vision.
(*Cons,* 35)

The habit of social and cultural exclusion emanating from fear or arrogance leads to a blind self-imprisonment. Here the dogs serve as an
ironic symbol: "In the morning, William found the gates open. Inside
the dogs snarled and raced up and down before the gap, up and down,
as if, for them, the pattern of closed gates was still barred across their
eyes" (*Cons,* 125).

These symbols of self-imposed isolation are just one small part of the
novel's broad pattern of symbols that interlace and resonate throughout
the novel, reinforcing, extending, and embroidering meanings. They
operate broadly and specifically, and they often comment ironically—
irony being the other major organizing principle of the novel—on
events and situations. The majority of symbols are drawn from nature,
and nature is presented as a powerful force of change. Framing the narrative, the drought and the storm operate as major structural symbols.
The drought, a time of hopelessness and cultural dearth for the country,
is relieved by the rains. The storm, which reawakens and revitalizes
African culture by resurrecting the black body (another major symbol),
predicts the triumph and healing of black power through cultural
integrity (the funeral), and sweeps away white dominance, symbolized
by the drowning of an Afrikaans couple in their car and by Mehring's
psychic disintegration. The symbol of the egg places the black world
closest to nature. They eat the guinea fowl eggs so determinedly conserved (despite nutritional needs of the black community) by Mehring; a
despairing Indian youth draws an egg-shaped peace sign on the water
tank; and Mehring's son Terry offers a sterile stone egg to his mother.
The oak and Spanish chestnut trees Mehring plants on his farm define
his Eurocentric vision for Africa, trees for future generations that, ironically, will not be his offspring. The symbol of dogs—nature domesti-
cated—operates in a variety of ways: The dogs' dependency on human
authority renders them blindly conditioned (Bismillah's dogs) or beaten
(compound dogs).

Sexual complicity, exploitation, and hostility within the white world
symbolically extend the issues of political and material exploitation, dys-

functional psychology, and violence: Mehring's love/hate relationship with Antonia, the fingering of the Portuguese girl, and his lust for his colleague's daughter. The material power of the white world governing everyone's lives is invested in technological symbols of luxury and exclusion like the airplane and the automobile, which ironically also function as the agent of white demise: The couple in the flood are drowned in their car; Mehring's industrialist colleague commits suicide in his car; and Mehring's Mercedes is the image around which his final descent into insanity and incoherence takes place.

Irony abounds, most notably in the title. All Mehring's efforts to own, conserve, and enjoy the farm backfire. In a novel where African notions of ancestry and connectedness gain increasing credence, Mehring has no home (a flat and an empty farmhouse) and no family (he is divorced, and alienated from his son), with no hope of heirs. Absence often implies presence in the novel: The body is absent in that it is buried, yet its presence is strongly felt. Conversely, Mehring's presence on the farm turns out to be superficial—he is largely and ultimately absent. Silence speaks: Mehring's most profound communication takes place in the silence of the third pasture. Speech, on the other hand, turns out to be meaningless: Mehring's repeated "no" to the woman really means "yes," and his rantings at the end of the novel are unintelligible. Nothing is actually something: Phineas's diviner wife who "don't see nothing" (*Cons,* 144) is the most culturally informed, while Mehring, who wants "for nothing" (*Cons,* 159), ends up with nothing. Gordimer shifts linguistic and social codes, exploring the role that language plays in identity formation. She reintegrates African identity through language and culture, while dissolving the white world's reality. His reference points all jumbled, Mehring can't even recall the meaning of a green light: "Jeers of horns are prodding at him. Blank" (*Cons,* 251).

Clingman regards this social coding or textuality as one of the novel's three most important features. He notes that the coherence of Mehring's character is dependent on a social, cultural, and ideological text that makes up reality, and when the reality frame or cultural "grid" changes, his character disintegrates. Also a significant feature for Clingman is the Zulu mythology, which, he believes, appropriates the text just as the body claims the farm. The relationship of politics and psychology is the third feature he highlights. Conforming to a classic Freudian pattern, Mehring's efforts to repress his complicity only result in greater psychic menace. Clingman holds that, typically, the site of

repression will return to consciousness in threatening ways. Only by
raising the repressed can the threat be properly buried (161–65).

Newman claims that the novel asserts and examines the complicity of
language and mimetic realism in maintaining colonialism: "If we accept
that there is nothing 'real' about realism, that realism is a linguistic creation, a code which fosters an easy, unthinking acceptance of its signs as
'natural,' we accept that language may operate on the side of the colo-
nizer" (55). She sees Gordimer's implosion of realism in the novel as "a
first step towards political decolonization" (55). Gordimer uses Zulu
myth to supplant the "text of public culture," and she translates colonial
desire into the language of sexuality (Newman, 56). Newman asserts
that the foregrounding of black consciousness in the novel provides a
critical perspective of the white psyche's fantasy projection of its conflicts onto woman and black man. Gordimer argues, she believes, that
true conservation of the land requires a regeneration of its language
(Newman, 67).

In 1985, Clingman called *The Conservationist* "probably the richest of
Gordimer's novels" (161). In 1993 Michael Wade still considered this
novel pivotal. Distinguishing between Gordimer's early and later work,
Wade holds that the early novels do not address a local South African
audience, but rather attempt to explain white South Africa to the European metropolis. He sees *The Conservationist,* however, as the novel that
frees itself of this colonial tendency, manifesting instead to a local audience the emotional emptiness at the core of the white South African
experience, and thereby helping to alter the group's myth of self. In this
way he sees Gordimer as instrumental in changing the consciousness of
her white South African readers. *The Conservationist* is a novel that
demands participation from its readers, South African or otherwise
(Wade, 109–10). To tap its rich depths, readers must learn more about
African culture and history. We must familiarize ourselves with texts
about Zulu mythology and language, revisit Eliot's "The Waste Land,"
and trace Osiris back to the Nile. As the reader must work to gain full
entry to the novel, so—the novel teaches—must the white South
African work to earn a place as African. Birth and wealth are not qualifi-
cations: In *A Guest of Honour,* Bray, an Englishman, earns his place as a
white African, while Mehring, born and raised in South Africa, loses his
heritage through bad faith. Gordimer admits the challenge the novel
poses for its readers:

> I chose to ignore that one had to explain anything at all. I decided that if
> the reader didn't make the leap in his mind, if the allusions were puzzling

to him—too bad. But the narrative would have to carry the book in the sense of what is going on in the characters' minds and going on in their bodies; the way they believed things that they did *really were*. . . . In other words, the novel was full of private references between the characters. Of course, you take a tremendous risk with such a narrative style, and when you succeed, I think it's the ideal. (*EG,* 148–49)

European literary markers like the use of interior monologue and the echoes of "The Waste Land" are reinterpreted and recontextualized to resonate with Zulu mythology. Asserting a call for a new and revitalized South Africa, the last two lines integrate South African past and future. They are a translation of the ANC's slogan, which was repeated after each item of the Freedom Charter was read out at the Congress of the People in 1955: "Afrika! Mayibuye!"—"Let it come back." They refer also to the body now buried: "He had come back. He took possession of this earth, theirs; one of them" (*Cons,* 266). The new South Africa summoned must—like this novel—draw from all its traditions to forge a nation of unity and harmony. It must endorse the African past as a way to direct and give meaning to the future, imbuing readers and citizens alike with an understanding of the invigorating integrative power of cultural traditions reexamined and reinterpreted. This is the heart of national consciousness about which Fanon speaks and which Gordimer envisions for her country.

Chapter Four

Living in the Interregnum:
Burger's Daughter and *July's People*

In 1979 Gordimer published *Burger's Daughter,* and in 1981 she published *July's People*. Both novels use the topic of revolution to explore whether white South Africans can have a place and a role in bringing about a new and equitable nation. Both novels examine the appropriateness and resilience of the family as an organizing unit in a society caught up in the avalanche of revolutionary change, but each focuses on a very different kind of white family. *Burger's Daughter* centers on a subject that had fascinated Gordimer for a long time, the role of the small group of white hard-core leftists, which she explores through the family of a dedicated long-term communist dissident, Lionel Burger. Gordimer has acknowledged that the Burger family is partly modeled on the life of well-known South African Abram Fischer, avowed dissident and leader of the banned South African Communist Party (SACP), who was sentenced to life imprisonment for treason in 1965 and who died 10 years later of cancer. Fischer was a member of a distinguished Afrikaner family: his father had been judge-president of the Orange Free State within the Union of South Africa, and Fischer himself was an advocate and queen's counsel. Brilliant and compassionate, Fischer rejected Afrikaner ideology in favor of communism, which he believed could bring about a just and nonracist society; in the eyes of Afrikaners, this made him an archtraitor to the *volk,* who would have showered him with honors and high office had he remained within the fold. This is the only time in her fiction that Gordimer focuses her story on an identifiable historical figure. She offsets that focus, however, by shifting attention to Rosa, Burger's daughter, and the next generation.

July's People, on the other hand, centers on a very different type of family. The Smales are a typical bourgeois white family with vague liberal pretentions who find themselves uncomprehending and unprepared when revolution—the one the Fischers and Burgers of the white world have been clandestinely working toward—erupts. The two novels' focus

[handwritten margin note: Bram Fischer]

on revolution in South Africa drives home the fact that profound change must and will take place; the families' different perceptions of that revolution determine the meaning such change will have for them. Both novels exemplify the most powerfully integrated writing of Gordimer's career: formally innovative, ideologically challenging, and personally moving. Gordimer was awarded South Africa's CNA Prize for *Burger's Daughter* in 1980 and again for *July's People* in 1981.

Burger's Daughter

In a mixture of fiction and fact, *Burger's Daughter* is set during the teenage and young adult years of Rosa Burger, born in May 1948, the month and year the National Party came to power in South Africa. In the late 1960s and 1970s the strongest political influence among young black activists in South Africa was the black consciousness movement, a movement that challenged the concept of nonracialism that was so central to the communist party doctrine by which Rosa's parents had lived. Black consciousness was a watershed between generations; it shifted the struggle against the South African regime from one that included all races fighting together for equitable integration to a black-centered struggle that shunned any contact or cooperation with whites whatsoever. This meant that Rosa would experience the movement's repudiation of white activists' efforts in the struggle (something her parents had never had to deal with), and she would face much greater uncertainty about how freedom would ultimately be won.

The radical subject matter of *Burger's Daughter* and its inclusion of quotations and documents from banned leaders and organizations brought swift reaction from the South African censors. The book was immediately embargoed and banned upon publication, but very shortly afterward, in an unprecedented move, it was unbanned by the director of the very committee that had banned it in the first place. The South African Publication Board's bizarre actions prompted a response from Gordimer. Her pamphlet *What Happened to "Burger's Daughter" or How South African Censorship Works* describes the bureaucratic obstacle course South African censors applied to the book. The furor surrounding these events, as well as the novel's enthusiastic reception abroad, makes it one of Gordimer's most renowned novels.

Rosa Burger's political and personal evolution—though framed by the family and political history of her father, who was leader of the

SACP—is most radically shaped in response to rising sentiments of black consciousness, which culminated in the Soweto Revolt of 1976. Rejecting all forms of political participation or affiliation with whites, proponents of the movement argued that no matter how radical their politics, all whites remained complicit in deep and persistent patterns of white supremacy. This challenge to the authenticity of politically active whites brought about a "white consciousness" among white students, an honest and self-searching response that seriously considered the point that black consciousness was making: Only by recognizing the possibility of embedded supremacism could whites work for an authentic alternative. Clingman reports that in the late 1970s Gordimer "showed herself much exercised by the question of 'white consciousness' as a response to Black Consciousness," and that "*Burger's Daughter* can be seen as a fictional way of working out the same problem" (176).

The novel opens with 14-year-old Rosa, dressed in her school uniform, waiting with an eiderdown and hot-water bottle among a group of people outside the prison where her mother is being held. The first of the novel's three parts introduces Rosa's background and quickly establishes the unusualness of the Burgers' family life because of their profound commitment to revolutionary change through the disciplined policies of the SACP. Introducing the reader to the little-known world of radical whites, this section of the novel describes Rosa's warm memories of her father's Sunday barbecues around the swimming pool for whoever turned up at the open house, and it recalls vividly her sense of Lionel's secure presence during the swimming lessons he gave to her, her brother Tony, and "Baasie" (Afrikaans for "little master"), the young black child who lived as part of the Burger family for a while. The Burger household of Rosa's youth welcomed all political dissidents and their hangers-on; it was a refuge and gathering place for a broad spectrum of people of all races bound together by political purpose. The descriptions of the Burger home capture the warmth and generosity of spirit for which Bram Fischer was known. Conventional family loyalties and care reform more broadly to affiliate along political lines. Rosa speaks of the intensity of the bonds between her father and two of his comrades:

> These two people represent an intimacy with my father greater than mine. They know what even one's own daughter is never told. . . . It goes beyond friendship, beyond association; beyond family relationship—of course. . . . How they all cared for each other's children, when we were little! In the enveloping acceptance of Ivy's motherly arms—she feels as if I were her own child—there is expectance, even authority.[1]

We learn also of the tragedies suffered by the family: young Tony drowns in the pool that gave so much pleasure to friends and visitors, and Rosa's mother, after a series of stays in detention, dies of multiple sclerosis. (Fischer's wife was drowned in a car accident and their son died of cystic fibrosis.) Rosa dutifully assumes the political role of her mother after her death; she works with lawyers and lovingly supports Lionel through his trial for treason, his life sentence, and his death in prison a few years later. During the trial, Rosa is befriended by a pale, feckless young man, Conrad, who is drawn to her by his curiosity about the Burger family. Feeling strangely free after Lionel's death, Rosa takes refuge at Conrad's cottage, a place expropriated for a freeway, but rented in the delay before construction. She lives "without official tenure at an address that no longer existed. . . . It was safe and cosy as a child's playhouse and sexually arousing as a lovers' hideout. It was nowhere" (*BD*, 21).

Here, during a brief affair, the intimacy of which soon shifts to the closeness of siblings, Conrad challenges the Burger creed of unwavering political commitment to others with his self-absorbed theories of psychological repression and the centrality of sex and death. Gordimer has said that *Burger's Daughter* is about "the human conflict between the desire to live a personal, private life, and the rival claim of social responsibility to one's fellow men,"[2] and it is this already simmering tension in Rosa that Conrad's challenges ignite.

When Rosa moves out of the cottage to live on her own again she avoids the old political crowd. During this time she experiences two peculiarly distressing incidents: At noontime in a city park where she lunches regularly, a hobo dies silently not far from her bench; later, driving through a derelict section of the black township after giving an African woman a ride home, Rosa witnesses the brutal beating of a donkey by the cart's drunk driver as his family cowers in terror on the cart. Unnerved and overwhelmed by the suffering she sees, Rosa concludes that she "no longer knows how to live in Lionel's country" (*BD*, 210). Heeding Conrad's observation that "even animals have the instinct to run from suffering" (*BD*, 73), she leaves for France. She uses the passport that she has persuaded the sophisticated and worldly Brandt Vermeulen, member of the Broederbond (the powerful Afrikaner political brotherhood), to extract from his friends at the Ministry of the Interior.

The second part of the novel deals with Rosa's time abroad, where she learns from her father's first wife, Katya, how to defect from Lionel's political way of life. Warmly welcomed by Katya and her friends into

the fairy-tale seaside village, Rosa is encouraged to pursue a private and
dreamily romantic existence that could never be a part of Lionel's politically driven world. Her love affair with erudite Bernard Chabalier is
emotionally enchanting, and they begin making plans for Rosa's permanent stay in France. During a brief trip to England, however, Rosa
becomes tentatively involved with politics. She attends a meeting of
South African exiles where—astonishingly—she recognizes a young
black man as Baasie, who had lived with her family as a child. Despite
his cool, off-hand manner, she asks him to call so they can meet some-
time. Surprisingly, she is awoken by a phone call much later that night.
Drunk and furiously angry, the young man delivers a tirade rejecting
any connection or claim of friendship Rosa may assume. He asserts his
separate, African identity by spurning the patronizing name Baasie in
favor of his given name, Zwelinzima ("suffering land") Vulindlela. Lionel
Burger's heroic renown infuriates Zwelinzima, whose own father,
among thousands of others, also suffered and died at the hands of the
apartheid regime. He hurls at Rosa the inappropriateness of the attention given to white Lionel for a fate that blacks continue to suffer daily
as a matter of course. The sickening shock of his phone call acts as a cat-
alyst, and Rosa, who "cannot explain to anyone why that telephone call
in the middle of the night made everything that was possible, impossible" (BD, 328), moves back to South Africa with a clearer sense of her
own commitment and mission.

The last part of the novel finds Rosa back in South Africa working as
a physical therapist at a black Johannesburg hospital. The Soweto
Revolt erupts shortly after her return, and Rosa ends up assisting not
disabled children, but the young students who have been brutalized and
mangled by the police. In a massive police sweep 16 months later, Rosa
is one of many dissidents jailed. Rosa, Clare Terblanche (whose parents
were comrades of the Burgers), Marisa Kgosana (whose husband is held
on Robben Island), and others, are held in solitary confinement in a
prison where intermittent communication among detainees of all races
is impossible to prevent. Like her father before her, Rosa is in solitary
confinement. Significantly, however, she lacks his heroic stature; she is
merely one among many activists who have been detained in their
struggle for change. Only her attorney knows that she will likely be
charged by the state for colluding with the charismatic Marisa Kgosana
(modeled on Winnie Mandela) to incite, aid, and abet the students' and
schoolchildren's revolt.

By challenging the whole idea of a self-negating historical or political commitment with more Freudian-based psychosexual theories that focus on the individual and the self, the novel takes seriously the human demand for a personal and private existence, and it seeks to reconcile the tension between these seemingly conflicting modes of being. Gordimer returns in this novel to focus on a certain humanism—epitomized in the personal kindness of Lionel's compassion for humans and animals and in Rosa's compassionate response to suffering—that Gordimer sees, not as an end in itself, but as a route toward commitment to a radical system for social change. Rosa explains the brand of communism that her parents practiced:

> Lionel—my mother and father—people in that house, had a connection with blacks that was completely personal. In this way, their Communism was the antithesis of anti-individualism. The connection was something no other whites ever had in quite the same way. A connection without reservations on the part of blacks or whites. The political activities and attitudes of that house came from the inside outwards, and blacks in that house where there was no God felt this embrace before the Cross. At last there was nothing between this skin and that. At last nothing between the white man's word and his deed; spluttering the same water together in the swimming-pool, going to prison after the same indictment: it was a human conspiracy, above all other kinds. (*BD*, 172)

The epigraph of the first section of the novel also attests to the subjective base of political commitment: "I am the place in which something has occurred" (Lévi-Strauss).

But Gordimer recognizes that as historical and political circumstances shift, so the precise understanding and nature of commitment changes; each person must come to his or her commitment anew. The historical circumstance of Rosa's young adulthood was the black consciousness movement, which refocused attention on the divisiveness of race in a new way; for the first time whites had to read themselves as raced, living in bodies defined by color and judged by it. As Rosa notes: "Lionel and my mother did not stand before Duma Dhladlha and [when asked what he would do if he were white] have him say dismissively: I don't think about that" (*BD*, 172). Bishop Desmond Tutu explained the significance of race for the participants of the struggle against apartheid: "However much [whites] want to identify with blacks it is an existential fact . . . that they have not been victims of this baneful oppression and exploitation. . . . It is a divide that can't be crossed and that must give blacks a primacy in determining the course and goal of the struggle. Whites must be willing to follow" (*EG,* 267). Tutu's analysis returns us to the ever-present dilemma of white participation in shaping the future of South Africa. The question becomes what role remains for a white middle-class South African woman and for whom would she be playing such a role. The novel examines whether there is a place in the struggle for Rosa and whether she can claim the struggle as hers at all.

The form and narrative of *Burger's Daughter* are structured in every way to express the quest of the novel. The bildungsroman facilitates Rosa's defection from her father's camp so that she may establish her own identity, an identity that will ultimately lead her back to her own political commitment. Unlike Clare Terblanche, who unquestioningly accepts the politics of her radical parents and enters the same pattern of revolving stays in detention, Rosa rails against the generational conformity of dissident families: "Other people break away. They live completely different lives. Parents and children don't understand each other—there's nothing to say, between them. Some sort of natural insurance against repetition. . . . Not us. We live as they lived" (*BD,* 127). Set free from family restraints after her father's death she pursues a private life, and it is her understanding and experience of the limitations of that life which enable her to rededicate herself to political activism once more. The dialectical pattern of challenge and probation (thesis, antithesis, synthesis) forms the three sections of the novel: Rosa grows up in the Burger heritage; Rosa rejects that heritage for a personal life after her father's death; Rosa finds her personal identity in political commitment and reunites with her heritage. According to Clingman, this pattern is a major part of the way Gordimer tries and tests a "consciousness of history" in all her work (179).

The novel pursues its resolution through a series of tensional relationships: past and present, South Africa and Europe, private and political, black world and white world, metaphor and history, and first- and third-person narratives. The narrative structure is central to the organization and meaning of the novel, and the alternating first- and third-person narratives provide the lenses through which we view contesting realities. The first-person narrative grants the reader insight into Rosa's internal and private realities, while the third-person narrative—a multivocal text that examines Rosa from every possible point of view—maintains external views of reality, and the contrast exposes the disjunction between inside and out. The function of the multivocal form has been debated, most notably by Clingman, who contests critic Robert Green's view that objectivity is ensured by the variety of external narratives, that there is "no necessary politics of the text *at all* in *Burger's Daughter*." Clingman holds rather that a multivocal text is as manipulable a form as any other and that seeing Rosa from every possible angle (sympathetically, hostilely, neutrally, among others) "has merely led to an apparently necessary outcome: that this is the destiny Rosa was born to, that this is the commitment she must undertake" (191). Hers is a commitment and engagement, however, without any of the glory of her father's position.

Rosa's first-person narrative addresses itself to a different absent consciousness in each part of the novel. She says that "without knowing the reason, at different stages in one's life, one is addressing this person or that all the time, even dreams are performed before an audience" (*BD,* 16). In the first section she addresses the absent Conrad to whom she admits: "If you knew I was talking to you I wouldn't be able to talk. But you know that about me" (*BD,* 17). In the second she speaks to Burger's first wife, now known as Madame Katya Bagnelli, a woman in whom Rosa can find no remaining trace of her connection to Lionel's life. In the last section Rosa speaks to her dead father, explaining her encounter with Zwelinzima and her return to South Africa.

But in addition to the three audiences Rosa addresses, there is a fourth, the reader, who is directly implicated by her use of the second-person *you*. This powerful strategy draws the reader, who begins to identify with the life views of all three addressees, vicariously testing each worldview as the novel progresses. In the last section Rosa takes care to point out the real reason for her return to South Africa, and she asserts the difference between her father's commitment and her own:

It isn't Baasie—Zwel-in-zima, I must get the stress right—who sent me back here. You won't believe that. . . .

I had met a woman in her nightdress wandering in the street. She was like anyone else: Katya, Gaby, Donna; poor thing, a hamster turning her female treadmill. . . . Nothing can be avoided. Ronald Ferguson, 46, ex-miner, died on the park bench while I was busy minding my own business. No one can defect.

I don't know the ideology:
It's about suffering.
How to end suffering.
And it ends in suffering. . . . Like anyone else, I do what I can. I am teaching them to walk again, at Baragwanath Hospital. They put one foot before the other. (*BD,* 332)

Rosa now classes herself among the ordinary; she is "like anyone else" and comments that it is "strange to live in a country where there are still heroes" (*BD*, 332). She recalls that it was Brandt Vermeulen who—because of her radical family—insisted on seeing her differently from other whites; he had raised the difficulty of regarding her wish to go abroad simply as a need to holiday "like anyone else" (*BD*, 187).

Zwelinzima, on the other hand, insists that Rosa *is* like everyone else, and challenges any inclination she may have "to think we could be different from any other whites" (*BD*, 332). There is truth in both views. For before Rosa can return to the struggle she must be forced to recognize the consequences of her whiteness, the unconscious assumptions whites make that lead her to persist in seeing Zwelinzima as the little black Baasie of her youth. Zwelinzima's confrontation forces her to expunge her childish fantasy image of him—bred from a certain white paternalism—that she has harbored all these years. During the telephone call, he establishes his independent existence when he insists that she see clearly: "Put on the light, Rosa. I'm talking to you. . . . You didn't put the light on, then. I told you to" (*BD*, 319). Rosa must stand on her own. It cannot be Baasie who sends her back to South Africa. She must accept the autonomy of her position and work, as best she can, toward her own redemption. She acknowledges that she is not exceptional. She lives like anyone else: she does what she can to alleviate suffering.

The challenge that the racial exclusivity of black consciousness posed for the nonracial inclusiveness of Burger's ideology is understood in the novel as part of a process, the necessity of change, history. Rosa admonishes herself for forgetting this when she is personally affronted by Zwelinzima's angry rejection. She recalls the political point of view of her father and the SACP:

> '*A war in South Africa will doubtless bring about enormous human suffering. It may also, in its initial stages, see a line-up in which the main antagonists fall broadly into racial camps, and this would add a further tragic dimension to the conflict. Indeed if a reasonable prospect existed of a powerful enough group among the Whites joining in the foreseeable future with those who stand for majority rule, the case for revolt would be less compelling.*' (*BD*, 329)

When Rosa can place Zwelinzima's response in the context of the historical process, she is free to commit herself to being one of the group of whites whose "stand for majority rule" would reduce the chance of war and its consequent enormous suffering.

Change, or the historical process, then, is inevitable. The course of such change, however, is charted by a vision of the future. Lionel Burger's vision was driven by the ideology of the Communist Party, but Rosa's is shaped more by her encounters with the human suffering and her wish to alleviate it in others. Despite her declared atheism, Gordimer grants credence in an interview to critic Conor Cruise O'Brien's view that redemption through suffering is a central motif in the novel, thus making it a profoundly religious book (*CNG*, 173–74). The novel is permeated with metaphors of suffering, and the process history (time and place) must contend with the transcendence of metaphor to convey this ever-present human condition. That Rosa knows suffering is inevitable is endorsed by Gordimer in an interview. She points out that Rosa learned in France from the frightened, disoriented old woman in the village street that "you get old, lonely, dotty. That you suffer. That Katya, running from political suffering, has simply postponed what is coming" (*CNG*, 174). Rosa decides to follow the example of her parents and their comrades; she suspends the personal—sex and emotion, which serve the self and the family—to commit to a cause outside herself.

Gordimer's close scrutiny of contemporary events, as well as her fusion of historical and political texts into the narrative of the novel, create what Clingman calls a textual collage, which faithfully reflects the radical consciousness of the times. He points out that Gordimer included quotes from a variety of sources: the pamphlet attributed to the Soweto Students Representative Council is a faithful reproduction of a pamphlet that appeared on the streets of Soweto during the revolt, and Duma Dhladhla's comment that black liberation cannot be divorced from black consciousness "because we cannot be conscious of ourselves and at the same time remain slaves" (*BD*, 164) is a quote from Steve Biko, who is quoting Hegel. In his speech from the dock, Lionel Burger echoes Bram Fischer, saying, just before sentence was passed on him in his trial: "What we as Communists black and white working in harmony with others who do not share our political philosophy have set our sights on is the national liberation of the African people, and thus the abolishment of discrimination and extension of political rights to all the peoples of this country. . . That alone has been our aim. . . . beyond . . . there are matters the future will settle" (*BD*, 26).

But the major written source for *Burger's Daughter*, according to Clingman, is an essay written by Joe Slovo, long-standing white communist and leader of the ANC's military wing, Umkhonto We Sizwe, titled "South Africa—no middle ground." It was first published in 1976, and it acknowledges the proud record of nonracialism of the SACP, the only party in the 1920s to incorporate blacks. Gordimer's own response to the Communist Party was somewhat mixed, but she has Rosa mouth a number of direct quotes from Slovo concerning the small group of radical whites and SACP ideology. Clingman notes two very obvious quotations taken from Slovo, who became minister of Housing in Mandela's ANC government in 1994, but died of cancer very shortly afterward:

> When Rosa talks of a small group of white revolutionaries who are supposed to have solved "the contradiction between black consciousness and class consciousness" (126), the phrase comes directly from Slovo. . . . Similarly, when she talks of the sixth underground conference of the SACP in 1962, at which Party ideology was finally evolved in the form of the thesis that "it is just as impossible to conceive of workers' power separated from national liberation as it is to conceive of true national liberation separated from the destruction of capitalism" (126), this account comes verbatim from Slovo. (Clingman, 186–87)

Using the quotations in their authentic form grants their sources the respect they deserve. It also presents opinions and documents banned in South Africa at the time, and gives voice to a historical and social presence otherwise silenced.

This faithful presentation of the ideology of others is tempered, however, by the humanism of personal suffering, and the body as a site of suffering is established right away as a central metaphor in the novel. The revolt of Rosa's own body frames the text: In the opening scene it counters instantly the third-person view of Rosa standing outside the prison with Rosa's first-person account of that moment when "real awareness is all focused in the lower part of my pelvis, in the leaden, dragging, wringing pain there" (BD, 15), and it moves toward closure after Zwelinzima's shocking phone call has sent her running to the bathroom where she "fell on her knees at the lavatory bowl, vomiting. The wine, the bits of sausage—she laid her head, gasping between spasms, on the porcelain rim, slime dripping from her mouth with tears of effort running from her nose" (BD, 323).

But the novel's most powerful metaphor of pain and suffering is the scene in the township when the donkey is beaten. It questions the possibility of ending any kind of suffering at all, and, in an oblique allusion to W. H. Auden's poem "Musée des Beaux Arts," it raises also the issue of the power of art to change anything. But while Auden's poem describes its observers of suffering as leisurely and disinterestedly turning away, Gordimer explains Rosa's turning away from suffering very differently. Rosa describes her response as "a sudden shift, a tumultuous upheaval, an uncontrollable displacement. . . . A shift that comes to me physically, as intestines violently stir and contract when some irritant throws a switch in the digestive tract" (*BD*, 196). The image of dislocated suffering, suffering distilled down to its essential agony, is encapsulated for Rosa in the donkey episode:

> I didn't see the whip. I saw the agony. Agony that came from some terrible centre seized within the group of donkey, cart, driver and people behind him. They made a single object that contracted against itself in the desperation of a hideous final energy. Not seeing the whip, I saw the infliction of pain broken away from the will that creates it; broken loose, a force existing of itself, ravishment without the ravisher, torture without the torturer, rampage, pure cruelty gone beyond control of the humans who have spent thousands of years devising it. The entire ingenuity from the thumbscrew and rack to electric shock, the infinite variety and gradation of suffering, by lash, by fear, by hunger, by solitary confinement. (*BD*, 208)

It is not this image of distilled pain that prompts Rosa to flee to Europe, however; it is rather her impotence before it. She is overwhelmed by her recognition of white culpability in the chain of suffering. Her inability to act without invoking the white authority, which creates black misery, paralyzes her, and she is unable to live in South Africa any longer. She admits:

> I could have put a stop to it, the misery; at that point I witnessed. . . . No one would have taken up a stone. I was safe from the whip. I could have stood between them and suffering—the suffering of a donkey. . . .
>   I drove on. I don't know at what point to intercede makes sense, for me. . . . I drove on because the horrible drunk was black, poor and brutalized. If somebody's going to be brought to account, I am accountable for him, to him, as he is for the donkey. (*BD*, 210)

The centrality of race and the body in *Burger's Daughter* gives Newman cause to read the novel as an interrogation that asks whether racism is a function of a political system like capitalism or whether it is a screen for more primary sexual insecurities, a product of sexual repression. Newman's discussion of the psychological and gender-related issues in the text balances more historically and politically deterministic readings. She notes that, like *The Conservationist,* a body again lies just below the surface of consciousness in this novel, only this time it's a white woman's body. Gordimer focuses, she believes, on the fantasies of the white subconscious in order to undermine their power (Newman, 69). In an analysis of the novel that relies on a variety of psychological theories of racism and colonialism with which she believes Gordimer was familiar, Newman traces Rosa's progress toward a personal and political autonomy that involves "coming to terms with the mythic masks which men have fastened over the female face . . . and correcting the errors of her own internal eye" (83).

Newman outlines the theories of Gordon Allport and Joel Kovel, who see racism as a product of sexual repression, and she discusses Octave Mannoni's theory, developed in *Prospero and Caliban,* which places more emphasis on the role of sexual fantasy in repression. Mannoni holds that the repressions of European men surface in the colonial situation, and that the roots of racism in a patriarchal system stem from the European male's rationalization of guilty incestuous feelings by projecting his own guilt onto black men. In *The Tempest,* Miranda is the only woman on the island, and Prospero justifies his hatred of Caliban by accusing him of attempted rape. Within the European psyche he identifies the conflicting needs of attachment and individualization, manifest in the infantile desire to revolt (against the parents) and—by projection of the child's unconscious images onto others—to dominate. Transferring troublesome and "dirty" sexual desires onto the "primitive" natives is easy because the more remote people are, the more easily they appear to attract our projections. The colonial lives happily among the natives to whom he grants no autonomous existence, using them only to reflect his "superior" self. In this respect, Mannoni notes the psychological importance of faraway princesses. The princess image, Newman warns, is one that Rosa almost assumes through her enchanted life in Europe and her guilty, though temporary, revolt against her father (70–71).

But a number of critics, particularly socialists, object to Mannoni's theories as an evasion of political problems, and Newman sees Gordimer's views on the psychology of racism aligning with those of Fanon, whose terminology she even adopts at key points (73). Fanon acknowledges that colonial man suffers from what Mannoni calls the Prospero complex, that is, the combination of unconscious neurotic tendencies of paternalism and of the racism that transfers the guilt of incestuous sexual feelings to a black man who is assumed to be "just waiting for the chance to jump on white women" (Fanon 1967, 107). But Fanon rejects Mannoni's lack of resolution, saying that "the collective unconscious is . . . the result of what I shall call the unreflected imposition of a culture" (Fanon 1967, 191), and he believes that unconscious neuroses can be made conscious and overcome. He holds: "It is just that over a series of long days and long nights the image of the biological-sexual-sensual-genital-nigger has imposed itself on you and you do not know how to get free of it. The *eye* is not merely a mirror, but a correcting mirror. The *eye* should make it possible for us to correct cultural errors" (Fanon 1967, 202). Unflinching self-scrutiny is the arduous path toward the genuine human love that Fanon (and Gordimer) believes is possible: "True, authentic love—wishing for others what one postulates for oneself, when that postulation unites the permanent values of human reality—entails the mobilization of psychic drives basically freed of unconscious conflicts" (Fanon 1967, 41). Fanon points out that "it is through the effort to recapture the self and to scrutinize the self, it is through the lasting tension of their freedom that men will be able to create the ideal conditions of existence for a human world" (Fanon 1967, 231).

In *Burger's Daughter*, Rosa painfully uncovers and confronts her unconscious prejudices and stereotypes through a process of self-scrutiny, and she learns to stand free in a world of autonomous beings. It was Rosa's ambivalence toward the body—created perhaps by her family's repression of her sexuality for political ends and indicated by her susceptibility to stereotype the "other" as exotic or, alternatively, as dirty and nasty—that led her, according to Newman, to disown her original attachments and replace them with surrogate brothers and mothers in a fantasy landscape. Newman notes that Rosa's memories of a meeting in a department store with the sensuous and beautiful Marisa Kgosana and of a bed-wetting episode with Baasie, whom she blamed for wetting the bed they shared as children, arise together to "suggest the twin racist strategies delineated by Kovel and Mannoni—the attempt to use blackness as a way to sensual liberation (Marisa), the attempt to blame 'dirty' actions on the black (Baasie)" (Newman, 74). But by the end of the novel Rosa's now open consciousness has defused these images, and Newman argues convincingly that "Gordimer employs the terms of the white racist subconscious in an attempt to free her art from Prospero's complex, and to direct it towards a world where 'You' is not a fantasy projection, but real" (74). Both Rosa and Gordimer can now affirmatively answer Fanon's rhetorical question: "Was my freedom not given to me then in order to build the world of the You?" (Fanon 1967, 232).

Gordimer's choice of a female protagonist who is the defecting daughter of an Afrikaner communist complicates the text's analysis of competing political and personal worlds in a number of ways. In Lionel's world, the private and the sensual is sacrificed for political ends. Rosa must pretend to be the beloved fiancée of detainee Noel de Witt in order to get messages to and from him for the movement. Her parents remain oblivious to the fact that she does, in fact, fall in love with Noel and must repress her feelings for him. Rosa is desexualized by the radical white community, which, in the beginning, sees her as a dutiful daughter and, at the end when she is back in South Africa, describes her as looking like "a little girl. . . . About fourteen" (BD, 360). Rosa's revolt against her father's world stems from her attraction to a world more intimate and sensual. Such a world proves dangerously seductive in all three of the incarnations Rosa encounters. Rosa fraternizes first with the obsessively self-absorbed world of Conrad, private and erotic, without politics or parental control. Second is the intimately seductive and powerful world of the State symbolized by Brandt Vermeulen, whose warm and comfortable intimacy belies the crudity of one of his otherwise tasteful and erotic artistic displays: "A life-size plastic female torso, divided down the middle into a blue and red side, with its vaginal labia placed horizontally across the outside of its pubis, like the lips of its mouth. The tip of a clitoris poked a tongue. The nipples were perspex, suggesting at once the hardness of tumescence and the ice of frigidity" (BD, 181–82). The third is the world of Rosa's love relationship with Bernard Chabalier of which the Bonnard paintings and the unicorn tapestry become the symbols.

Life with Bernard would perpetuate a world of fantasy that would pluck Rosa from her historical destiny and trap her out of time in an unreal place. As Rosa herself observes: "There's nothing more private and personal than the life of a mistress. . . . Bernard Chabalier's mistress isn't Lionel Burger's daughter; she's certainly not accountable to the Future, she can go off and do good works in Cameroun or contemplate the unicorn in the tapestry forest" (BD, 304). The Bonnard paintings—favorites of Bernard—exemplify an art untouched by time or history. He comments, "There was the growth of fascism, two wars—the Occupation—And for Bonnard it is as if nothing's happened" (BD, 286–87). His human subject "hasn't any existence any more than the leaves have . . . No past, no future . . . c'est un paradis invente" (BD, 287). Katya had prepared a room for a Rosa of her imagination:

> A big jar of lilac, scent of peaches furry in a bowl, dim mirrors, feminine
> bric-a-brac of bottles and brushes, a little screen of ruched taffeta for
> sociable intimacies, a long cane chair to read the poetry and elegant mag-
> azines in, a large low bed to bring a lover to. . . . Rosa Burger entered,
> going forward into possession by that image. Madame Bagnelli, smiling,
> coaxing, saw that her guest was a little drunk, like herself. (BD, 229–30)

The tapestry series titled "La Dame a le Licorne" that Bernard had so
wanted to show Rosa, seems to capture the essence of the life that
tempts her. But in an excellent discussion of the significance of the six
tapestries, Newman argues that Gordimer leaned on a contemporary
interpretation of renunciation—rather than celebration—of the pleasures of life, and so used the tapestries to encapsulate Rosa's ultimate
rejection of a pleasure-filled private life with Chabalier (81–83). The
tapestries use the medieval fantasy landscape of islands, flowers, mirrors
with a tame lion, a lovely lady, and a unicorn. Numbers one through five
depict the five senses, with the first being sight. In the first tapestry
Gordimer describes a lady holding a mirror in which a unicorn is
reflected, but then she merely lists the next four tapestries as depictions
of hearing, smell, taste, and touch. Her focus is on the sixth, the most
difficult to interpret, and it "shows the Lady before a sumptuous pavil-
ion or tent amusing herself with a box of jewels." The unicorn is

> holding aside with a hoof one of the flaps of the tent . . . . A legend is
> woven in gold around the canopy of the tent, *A mon seul desir.* . . . Such
> harmony and sensual peace in the age of the thumbscrew and dungeon
> that there it comes with its ivory spiral horn
>   there she sits gazing . . .
> Sits gazing, this creature that has never been. (BD, 340–41)

Newman explains that the lady is not receiving the necklace, but replacing it in the box. *A mon seul desir* ("by my own free will") suggests that
the sixth tapestry shows the woman exercising the free will to resist the
power and control of the senses. The necklace can be seen to renounce
the passions that may interfere with our ability to act morally. Previous
interpretations understood the tapestries as celebrating the senses, as
embodied in a beautiful woman, but now the sixth panel has corrected
the eye of the observer. The tapestries indicate that Rosa deliberately
chooses to abandon the sensual pleasures of life with Bernard, for it
seems he loves an image of Rosa to which she does not entirely corre-

spond: "Rosa Burger may become, like the lady, a gazer into a hand-held mirror which reflects back to her only an unreal and mythical creature, a woman who has only existed in the projections of others. In returning to South Africa, however, Rosa chooses not to be such an image, an object to be displayed and desired, a figure in an erotic or political iconography" (Newman, 83).

Like the lady replacing the necklace, Rosa resists the protective cocoon that Chabalier would cast around her. By refusing either to succumb to Chabalier's aesthetic fantasy world or to blindly follow her father's ideology, she rejects the paternalism (to which Bray and Rebecca fall prey in *A Guest of Honour*) so subtly embedded in her relationships with men. Instead, she courageously forges her own humanistically motivated path toward an unshakable and solitary political commitment. Europe remains a fantasy land for Rosa; South Africa is reality and home.

July's People

Gordimer's eighth novel, *July's People,* takes as its topic the apocalyptic event of a fractured nation in open and total revolution. It was the event most feared, most anticipated, almost willed, by South Africans and others around the world during the apartheid era. Would there be a bloodbath? But as she does with the topic of the interracial affair in *Occasion for Loving,* Gordimer deflects the obsessive and prurient fascination with sensation. She points the reader to the true concern of the novel: an unflinching analysis of white bourgeois South Africa, displaced and stripped of its context, that exposes the determining role economics plays in shaping and maintaining stable identities. It is the epigraph of the novel, drawn from Italian Marxist Antonio Gramsci, that shifts the focus from revolution—which is merely the setting—to the dilemma of the present: "The old is dying and the new cannot be born; in this interregnum there arises a great diversity of morbid symptoms." The context of revolution strips away the cardboard mask of bourgeois life to reveal the hollow emptiness behind it. While ironically invoking European literary traditions for greater resonance (Shakespeare's *The Tempest* comes to mind), the novel is decidedly African. It addresses a South African audience about a South African issue in a South African social and linguistic setting. The impressionistic style of the novel's narrative facilitates one of Gordimer's most powerful demonstrations of how the slightest nuance of intimate behavior and idiom is shaped and forged by the economic and political realities of one's situation. This novel—read more than any of her other novels in university programs across the world—is one of her most integrated and outstanding literary achievements.

At the time Gordimer was writing this novel, white South Africa was coming to terms with the lessons that black consciousness had dealt. The Soweto Revolt was over, and new ways were needed to continue the struggle. Political organizations were springing up everywhere: the black trade union movement was growing, and the ANC renewed its commitment to a nonracial South Africa. Government crackdowns remained vicious, yet civil disobedience and disregard for the regime were growing. Gordimer herself seemed to be searching for an avenue of action. In her search for a place as artist and citizen, she increases her battle against censorship and addresses her responsibility as an artist in helping to forge a single common culture of the future, for, as she says, "art is at the heart of liberation."[3] Her portrayal of the white children in *July's People* as the characters who readily adapt to African culture locates her faith for a common future beyond the present South African generation.

July's People tells the story of Maureen and Bam Smales and their family, who escape the burning, war-torn city for the rural African village of their domestic servant, July. At July's suggestion, Maureen and the three children—all huddled in Bam's *bakkie* (pickup truck)—are led by July with Bam at the wheel to July's family home, the home where July has spent his holiday from his job in the city each year. They find themselves accommodated in a hut, stripped of all but a handful of things from their suburban life in Johannesburg. In an Admirable Creighton reversal of roles, the Smales try at least to be good guests, but find that neither they nor July can escape the roles they have inhabited for so long. Without the power that their economic and material status conferred on them, the Smales' identities crumble and they soon become bitter strangers to one another. They cling pathetically to the symbols of power from their previous life—the car, the radio, the gun—each steadily usurped or lost to the African community. Bam, a mere shadow of the white master without his props, helps a bit around the village (he puts up a water tank) and takes care of the children. Maureen—prevented from helping the village women by July—is forced to reassess her past. The Smales children, on the other hand, make friends with the African children and quickly adapt to their new way of life, absorbing African customs and courtesies unconsciously. They represent the hope for the future. But it is the relationship between Maureen and July that dominates, spiraling out of control until they are locked in intimate psychological battle. At the end of the novel, when Maureen hears the throb of a helicopter engine as it lands in the veld beyond, she runs toward it, not knowing or caring which army will be at the controls.

July's People is Gordimer's first major venture into describing rural African life. Considering her view in 1980 that—because of apartheid—"there are areas of black experience that no white writer can write about" (*CNG,* 168), it was a particularly bold and successful move. She succeeds in demystifying and deromanticizing rural black culture, exposing the fissures in village life that differences in experience, generation, and gender create. The chief, young Daniel, who steals the gun, Martha, and July all serve to dramatize the complexity of the village community, dispelling any illusion of ideological homogeneity. The role of economics in structuring our sense of self, even our sexual identities and values, is graphically brought home by the dependence of Bam and Maureen's sex life on the luxury of the master bedroom, compared to July's situation, which dictates a standard of split loyalties (town lover and village wife) due to the realities of migrant labor. "The balance between desire and duty is—has to be—maintained quite differently in accordance with the differences on the lover's place in the economy."[4]

Maureen and July's relationship is defined by economics. In white South Africa's eyes, she is madam and he is "boy." The intense, unacknowledged intimacy of the madam/servant relationship is aggravated by white ignorance of and indifference to African culture, an indifference afforded by white economic status. In a country where domestic servants are overwhelmingly female, Gordimer deliberately shifts gender. That July is male intensifies the cultural collision in the novel, for he represents a patriarchal system in which women do not openly challenge their husband's decisions. When his wife, Martha, expresses her unease at the white family's presence, July—feeling his new power—dictates: "If I say go, they must go. If I say they can stay . . . so they stay" (*JP,* 82). Maureen, on the other hand, represents a class and culture in which women affect an independence while remaining comfortably supported by the white male economic structure. She is not used to playing a subservient role to men, particularly black men. When July commands that the whole family visit the chief after Maureen has told him only Bam will go, we are told: "She was unsteady with something that was not anger but a struggle: her inability to enter into a relation of subservience with him that she never had with Bam" (*JP,* 101).

July and Maureen are ordinary, peace-loving people who have maintained harmony within the white system—despite economic and cultural differences—by adhering to a set of patterns and roles when dealing with each other. Gordimer holds:

> All this role-playing that is done in a society like ours—sometimes the role is forced upon you. You fall into it. It's a kind of song and dance routine, and . . . my characters find themselves acting out these preconceived, ready-made roles. (*CNG,* 116)

July, who is forced to play the role of affable servant to survive, and Maureen, who enjoys the convenience of a servant, are fairly average South Africans. Neither has the makings of a martyr or a revolutionary hero. Maureen is not a Rosa Burger or a Helen Joseph; rather, she hearkens back to a possible adult version of Helen Shaw of *The Lying Days.* July is not a Baasie or a Biko; his predecessor is Jacobus of *The Conservationist.* Maureen assuages her conscience by joining various liberal organizations and by being a good madam; she takes care of July when he is ill and pays his fine when he is arrested. July preoccupies himself by playing Fahfee to make a few extra rand and by being a good "boy"; he takes care of the house and never steals from the liquor cabinet. Both are concerned with avoiding conflict to maintain their relative social and economic status: July must provide for his wife and clan in the village as well as for himself, and Maureen values the privilege of leisure that July's needs ensure.

The roles of gracious madam and good boy are so ingrained that they persist even in the rural village where they no longer apply. When Maureen sees July trying to fix the *bakkie*'s exhaust, she reaches for the stock response: "There is always something to say: the formula for the roadside breakdown.—What's the trouble?" (*JP,* 94). Later, hearing from Maureen about the heavy fighting in the city, July, too, has his ready response:

> For him, too, there had always been something to say: the servant's formula, attuned to catch the echo of the master's concern, to remove combat and conflict tactfully, fatalistically, in mission classroom phrases, to the neutrality of divine will.—My, my, my. What we can do. Is terrible, everybody coming very bad, killing . . . burning . . . Only God can help us. We can only hope everything will come back all right. (*JP,* 94–95)

In Johannesburg Maureen assumed that July's ineptness with mechanical things meant that his ego was vulnerable. She patronizingly protected him from Bam's criticism. In the village, July, still playing the thoughtful servant, brings two pink glass cups of tea for Bam and Maureen. The song and dance routine is, however, the proverbial vicious circle. Its polite evasions are designed to protect whites from the ugly reality of the economic system they support; blacks are trapped into participation. They are collaborators for the sake of economic survival and an uneasy peace.

Domestic familiarity has intimately attuned July and Maureen: they can interpret each other's slightest nuance of behavior. But despite this intimacy, Maureen knows little or nothing about July's background or culture. It is July who has had to make the cultural adaptations. Like Bismillah's dogs in *The Conservationist* that snarl at the gates even though they are no longer closed, Maureen remains blinkered within her sphere of "decency." She does not see in July's mechanical ineptitude the economic inequality that created it. Rather, she sees a childlike ego in need of protection. Such misperceptions—the blind veneers of tact that govern whites' relationships with blacks—have ill-equipped the Smales for the unknowns and tensions of the unthinkable situation in which they find themselves. They are runaways with nothing, hiding in their servant's *kraal*. Their social and cultural codes belong to the powerful world of the white man, and they are left helpless and inadequate in a culture and situation they cannot interpret. When July, who is slowly switching codes, sees the impotence of Maureen and Bam, he begins to shake free of his song and dance. He

> who had seen the white woman and the three children cowered on the floor of their vehicle, led the white face behind the wheel in his footsteps, his way the only one in a wilderness, was suddenly aware of something he had not known.—They can't do anything. Nothing to us anymore. (*JP*, 21)

When July feels his new power and Maureen and Bam must face that theirs is almost gone, no ready-made roles can cope with the deadly struggle that surfaces. July senses their resistance to his appropriation of the *bakkie* and the battle begins in earnest. Though they clash over only the *bakkie* and the gun, all technological objects—including the radio and helicopter—function as symbols of the transference of power. The *bakkie* and gun are Bam's, and he is—by extension—a symbol of the exploitative system that backs the Maureens of the apartheid world. But in the domestic sphere Maureen is executor of that power, and it is through her that July experiences it most directly. Dependent on the system, Maureen is effective only as long as the system holds. When Bam and the radio crumble and her support is gone, Maureen must fend for herself. The crisis of collapse coincides with the disappearance of the *bakkie*: "She was someone handling her being like an electrical appliance she has discovered can fling one apart at the wrong touch. Not fear, but knowledge that the shock, the drop beneath the feet, happens to the self alone, and can be avoided only alone" (*JP,* 41).

From this time in the novel, Maureen is symbolically linked with the solitariness of a cat. July's covetousness of the *bakkie* has alerted Maureen to a fundamental threat. She feels trapped, and her response is instinctively feline: tense, alert, independent, predatory, and cruel. July senses the battle. For 15 years July and Maureen have been locked together in a bizarre domestic intimacy, and their psyches have been shaped by the experience. Though apartheid's barriers limited some communication, they have been absorbing each other's "vibes"—as Gordimer put it—for years.[5] Like lovers, they instinctively know each other's vulnerabilities, weaknesses, and boundaries—where to touch to cause pain. With the restraints of the old system gone, they begin to use their intimate knowledge, not to maintain harmony, but as weapons of destruction.

The battle begins over the control of the car keys. When July explains his appropriation of the *bakkie* quite logically as a need to fetch supplies (he considerately brings new batteries for the radio—their only link with the outside world), Maureen taunts him with ploys, first to get the keys back, then with a show of returning the keys to him:

—Here are *your* keys.—
   For an instant his hands sketched the gesture of receiving and then were recalled to themselves and the thumb and fingers of his right hand simply hooked the bunch, with a jingle, from her fingers. (*JP,* 68–69; emphasis added)

The sarcasm of *your keys* is deflected by July's refusal to "receive" them, by the way he checks his ingrained dependence and subservience, simply taking them from her fingers. They square off and face one another:

He stood there, his stolidity an acceptance that he could not escape her, since she was alone, they were one-to-one; hers an insinuated understanding that she had not refused to come to him but wanted them to meet where no one else would judge them. The subtlety of it was nothing new. People in the relation they had been in are used to having to interpret what is never said, between them. (*JP,* 69)

But July states the unsaid this time; he tells the truth: "You don't like I must keep the keys. Isn't it. I can see all the time, you don't like that" (*JP,* 69). Maureen protests feebly that they always trusted July with their home and keys in Johannesburg, but July exposes the phoniness of that trust:

> —Myself, I'm not say you're not a good madam—but you don't say you trust for me.— It was a command. —You walk behind. You looking. You asking me I must take all your books out and clean while you are away. You frightened I'm not working enough for you? (*JP,* 70)

This truth—previously unrecognized, unadmitted—cuts Maureen to the quick and illustrates the hypocrisy of the white liberal. But July, angry and hurt himself, twists the knife. He calls himself "your boy who work for you," insisting on the validity of the term that denotes an economic relationship, while knowing Maureen's guilt-ridden aversion to the term. "The absurd 'boy' fell upon her in strokes neither appropriate nor to be dodged. Where had he picked up the weapon?" (*JP,* 70). Maureen retreats to the liberal refuge of individual friendship in an attempt to bridge all differences; she suggests they can pass the key back and forth as friends now. But July will acknowledge only the old economic relationship. He pushes the keys back at her, generating a vicious backlash from Maureen. Frustrated by his rejection, she angrily speaks the unspeakable:

> —If all you can think about is what happened back there, what about Ellen?—
>
> The name of his town woman fell appallingly between them, something neither should dare take up. . . . they had stepped across fifteen years of no-man's land, her words shoved them together, duellists who will feel each other's breath before they turn away to the regulation number of paces, or conspirators who will never escape what each knows of the other. (*JP,* 72)

In their second major clash, it is July who delivers the *coup de grâce.* Maureen is frustrated and surprised when July insists that she not join the African women's work parties collecting wild spinach, especially since she imagines (probably erroneously) that she is beginning to communicate with them. Hitting below the belt, she insinuates in a snide comment that July is afraid she will tell his wife, Martha, about his town lover, Ellen. But aware of Maureen's greatest fear, July is ready with his weapon:

But he silenced her: —Yesterday night someone's come.—

The whip cracked over her head. Deep breaths slowly pumped her chest; she was aware of the pulse showing in her small, flat, left breast under the T-shirt: fear in there. —Police? Who come?— He left her to it a moment. —Someone from the chief. (*JP,* 100)

Maureen's barb has earned her this little torture, but July's objection to her work in the fields is not so easy to understand. Though his story is told, July's motives are never given in the novel. July's identity as an urban black has granted him a certain status among the villagers, but it simultaneously severs him from village culture. His big city status is derived from Bam and Maureen's status, and Maureen's attempts to assist on the settlement only degrade him. He prevents her also from doing her laundry and Bam from collecting wood, all traditionally women's work, which is considered inferior. Bam's technological know-how with the water tank and the gun, on the other hand, enhances July's status in the eyes of his people. Bam is displayed to friends at the beer party where he must drink from a mug, rather than a clay pot like the locals, while July strides about "declaiming proprietarily an anecdote that obviously referred to this man who had been his employer, the guest and stranger" (*JP,* 35).

The Smales are blind to their cultural transgressions, and consequently July's hope that they may add to his prestige backfires. His wife and mother are not impressed by them; this is not how the all-powerful whites should be. The Smales become a complication and a burden, and Martha suggests that July could do very well without them. After the fighting is over, she naïvely tells July, he "could have a shop here, sell soap and matches, sugar . . . And now you can drive. For yourself" (*JP,* 135). But July, too, is adrift from his culture. His authority in the village has derived from his ability to provide money, and the Smales are his source of money. To be rid of them is to be—ironically—rid of his source of authority in the village. Notably, during the Gumba-Gumba festivities, July retreats to the roofless old hut where the *bakkie* is hidden. The broken hut, symbolic of July's break with his traditional past, protects the vehicle, a symbol of July's connection with his urban past and his aspirations for the future.

Here Maureen seeks July out to challenge him about the theft of the gun. July, who smells her cold cat smell, resists the burden of responsibility for recovering the gun. Maureen's authority, Bam, is helpless, and July, her next hope for support, refuses to shoulder her problem. Impotence drives Maureen to hurt and destroy. She accuses July of stealing items from her house. In a scene that is indisputably the most powerful in the novel, he bursts out at her in his own language. It is here that she finally grasps his absolute rejection of her:

> She understood although she knew no word. Understood everything: what he had had to be, how she had covered up to herself for him, in order for him to be her idea of him. But for himself—to be intelligent, honest, dignified for *her* was nothing; his measure as a man was taken elsewhere and by others. She was not his mother, his wife, his sister, his friend, his people. (*JP,* 152)

July is "done" with Maureen, and she knows it. He has made his choice. Maureen at last understands and faces this indictment. But she is not done with him yet. If she must face the truth, then so must he:

> She told him the truth, which is always disloyal. —You'll profit by others fighting. Steal a bakkie. You want that, now. You don't know what might have happened to Ellen. She washed your clothes and slept with you. You want the bakkie, to drive around like a gangster, imagining yourself a *big man,* important, until you don't have any money for petrol, there isn't any petrol to buy, then it'll lie there, July, under the trees, in this place among the old huts, and it'll fall to pieces while the children play in it. Useless. Another wreck like all the others. Another bit of rubbish. (*JP,* 153)

Their relationship is destroyed by the truth. Maureen is left in a vacuum, her identity shattered. All social codes from which she previously drew her sense of self are gone. July, who was the last vestige of the social context from which Maureen's identity was drawn, turns into a stranger who discounts her absolutely. July, too, is alienated. He becomes a nuisance to Martha, who—used to living without him most of the year—needs his income more than his presence. He is lured by the white man's goodies and power, yet—due to past inequities—he is in no way able to take on their power. But at least July—with roots in African culture and land—has hope of regenerating his African identity. Maureen is cast totally adrift.

In the final scene, when a helicopter arrives, Maureen runs toward it. Critics have variously interpreted the significance of her flight. For Clingman and other critics, this is her first authentic choice. Maureen accepts that she is not one of July's people, and she confronts her collusion with the apartheid system without regard for the consequences. She cannot know what fate awaits her: white government forces that may take her to relative safety, or black revolutionary forces that may capture or kill her. She is prepared to face the consequences of her existence. In this final scene, Maureen's crossing of the river is described in images of rebirth and balance. Her sprint from the village does not appear to recall the delirium of the earlier flight from Johannesburg in the *bakkie*, as some critics suggest. Maureen recognizes she has no place in the black settlement. She carefully maintains her balance in the river by imitating the African women she has seen crossing, pulling herself to safety by the life-giving roots of the huge fig tree, "landmark of the bank she has never crossed to before" (*JP*, 160). This river is her Rubicon, and once crossed, "she runs; trusting herself with all the suppressed trust of a life-time" (*JP*, 160). Gordimer states in an interview:

> We whites have been brought up on so many lies; we've been led up the garden path, or sold down the river by our ancestors in South Africa. In other words, whites have developed a totally unreal idea of how they ought to live, of their right to go on living in that country. Consequently, they must undergo a long process of shedding illusions in order to fully understand the basis for staying in South Africa. Unfortunately, there aren't enough people who have the will to attempt this. It's hard to peel yourself like an onion, without producing a lot of tears in the process. (Boyers, 28)

It is July and Maureen who have peeled each other like onions, shedding illusions. But for Maureen the truth has come too late.

While the authenticity of Maureen's act may hold redemptive significance for her personally, her fate (and the fate of whites like her) is of no consequence to the South Africa of the future. Like Mehring of *The Conservationist,* whether she survives or not is irrelevant to the story of a new nation. Hope for a common future lies in a time of greater equity. It is to this hope that Gordimer turns in her next novel.

Chapter Five

Apprentices of Freedom:
A Sport of Nature, My Son's Story,
and *None to Accompany Me*

In 1988, Stephen Clingman stated of Gordimer's artistic evolution: "Beyond division and dichotomy hers is a quest for wholeness, the vision of which imaginative writing can offer, and which remains a political ideal" (*EG,* 8). But as early as 1981, when the ideas for *A Sport of Nature* must have been germinating, Gordimer herself spoke of a new kind of literature which would stake her place as a white artist in "a real indigenous culture of the future by claiming that place in the implicit nature of the artist as an agent of change."[1] She described South African art as "didactic, apocalyptic, self-pitying, self-accusatory." Like James Joyce, she asserted that the South African artist should seek to escape the shackles of the nightmarish historical moment, for "when we posit a post-apartheid art—and we must right now—then we switch off the awful dynamism of disintegration and disaster" (Apprentices, iv). *A Sport of Nature* is Gordimer's fictional call to this duty.

A Sport of Nature

A Sport of Nature is the most historically and geographically panoramic of Gordimer's work. It can also be considered the most ambitious of her novels. Spanning not only the full period of the history and politics of the National Party's apartheid regime, it also covers the entire period of Gordimer's artistic publishing career, from the late 1940s to its publication in 1987, and then expands into the future. While ostensibly about revolution, *A Sport of Nature's* panoramic overview of the armed struggle serves more as a springboard into the future. The novel reflects Gordimer's astute and reflexive historical consciousness, and it asserts her call for artists to shape historical conditions by positing a new, postapartheid art. It can be read as Gordimer's personal and artistic refusal to submit to the logic of oppositional forces in South African history. Attempting to shift art—via fiction and the imagination—beyond the colonizing bounds of contemporary history and into the future, Gordimer changes the focus from the morbid present to the creative possibilities of a postapartheid South Africa. "Fiction," Gordimer has said, "is a way of exploring possibilities present but undreamt of in the living of a single life" (*EG,* 2). Remaining resolute in her commitment to act on history's course herself, Gordimer is still aware that her urge to persuade artists to break out of the confines of history into a creative and imaginative future is itself ironically driven by historical circumstance.

Gordimer's need to shake art free from historical control accounts for the fairy-tale quality of the story. This quality is deliberate and signals the need to read the novel metaphorically. In a shift away from issues of class and toward race (a shift that troubles some critics), Gordimer tells the story of a young white teenager. She turns the colonial adventure novel on its head by using a female protagonist. A female bildungsroman, *A Sport of Nature* follows the adventures and coming of age of Hillela Capran, who has been deserted at age four by her mother for a Portuguese lover. After being expelled from her Rhodesian boarding school for befriending a "coloured" youth, Hillela is again abandoned, this time by her ineffectual father, to the care of her two upper-middle-class Jewish aunts (one a rich materialist, the other a liberal) in Johannesburg. When caught sleeping with her cousin, Sasha, she is ousted from the sanctuary of her liberal aunt's home, and she moves through a series of adventures, sexual and otherwise. She works at a number of odd jobs and explores various relationships—one of which leads her to flee with a phony white activist into independent Tanzania. When he, too, abandons her, she is "rescued" by South African revolutionaries working in exile, a fate that propels her eventually into marriage and motherhood with a black South African revolutionary organizer, Whaila Kgomani. After her perfect "rainbow" marriage is shattered by his brutal assassination, Hillela learns the need for commitment to the liberation cause for which she now works untiringly. As a result of her work, she meets and almost marries a white American, Brad, whom she passes up finally for marriage to a black African general—soon to be successful president— of an unidentified independent African country. The general ultimately becomes president of the Organization for African Unity (OAU), and he and Hillela preside happily over the independence ceremonies celebrating the new nation of South Africa.

Unlike a one-dimensional fairy tale, *A Sport of Nature's* innovative structure instantly complicates the narrative. Written as a kind of biog-

narration

raphy, the mysterious narrator ostensibly sets out to recover the "true" Hillela. This recovery of the "truth" is deliberately subverted by the text's biographical frame, for the accounts obtained about Hillela from a variety of sources are contradictory and incomplete; these accounts are clearly colored by each reporter's ideology and place in time. The structure frustrates the reader's attempt to "know" Hillela, for, as the narrator notes: "Everyone is familiar with memories others claim to have about oneself that have nothing to do with oneself. In the lives of the greatest—there are such lacunae—Christ and Shakespeare disappear from and then appear in the chronicles that documentation and human memory provide."[2] Intertextually rich, the novel incorporates historical figures like Mandela, Nkomo, Luthuli, and cameo appearances of fictional characters like Gordimer's own Rosa Burger from *Burger's Daughter.*

Hillela poses special problems for conventional readers. She seems touched by little; she is easy and adaptable, with a sensuality and amorality that puzzles and even threatens many readers (critics refer to her as "slippery," a "malleable waif," an "engaging opportunist," and an "innocent"). But the confusion is deliberate, for the structural frame of pseudobiography resists knowing or fixing Hillela. Unlike a Maureen Smales, whose identity and values have been firmly set according to her predictable social circumstances, Hillela has known only instability and change. She has been released from the social codes that fix the identity of a Maureen, and granted a freedom without which the transitions she makes would be impossible. It is this freedom that makes Hillela a " 'sport of nature': a plant, animal, etc., which exhibits abnormal variation from the parent stock or type . . . A spontaneous mutation; a new variety produced in this way."[3] But the reader cannot follow her shifts and changes without feeling some challenge, and no sooner do we judge Hillela than we realize we have allied ourselves with another less than admirable character in the novel: hypocritical aunt Pauline, sexist Arnold, a pretentious English couple, or bitter Brad. While the text evades a "rational" moral judgment of Hillela, it nevertheless urges us to feel Hillela's engaging energy via scenes of genuine sensual love. By withstanding the inclination to judge and by reading her metaphorically instead, the reader comes closer to comprehending the dynamic of creative energy that will generate a postapartheid art. Just as Hillela is a character in the text called a novel, so is the artist a character in the text called history. The metaphorical resonance set up by this reading unlocks the real significance of Hillela, who thus, as in all good fiction, ceases to be merely entertaining. Clues to her metaphorical dimension are found in her name changes throughout the novel: She rejects the name Kim, as she does the colonial past; she assumes Hillela while—like Rabbi Hillel who was president of the Sanhedrin at the time of Christ—she searches for a place and an identity; and her general bestows on her the African name Chiemeka (Igbo for "God has done very well") when she finds a stable home in Africa.

The action of history is evident both on Hillela as a metaphor for the white artist and on Gordimer, who has said: "I have to offer you myself as my most closely observed specimen" (*EG*, 264). Like Gordimer, Hillela's consciousness is transformed rather late in life. Both experience "a series of transgressions, an overstepping of successive boundaries" (*EG*, 4). In Gordimer's case, the first transgression was reading, the second, writing. In Hillela's case, the first was breaking the color bar (her friendship with a Coloured youth), the second was incest (sleeping with her cousin Sasha). These activities send them both "falling through the surface of South African life" (*EG*, 26), shifting them beyond the boundaries of conventional white South African culture. Granted outsider status essential for their transformation, they begin an inexorable move toward an African perspective. Hillela's move is predicted early by such signs as her curly black hair, which, as some Africans do, she straightened at one time; her affectionate naturalness with the servants, Jethro and Betty; her partying in the Coloured townships of Fordsburg and Pageview; and, ironically, her exposure to black opinions through her liberal aunt, Pauline. Hillela's growth through her life's experiences echoes the ideological shifts in Gordimer's novels. Hillela first valorizes the personal in her interracial marriage to Whaila, but rejects individual humanism after his assassination. She learns that personal love "can't be got away with"; it isn't enough. "The only love that counts is owed to them" (*SN*, 232). In her political work after Whaila's death, Hillela enacts Gordimer's search for a committed supportive role and place for whites in the transfer of power from white to black hands. Hillela's second African marriage, to the president of the OAU, conjures Gordimer's pan-African vision to which she sees the new nation of South Africa belonging. It also reflects Gordimer's conviction that through alignment with revolutionary forces the artist has a role to play in building a new nation. Gordimer has said that the white writer "has to find a way to reconcile the irreconcilable within himself, establish a relation to the culture of a new kind of posited community, non-racial but conceived with and led by blacks" (*EG*, 278). She is determined to "find [her] place in 'history' "(*EG*, 278).

After exploring the breakdown of communication in *July's People,* in *A Sport of Nature* Gordimer seeks a restorative language, and to find it she relies on the metaphorical language of art. Metaphor, Daniel Schwarz notes, is by definition "synchronic and knows no boundaries . . . for metaphor brings into existence something that is absent simply by declaring its presence."[4] Quoting Derrida, Schwarz notes also that "logic is only slavery within the bounds of language. Language has within it, however, an illogical element, the metaphor. Its principle force brings about an identification of the non-identical; it is thus an operation of the imagination. It is on this that the existence of concepts, forms, etc., rests" (Schwarz, 14). Operating imaginatively, the artist can create new forms, new visions through metaphor, a language all artists and readers can share. Metaphor escapes the logic of time and space, the logic of history; it is the language of utopian ideas. As Sasha—Hillela's cousin and the only white character who understands her—says when speaking of South Africa's problems:

> Instinct is utopian. Emotion is utopian . . . It's all got to come down, mother. Without utopia—the idea of utopia—there's a failure of imagination—and that's a failure to know how to go on living. It will take another kind of being to stay on, here. A new white person. Not us. The chance is a wild chance—like falling in love. (*SN,* 187)

The wild chance of which Sasha speaks is the sport of nature, a unique individual reproduced spontaneously from conventional stock. Hillela, our sport of nature, is portrayed as a highly sensual and sexual being. The language of the body is her form of communication, as universally communicative as metaphor. It is through her sexuality that Hillela gains political awareness, most particularly through her interracial marriage to Whaila. This relationship raises the perennial theme of interracial sexuality in the novel, a theme that has permeated white South African writing since the earliest publications. Just as the enduring theme of attitudes toward the land in *The Conservationist* resonates ironically with Olive Schreiner's *Story of an African Farm,* so Gordimer intends *A Sport of Nature* to resonate ironically with the work of another South African writer, Sarah Gertrude Millin, who has written quite differently about interracial sex. Preaching racial purity in the early 1900s, Millin espoused that those who deny having "colour consciousness are, biologically speaking, sports." She claimed that color consciousness is a "profound feeling (call it instinct or call it acquired prejudice)" that can only be overcome by another biological force, such as sexual desire.[5] Gordimer ironically inverts the negative value Millin places on color consciousness and makes it desirable. She portrays Hillela's color consciousness as one that delights in difference and that unites with her sensuality to brand her as a sport of nature. The old colonial attitudes are debunked in this ironic comparison, and Hillela is the only white person in the novel who is fully integrated into the African community.

For critics, however, the most controversial aspect of the novel remains Hillela's open and uninhibited sexuality. Set outside the boundaries of South Africa, the interracial relationship between Hillela and Whaila differs markedly from that of Gideon and Ann in *Occasion for Loving;* it is freed from the constraints of apartheid's legal discourse on race and sexuality:

> The laws that have determined the course of life for them are made of skin and hair, the relative thickness and thinness of lips and the relative height of the bridge of the nose. . . . The laws made of skin and hair fill the statute books in Pretoria; their gaudy savagery paints the bodies of Afrikaner diplomats under three-piece American suits and Italian silk ties. The stinking fetish made of contrasting bits of skin and hair, the scalping of millions of lives, dangles on the cross in place of Christ. Skin and hair. It has mattered more than anything else in the world. (*SN,* 177)

The suspension from apartheid's interference grants the relationship a freedom that is reflected in the taboo-breaking description of the openness and sensuality between the couple:

> [Hillela] never tires of looking at his hands.—Not wearing anything. They're you. And they're not black, they're all the flesh colours. D'you know, in shops—and in books!—"flesh colour" is European's colour! Not the colour of any other flesh. Nothing else! Look at your nails, they're pinkish-mauve because underneath them the skin's pink. And (turning the palm) here the colour's like the inside of one of those big shells they sell on Tamarisk. And this—the lovely, silky black skin I can slide up and down (his penis in her hand), when the tip comes out, it's also sort of amber-pink. There's always a lot of sniggering about the size of a black man's thing, but no one's ever said they weren't entirely black. (*SN,* 178)

It is the first time in Gordimer's fiction that an interracial relationship moves beyond the bounds of apartheid, both figuratively and literally. But by eroticizing Hillela's sexuality, by impassioning her lovemaking with Whaila, and by expressing her unabashed curiosity and wonder over intimate racial differences, Gordimer has unleashed a flurry of agitation among critics and characters. Hillela is at once a "natural mistress," "an innocent"; she is "manipulative" and "her field is men." Since there has been no category, no discourse, in South Africa for this kind of loving interracial relationship, it remains deeply resisted. *A Sport of Nature* challenges the reader to recognize racial differences as positive and interesting, as we do differences in hair and eye color, rather than to affect color-blindness. Reading difference individually and quite naturally as part of the fascinating diversity of our world resists the negative power of racist discourse and provides the reader with a tantalizing glimpse of a culture that celebrates difference.

But as Gordimer has shown in all her work, the politics of sex and power in South Africa are inextricably intertwined. Through apartheid, then, the body becomes enormously significant. She speaks of

> a particular connection between sexuality, sensuality, and politics inside South Africa. Because, after all, what is apartheid about? It's about the body. It's about black skin, and it's about woolly hair instead of straight long blond hair . . . The whole legal structure is based on the physical, so the body becomes supremely important. (*CNG,* 304)

Sex, therefore, becomes the intersection, a disputed territory, of the public and the private. Gordimer's use of sexuality both as a concept and as a device in her work is clear in her earlier fiction. She has retained the right, as Dorothy Driver puts it, "for women . . . to be sexually attractive and vital beings, without being therefore classified as 'merely' feminine."[6] She recognizes that sexual communion often provides for women an entree into "the life under the surface of things," into the world with political ramifications. When Gordimer explains that "having the revolutionary temperament, the daring, usually goes along with very sexually attractive personalities, strong sexuality in both men and women" (*CNG,* 278), she seems to be saying that sexual and revolutionary energy rise from the same site. She refers to her own induction into the world via sexuality, calling it her "Rapunzel's hair" (*CNG,* 153). Hillela is Gordimer's most striking fictional equivalent here, a figure Gordimer admitted would probably "annoy some feminist circles very much" (*CNG,* 293). Yet despite views on sexuality that may make feminists bristle, Gordimer demonstrates that in South Africa the life of the body makes sex a political act, which frees her use of sex in fiction, both literally and metaphorically, for political ends.

Not exactly — still patriarchal

Read metaphorically, then, *A Sport of Nature* becomes Gordimer's imaging of a new kind of culture based on holistic politics that include the politics of the body; it is the artist's attempt to make whole the disintegrated consciousness of apartheid, to create a new integrated African consciousness. As Reuel, Hillela's second husband, says: "It's all part of my African-made—work, lovemaking, religion, politics, economics. We've taken all the things the world keeps in compartments, boxes, and brought them together. A new combination, that's us. That's why the world doesn't understand" (*SN, 266*). But the idealism of Gordimer's vision is complicated by an ironic tone that determinedly finds its way into the novel; it disrupts coherence and spawns competing interpretations. Reuel, for example, is described with larger-than-life exaggeration that hints uncomfortably of an undercutting irony: "The commanding shine that was always on his full face and majestic jowl used the dim theatrical lighting of the bar as a star performer attracts the following beam of a spotlight" (*SN, 265*).

Gordimer has commented on the tension between what she calls ironic writing and inspirational writing, and she admits that irony has often been her method. "I find irony very attractive in other writers," she claims, "and I find life full of irony, my own life and everybody else's" (*CNG, 172*). She sees irony as a corrective, a rein, to the inspirational or the ideal in a work, and it is perhaps an irresistible overcorrection—too hard a tug on the ironic reins—that undercuts the inspirational vision toward which *A Sport of Nature* seems to strive. Irony abounds in this novel. Whites who remain in South Africa after liberation are materialist Olga's two sons, an international banker, and a wine connoisseur. They are part of the neocolonial stronghold with whom Hillela's husband and other politicians must contend. Sasha, whose activism landed him in jail, is, sadly, absent at liberation. And Hillela's daughter, Nomzamo, named for Winnie Mandela, has been co-opted by western commercialism to model as "Nomo" for the covers of glossy magazines. If metaphor is the language of utopia, irony is designed to deflate. Equivocating between earnestness and irony, between metaphor and reality, between sexuality and revolution, between utopia and corruption, between socialism and neocolonialism, the novel struggles for coherence. Critic Richard Peck concludes that Gordimer, "as if uncertain what to think, . . . so distances herself from the new [revolutionary] approach that it is not clear whether she has endorsed it or condemned it";[7] and Dominic Head points out that the question of interpretation "is a central problematic for the novel."[8] Newman comments on what she calls "a choice between fervor and irony" (96), claiming that Gordimer recognized irony as the price for aiming high. The reportorial style of the novel, Newman believes, lends it a mock-historical tone, "implying that only time will tell whether 'mock' or 'historical' should be the key emphasis" (96).

Newman also examines, in particular detail, the mythical elements of the novel, indicating the power of mythical symbols as carriers of political change. She traces Hillela—revolutionary heroine or sexual adventuress—through her various fairy-tale incarnations of Sleeping Beauty (SN, 138), Cinderella (SN, 159), hetaira from *Arabian Nights* (SN, 148), and Goldilocks (SN, 155). Newman also explains the significance of the African myth of Qamata, the supreme Xhosa god, referred to in the novel when Hillela's journalist boyfriend, Rey, is questioning a group of black activists (SN, 115–16). Qamata was linked to Poqo ("alone" in Xhosa) in November 1967 through the testimony of an activist who claimed to have joined Poqo and its "sort of church Qamata" (Newman, 97). Poqo was a black organization (loosely affiliated with the PAC) associated with revolts in the Transkei in the 1950s and 1960s; its advocacy of violence against whites and reports of oaths taken by members, conjured for some whites parallels to Mau Mau in Kenya. Qamata was rumored to be an "African god . . . that can chase away the god of submission, the Christian god who says 'thou shalt not kill', and makes killing a sacrifice for freedom" (Newman, 116). But Newman points out that Gordimer also introduces a note of ambivalence to the positive power of myth by linking Qamata to a nineteenth-century Xhosa revolt that ended in disaster for the Xhosa people. An earlier prophet had foretold that the ancestors would rise out of the sea to sweep the whites away, so to propitiate the ancestors the people had slaughtered their cattle. When no resurrection took place, the people turned on each other. Whaila is repeatedly associated with the gods—"the disguised god from the sea" (SN, 198) and the "obsidian god from the waves" (SN, 216), but he is also linked to the nineteenth-century disaster by his emergence from the sea. This ambivalence is furthered by the invocation of the real-life African hero, Nkrumah. Nkrumah had developed the deep-sea harbor at Tema, described in the novel as holding "half-circled the power of the sea" (SN, 193). Despite his formative role in advancing black economic and political power in Africa suggested so evocatively in this image, Nkrumah was destroyed by the very people who declared him a god. Through undercutting irony, Gordimer destabilizes power, exposing its capricious and fickle nature, and foreshadows Whaila's untimely demise.

But not all critics read the novel ironically. Acknowledging that *A Sport of Nature* has "puzzled and perturbed its readers perhaps more than any other of Gordimer's works since the 1950s" (Wade, 124), Michael Wade's irony-free comments deserve some attention. Seeing the need to revise the perception of self and other as central to the novel, Wade draws on critic John Cooke's identification of family and childhood as the most significant experiences shaping Gordimer's work. Wade holds that Gordimer's own repressed Jewishness and her problematic relationship with her mother have not been adequately worked out until this novel. He believes that by freeing Hillela of the "massively repressive figure of the mother," Gordimer "reinscribes her own childhood and adolescence in terms of desire" (Wade, 126). He finds that Hillela's growing up "is described, relentlessly as Jewish" (Wade, 127), a focus noted as remarkable after such a long and surprising absence of the Jewish theme. This focus suggests—in Wade's view—the liberation of an area of repression in Gordimer's psychic organization, freeing her to prepare "the way for a radically new treatment of marriage" (127). In both of Hillela's marriages, the fulfilling quality of the marriage bond is presented as liberating. Wade sees the parameters of change in *A Sport of Nature* as "the free woman, independent of the landscape but acknowledging some kind of meaning in her origin; the transcendent marriage; the successful use of power; and realization of the most cherished telos, the liberation of South Africa" (Wade, 128). Hillela's pledge to dedicate her life to "looking for ways to free Whaila" (*SN*, 249)—now a symbol of the black South Africans—becomes for Wade "an act of perception which moves reflexively from Hillela, the white girl, to the other, the black man, and back to herself." Wade concludes that "what Gordimer brings to consciousness is the black component in white identity" (128–29).

Similarly, critic David Ward sees *A Sport of Nature* as "answering to the way in which black politics have re-formed white" (Ward, 134). He suggests that while *Burger's Daughter* addresses the problems posed by the black consciousness movement, *A Sport of Nature* responds by imagining a new and complementary way for whites to find their place in the ever-evolving present. Rosa Burger and Sasha follow the effective, but well-worn, tradition of resistance; Hillela, however, becomes a newly imagined route to an emerging freedom only now possible by the progression of history. Hillela's deepening integration into the life of black Africa fits Steve Biko's definition of integration: "Free participation by all members of a society, catering for the full expression of the self"

From chronicle to prophecy

rather than the old "breakthrough into white society by blacks" (Ward, 133). Ward notes that Gordimer's fiction "steadily moves away from chronicle, with its dependence on actual historical event, to prophecy, the attempt to capture and direct a future. A leap of imagination begins to border upon dabbling in magic" (Ward, 134).

Whether this leap is large enough, whether its magic works, or whether through undercutting irony or other ambiguities it falls short of its transformative goal, is the issue that preoccupies critics. As ambitious in its scope and its vision as the utopian world it projects, the novel succeeds in its shortfall. For as Sasha notes: "Utopia is unattainable; without aiming for it—taking a chance!—you can never hope even to fall far short of it" (*SN*, 187). The South African 1994 elections and independence celebrations remain as testimony to a society's transformative capabilities.

My Son's Story — *feminist novel?*

Gordimer's tenth novel, *My Son's Story,* represents a substantive shift in focus. While *A Sport of Nature* centered on race, this novel wrestles with issues of gender in the building of a new nation. It represents a shift from Gordimer's earlier view that only after the race struggle is won may the feminist battle be fought. It endorses instead the view of women like Mamphela Ramphele, the current principal of the University of Cape Town, who have long held a socialist feminist view that "key oppressions of sex, race and class are interrelated and the struggles against them must be coordinated."[9] Critics like Dorothy Driver and Karen Lazar hold that strong and consistent feminist concerns are embedded in all of Gordimer's work. In *My Son's Story* these concerns are central, making it Gordimer's first unequivocally feminist novel.

Gordimer's history on the issue of feminism is instructive. She has consistently denied that her work is feminist. A feminist novel, she holds, is one "conceived with the idea of proving something about women" (*CNG*, 297). She says she is a writer who happens to be a woman, not a "woman writer," that is, "somebody who is setting out to make a point about being a woman" (*CNG*, 278). She has in the past called feminist issues "piffling" and has asserted that feminism has no role to play in South African politics (*CNG*, 203). But critics have identified ambiguities and contradictions in her work which challenge her stance on feminism. Sheila Roberts states that in her fiction Gordimer has "by-passed the decades of the feminist movement's greatest literary activity, and has since the fifties established female protagonists whose lives must be taken seriously."[10] Dorothy Driver comments that throughout her fiction Gordimer

> makes enough statements for us to acknowledge her interest in the debased status of women in society, and her recent admission [1981] that she has become "much more radical" both "as a woman and a citizen" . . . authorizes us not simply to look for a recent development of feminist thought but to doubt that this feminist impulse has ever been absent. (Driver, 184)

agree or not?

NG is male-identified.

2 imp

Karen Lazar claims that it has been Gordimer's ignorance of feminism and its various strands that account for her rejection of it. She reveals that in a 1988 interview Gordimer acknowledged learning about a "harder, thinking feminism" that sees itself as "part of the whole issue of human rights, and understands very well that black women have certain problems that no white female has."[11]

feminism

There is no question that feminism in South Africa is complicated by the politics of race, sexuality, and cultural discourse. Gordimer has based her view that the struggle against racism is primary in South Africa on her belief that racism is stronger than sexism. White women, she asserts, have far more in common with white men than with black women, while black women identify not with their white sisters but with the oppression that black men suffer. She severely indicts white women for their complicity in the white system, claiming that despite their uneasiness about black conditions, they too often take shelter in their bourgeois marriages, either for fear of losing their privileges like Maureen Smales in *July's People* or after warnings from their husbands about "getting involved" like Flora Donaldson in *Burger's Daughter* (*CNG*, 166). But this critique can be read as a feminist summons, a call for white women to come out and fight against the white patriarchy for racial equality in South Africa (like Hannah does in *My Son's Story*); for, as we have seen, Gordimer's novels often have at their center the issue of a female protagonist's growth in social consciousness and responsibility. Susan Gardner notes that Gordimer is to be commended by feminists for illustrating

Fem NG

> the ways in which white women participate and benefit by racial oppression, for losing that Eurocentric vision against which black feminists like Gloria Joseph rail, for insisting, not on women's passivity, but on their responsibilities.[12]

imp

Driver explains that Gordimer "asserts the metaphorical relation between sexism and racism but makes the apparent common ground dependency rather than oppression" (Driver, 196), a stance that allows her to be less sympathetic toward white women.

The complications that race and sexuality bring to feminism in South Africa have been eloquently commented on by critics, but the role that cultural discourse plays deserves greater attention. Clifford Geertz and Michel Foucault both assert that language (among other signifying systems) does not simply reflect thought or experience, but rather culturally produces or creates, as it were, our social and emotional experiences. Foucault defines discourse as "those practices that systematically form the objects of which they speak."[13] Analysis of discourse, as Foucault sees it, must look at more than speech and recognize the local, contradictory, and fragmentary nature of discourses, and it must insist that discourses be understood in relation not just to social life, but to power.[14] The multitude and flux of cultures or subcultures based on race, ethnicity, class, or gender in South Africa—each with their own discourse that may or may not challenge the dominant discourse—result in a complex and confusing society with no cultural unanimity. Gordimer's recognition of conflicting discourses among women, for example, accounts for her sharp critique of white bourgeois women who, to gain any moral credibility in the struggle against apartheid, must first be stripped of their cultural context and moorings—in other words, stripped of their social discourse—so they are free to learn the alternative discourse of the struggle. Maureen Smales exemplifies such a stripping process, while Hillela Capran—cast out of her white colonial culture—learns the discourse of, and is admitted to, the revolutionary community in exile. In her fiction, Gordimer asks not only what the cultural meanings of emotions are and how emotional configurations might be related to social and political life but she also asks what Lila Abu-Lughod says we must ask: "How [are] emotional discourses implicated in the play of power and the operation of an historically changing system of social [and political] hierarchy?" (Lutz and Abu-Lughod, 15). This question becomes the central focus of *My Son's Story*.

The novel is set in the early 1980s, when petty apartheid laws are being dismantled and South Africa faces international sanctions designed to strangle the economy and so force political change in the country. *My Son's Story* tells the tale of a respectable Coloured schoolmaster who, after correcting the spelling errors on the placards of his demonstrating students, is drawn out of his comfortable though poor bourgeois family existence through his principled identification with the increasing militancy of his students. Sonny, the schoolmaster, turns out to be a surprisingly good speaker, and he is recruited into, and then rises through, the ranks of the banned ANC until he loses his government teaching job and is detained in jail for two years. His refined and lovely wife Aila, his bright son Will (named after Shakespeare), and his lively, pert daughter Baby have been protected from political implication through Sonny's faithful adherence to the rules of silence in the movement. In prison Sonny is visited by Hannah, a fleshy, blonde activist for an international human rights agency, who becomes his focus, first for friendship, and later, upon release, for a joyous but increasingly obsessive love affair. The affair is discovered unwittingly by 15-year-old Will one day when he stumbles upon his father and Hannah at a theater, and he becomes an unwilling accomplice in order to protect his mother. The affair continues, a destructive force at the center of the family as they all eventually intuit what is going on. Baby parties, takes drugs, attempts suicide, and leaves home; Will feels anguished and trapped. Only Aila seems to maintain her quiet, good, homebody wifely composure. Alienated from Sonny, Aila becomes a confidante for her daughter, who eventually announces her clandestine involvement in the struggle, which requires her exile in Zambia with her activist boyfriend (soon to be her husband). Aila's consequent trips to Zambia to visit Baby, who soon has a child, lead to her own unexpected involvement in the movement, an involvement revealed only late in the novel, much to the astonishment of Sonny and Will as well as to the reader, through her arrest. Sonny's status within the movement has by this time declined, and Hannah is moving on to a job promotion in another country. After a display of confidence and competence worthy of any comrade during her political trial, Aila leaves Sonny and Will confused and alone when she skips bail to live in exile. She is permanently lost to them both.

Given Gordimer's definition of a feminist novel as one that "sets out to make a point about being a woman," *My Son's Story* must be considered feminist. Gordimer sets the novel at a time when the legal system of apartheid is crumbling and some integration is taking place: the movie theaters are integrated and Sonny is moved by the ANC—as a form of protest and not without incident—into a white working-class suburb. Though she chooses—in her de-emphasis on race—not a black or white family, but a "Coloured" family (she has said that for her the Coloureds stand "in some subconscious way" for all South Africans),[15] Gordimer has not yet relinquished the issue of race. Apartheid's poison still lingers, most distressingly in the psyche of young Will. He says, thinking of his father's white lover, "The wet dreams I have, a schoolboy who's never slept with a woman, are blonde. It's an infection brought to us by the laws that have decided what we are, and what they are—the blonde ones."[16]

Despite lingering racism, the novel is a story about gender relations examined within the domestic structure—but it has far-reaching implications for the nation as a whole. It was Frantz Fanon who said that "the family is a miniature of the nation. . . . the characteristics of the family are projected onto the social environment" (Fanon 1967, 142). Even the title, *My Son's Story,* acknowledges the tangled family relationships and suggests that the novel is the story of Will, the son, or perhaps of Son/ny, the father. Though the personal pronoun *my* could refer to Sonny, who has a son, Will, it seems rather to refer to Aila, who is mother to son Will and wife to husband Son/ny. The novel has at least two narrative voices: One clearly is the angry voice of young Will, while the unnamed third-person other is a more reflective, detached voice, one able to appreciate Hannah's decency, understand Will's anger, and recognize Sonny's strengths and vulnerabilities. Susan Greenstein holds that the second voice is "Will himself, slightly older than the angry adolescent, and having authored his first novel."[17] Narrative voices aside, the central authority in the novel is slowly usurped by Aila. Her presence, quiet and unfathomable, comes to dominate the novel. Gordimer has said that in the clandestine atmosphere of South Africa, " you just never know, really, to whom you're talking" (*CNG,* 257), and it turns out that not even Sonny and Will knew to whom they were talking when addressing their own wife and mother, respectively. The novel, then, uncovers the limiting and sexist assumptions that restrict both son and husband from understanding Aila (and Baby, for that matter, who must go into exile and have a baby of her own to claim her womanhood), and the story becomes the tale of Aila's (and Baby's) liberation from their oppression.

The sexism permeating the novel is evidenced in both men's inability to "see" Aila for who she is and for who she becomes, and to know her strengths and possibilities. Their vision is clouded by their preconceived notions of women and by their admiration for her beauty and her feminine refinement. She is valued (and blamed) for her nurturing care, her domestic skills, her quiet supportive manner; she is also viewed as inept and in need of protection in her dealings with the outside world. When Sonny learns of her planned trip to see Baby in Zambia, he recalls, perplexed, that she "never had much relish for journeys, she didn't know how to deal with officialdom; she had found it difficult even to speak in the presence of his warder" (*MSS*, 149). Will, on the other hand, assumes Aila cannot handle the truth about Sonny's affair. He fears that his guilt of complicity manifests itself in his behavior and will alert Aila to the problem from which he feels he must protect her:

> If I kept out of her way she would know something was wrong, thinking in her innocence this would be something concerning me. And if I try to be with her, to cover up that he wasn't—that might set her thinking, and I didn't want her to think, I didn't want my mother to think about him in any other but her gentle, trusting way. (*MSS*, 59)

Just how blind Sonny and Will have been in their perceptions of Aila as woman, wife, and mother is measured by their shock when they learn of her involvement in the struggle, an involvement more dangerous and daring than Sonny's—one with weapons rather than words. When Will discovers—much earlier than Sonny does—Aila's other life through her passport photos, his response is telling: "Where is she going? Is she going to leave him? Wild idea . . . my mother! . . . So I know nothing about her" (*MSS*, 146). And when Sonny finally discovers her activism, he admits:

> Yes, there was a blank in his chronology of her life; he knew little of the changes in her for which, he believed, he was responsible. . . . He knew he was having difficulty in accepting Aila as comrade. He had consciously to rid himself of an outworn perception of Aila. Consciously; that was the problem. (*MSS*, 257)

Will sees more than his father does. He at least understands how little he knows about her, and he knows, after her symbolic haircut (she crops her long, luxurious feminine hair into a short, boyish style) that she is free of conventional family ties. "She never came back," he says. "Cut loose. She was gone for good: my mother" (*MSS*, 168). He also acknowledges: "I realize I don't know enough about women" (*MSS*, 176), a realization Sonny never quite reaches. Nevertheless, Will remains trapped in patronizing and sexist behavior, an indication that changing deeply and emotionally ingrained behavior means changing patterns of power relations as well. Before Aila is arrested, Will picks up a woman at the beach for sexual experience, which he describes in terms of male power and dominance: "I went down to Durban on the motorbike and picked up a girl on the beach the first day. It was easy. Some of the beaches are open to all of us now. So I've lived with a woman for six days, fucked her and slept in the same bed with her, and don't ever want to see her again" (*MSS*, 136). He also dismissively refers to his girlfriend as "a nice enough little thing" (*MSS*, 184).

Wills misogyny (my word)

While the men in this novel start out as the authorities, the speakers in the novel, their position of centrality does not continue. Narrator/author Will's story is dislodged, thrown off course by Aila's story; the men's story is overtaken by the stories of women who refuse to be trapped by the sexist male narrative. Sonny—portrayed as orator, master of language, ANC spokesperson—is displaced by Aila as the real revolutionary, the committed activist. He experiences the thrill of male power when Hannah and Aila are present at the same function: "He became eloquent, his nostrils round with conviction, he had never expressed himself more forcefully than while, the first time, instead of keeping the two women fastidiously apart within him, he possessed both at once" (*MSS*, 93). But Sonny's position is undermined by the imbalance his need for Hannah creates in his political life; the private need usurps the political. Through an incident when police open fire at a political funeral ceremony that he and Hannah attend, Sonny realizes that his need for Hannah has eroded his political will. Fleeing with the others from the gravesides, he sees a man fall, hit in the head by a bullet. Instinctively he turns to aid his comrade, but checks himself and runs on to protect Hannah. Later he questions whether saving Hannah is in accord with his value of living for more than oneself. He admits:

> To run or to stop: a choice between them. Who was to say which was the most valuable? But this woman whose hand was curled against his neck, wasn't she oneself, his need?
> Saved himself.
> Now he had something he would never speak, not to anyone, certainly not to her. (*MSS*, 126–27)

Hannah, on the other hand maintains political balance. She loves Sonny dearly, but remains someone "for whom the people in the battle are her only family, her life, the happiness she understands" (*MSS*, 67). After Aila has skipped bail and Hannah has taken a new assignment (both leave Sonny to take up further political work), Sonny considers the ironic repercussions that the repeal of the Immorality and Mixed Marriages Act (which outlawed interracial sex and marriage) has meant for him:

law

> He found himself thinking—insanely—that if the law had still forbidden
> him Hannah, if that Nazi law for the "purity" of the white race that dis-
> gustingly conceived it had still been in force, he would never have risked
> himself. . . . Because needing Hannah, taking the risk of going to prison
> for that white woman would have put at risk his only freedom, the only
> freedom of his kind, the freedom to go to prison again and again, if need
> be, for the struggle. . . . That filthy law would have saved him.
>   *Out of the shot and danger of desire.* (MSS, 263–64)

law

While Sonny wrestles with his tangled secret private life, Aila slips in
and takes center stage. Sonny is needed no longer. Watching her prepare
for her trial, he tries to reconnect with her, to understand, but he has a
"sense of stretching his fingertips at something that was disappearing
from his grasp" (*MSS*, 239). His impotence is mirrored in his attempts
to reawaken her passion, but "he knew—now with his greater experience of what women can feel, in love—that she faked her pleasure . . .
she was thinking of something else. . . . Something bigger than self
saves self: that had been the youthful credo he had taught his shy bride"
(*MSS*, 242–43). Baby, too, finds her place in the world. Learning from
her mother's experience, she involves herself in the struggle early. She
finds a center, and only then, in a relationship of equality (unlike her
brother's relationship), she marries a fellow revolutionary.

IMP   The novel, then, becomes one about women who find their voices
through the course of political action. Aila and Baby move from passive
domestic roles to active political ones, while the men, Sonny and
Will—hampered by assumptions of their power and centrality, their
sexual competitiveness, and their egos—are marginalized. Both are left
impotent: Will has a story he "can never publish" (*MSS*, 277) and
Sonny—with shrinking gums, enlarged prostate (*MSS*, 264), and his
"bundle of sex" hanging like something "disowned by his body" (*MSS*,
169)—is shut away in detention again. Early in the novel when Baby
attempts suicide, the paternalistic pattern of traditional sexual identities that bond father and daughter and align mother and son is identified by Will. He realizes that Baby knows about Sonny's affair with
Hannah:

> Had she, all this time, been taking his part against my mother? As I tried
> to shield my mother against him? Female against female. Male against
> male. So what could we have done for her. To stop her cutting her wrists
> when she couldn't manage. (*MSS*, 62)

As the novel unfolds, however, this pattern shifts to another in which gender identity bonds mother and daughter. Their solidarity aids in their liberation from the limited gender-role expectations of Sonny and Will.

But Gordimer is not unrelenting in her critique of Sonny or Will. The intrigue of politics and power contorts and divides, its secrecy and deception alienate and manipulate, and its perpetrators are also its victims. Sonny pays for his dishonesty, his blindness, in his relationship with Aila by losing touch with her. He cannot know her anymore. At her political trial he wonders:

> But where did she get this from, know how to conduct herself, how to talk to her lawyer, put up a front that gives nothing away—not even to an old political lag who also happened to be her husband. Prison-wise. Aila prison-wise. His Aila; he made the claim to himself. In himself he ignored the crevasse of years he had opened between them and thought of them as Aila-and-Sonny, who together learned how to live, to whom nothing was faced, decided, dealt with that was not conjoined in the little house outside Benoni. (MSS, 234)

Sonny's alienation from Aila is attributable to his patronizing stereotyping of her. Developed in a traditional community where "in his kind of family women cooked and cleaned" (MSS, 163), Sonny and Aila's marriage discourse had embraced bourgeois values where

> for the uplift of the community he approached the Rotary Club and the Lion's Club in the white town that they might graciously send their doctors, lawyers, and members of amateur theatre and music groups to lecture or perform in the school hall. (MSS, 9)

His attraction to and communication with Hannah, however, results from political circumstances. Sonny's involvement in the struggle teaches him a new revolutionary discourse, one he feels restricted from passing on to his family because of the ANC codes of silence. Aila consequently is shut out, denied access to the language that remakes Sonny, the discourse of which he is now master. After visiting Sonny in prison, Will observes that being "in prison for the cause of freedom has made him someone elect, not to be followed in his private thoughts by ordinary people. Like herself. Like us" (MSS, 45). While Aila and Sonny had once needed no language to communicate, now at the breakfast table "the inconsequential talk was contained in the silence between them that all gathered there heard" (*MSS*, 100). It is this alienation, set against the energy, commitment, and excitement of his new life in the struggle that makes Sonny vulnerable to the affair with Hannah. He compares Aila and Hannah's visits to his prison cell:

> The silences between Aila and him that were so comfortable, natural in *Aila* their closeness, at home, were now a real silence without communication of any kind. . . . They had had love-names, tender and jokey euphemisms for what was hard to express, key words that recalled events in their life together or the antics of one or other of their children—who could expect Aila to put love-talk to the use of a prison code? (*MSS*, 48)

Hannah, on the other hand, is ingenious at the discourse of the struggle:

> Talking about food she was letting him know that in another prison some of the comrades were on a hunger strike, and apparently innocently relating the weather report she was able to indicate—remarking which cities were receiving heavy rainfall—where many other comrades were being held. (*MSS*, 49)

Hannah is also fluent at literary discourse, and her Shakespearean allu- *Hannah* sions loaded with revolutionary import—"you find sermons in stones" (*MSS*, 49)—are yet another kind of message that Sonny is elated to be able to recognize. He responds with a clear knowledge of his beloved Shakespeare: "And good in your kindness in coming to see me" (*MSS*, *Rox* 50). One cannot escape the irony that the revolutionary discourse used between Sonny and Hannah is in part couched in nuanced references to sixteenth-century European Shakespeare. The reader should also not miss the ironic allusion of the epigraph to Sonnet 13. The male speaker of the sonnet urges his handsome and loving companion to procreate so that the image of his beauty may not be lost to the world. The woman, or wife, who is to bear this copy image, is not even worthy of reference *Shakes* in the sonnet. She is merely the vessel to perpetuate this male line. That *mps* Aila renounces her roles of wife and mother comments directly on the *Sonny* import of the sonnet and links it with the scant regard for her that *& Aila* Sonny displays.

Sonny's failure lies not so much in his vulnerability to Hannah as in his underestimation of Aila's ability to change, to learn, to join him. His perceptions of traditional gender roles and of Aila's assumed acceptance of them trap him, and strand her, for the novel makes abundantly clear Aila's inner strength and intelligence and her capacity for change:

Aila understood everything, even the things [Sonny] didn't intend to bring up all at once; he could keep nothing from her, her quiet absorbed his subsumed half-thoughts, hesitations, disguising or dissembling facial expressions, and fitted together the missing sense. Because she said little herself, she did not depend on words for the supply of information from others. (*MSS*, 42)

But Sonny remains captivated by Hannah, who—educated, literary—is a lover of language as he is. In her letter to him in prison, she uses the phrase "happy for battle" and he is "stirred." The message confirms "a language of shared reference between himself and the writer of the letter." It represents "something particular not only to his present situation in prison, but to a whole context of thought and action in which that situation was contained" (*MSS*, 56). This shared political discourse that grants Sonny and Hannah a certain power over Aila heightens Sonny's elation: "That phrase, so simple, so loaded, audacious, such a shocking, wild glorious juxtaposition of menace and elation, flowers and blood, people sitting in the sun and bodies dismembered by car bombs" (*MSS*, 56).

It is the thrill of Hannah's mind, the thrill of communication, that draws Sonny to her physically. It is a relationship founded on precisely the opposite of adolescent Will's racial reading of the affair. They share a discourse based on ideology, politics, literature—not race. But while they revel in the passion this generates, Aila, too, is learning a new discourse, a feminist discourse of self-reliance, self-esteem, and self-assertion. While Sonny has deluded himself into believing that "at least he had been able to provide Baby with a room of her own for the process of becoming a woman" (*MSS*, 57), it is, ironically, Aila who is building a Woolfian room of her own. When Sonny tries to revive the old domestic discourse with Aila, he is stunned to find that she no longer speaks that language. She has changed and is thus lost to him.

The novel calls the conventional family structure into question, and it invokes the Reichian view that patriarchal family patterns repress our liberating instincts, discussed by Newman in relation to *A Guest of Honour* (Newman, 40–41). To succeed, a revolution must extend not only to the economic and political spheres but also to the repressive morality of everyday life as well. Newman quotes Philip Rieff's comment that

habits of domestic living are concrete ways in which ideology internalises authority. Unless a revolution conquers the bedroom it cannot conquer; without a rearrangement of intimacy, men will continue to identify

check

themselves, if not with old rulers, then with old rules of conduct. (Newman, 41)

The family is seen as the factory in which the state's structure and ideology are molded; however radical the revolution, so long as the conventional family persists, authority creeps back, and the revolution fails. Alienated from Sonny by his affair with Hannah, Aila learns to rearrange her intimate world, but Sonny still clings to the old rules of conduct. His reliance, first on Aila's respect for his authority as patriarch, then on Hannah's reinforcement of his political growth and worth, makes him blind to the meaning of Aila's change: "He had noticed she'd cut her hair, that's about all—women's whims. Meant little to him at the time" (*MSS*, 257). But after her arrest, when she exhibits no need for him since all is taken care of by herself and the movement, it slowly dawns on Sonny: "Perhaps he flattered himself Aila had needed to suffer his love of another woman to change. Perhaps it had nothing to do with that, with him. Perhaps she had freed herself just as he had, through the political struggle" (*MSS*, 258). When the ANC leaders make the decision that Aila will skip bail, Sonny is not consulted. He reflects that "she did not need him, even for that" (*MSS*, 262). It is when the Sonny's of the world have been stripped of their illusions of importance that hope for a new and equitable nation becomes a possibility. After Aila leaves, "he continued to work for the cause now. . . . He lived like so many others of his kind whose families are fragmented in the diaspora of exile, code names, underground activity, people for whom a real home and attachments are something for others who will come after" (*MSS*, 265).

And it is when the young Wills of the world mature beyond their superficial objectification of women that hope for the future lies. The father's house must be destroyed before the son can rise in his own right, and it is only when Sonny's house in the white suburb is burnt down that Will is—in a sense—set free. Though he tries initially to defend the house from chanting crowds, screaming "This is my father's house" (*MSS*, 272), he understands later, as he and Sonny stand in the smoky debris, that everything that has claimed Sonny, and therefore himself, is gone:

> Flocks of papery cinders were drifting, floating about us—beds, clothing—his books?
> The smell of smoke, that was the smell of her.
> The smell of destruction, of what has been consumed, that he first brought into that house. (*MSS*, 274)

Sonny's image of the phoenix that rises from the ashes as the symbol of hope for his people is also a symbol of hope for Will. At the end of the novel, Will makes two claims. One is: "But I'm young and it's my time that's come, with women. My time that's coming with politics" (*MSS*, 276). The other is:

> I was excluded from [politics] . . . but I'm going to be the one to record, someday, what he and my mother/Aila and Baby and the others did, what it really was like to live a life determined by the struggle to be free, as desert dwellers' days are determined by the struggle against thirst and those dwellers amid snow and ice by the struggle against the numbing of cold. (*MSS*, 276)

Will's time with women (rather than sex objects) still lies in the future, though certainly by the end of the novel both time and women have done much to educate him. Aila is no longer "mother" to Will. Rather, he calls her Aila, a woman in her own right without the familial claim. The "nice enough little girl" who is "not important" (*MSS*, 184) to Will becomes the "smart little garment-factory girl" who, on her way to work, delivers the message from an ANC leader regarding Aila's whereabouts. Will can no longer view this young woman in quite the degrading light he viewed his girlfriends. He admits that "in the midst of the strain and the tension of those moments there was an incongruous aside, in my feelings; pride in the fact of the unguessed-at commitment of our people to the struggle, hidden under this cheap appearance" (*MSS*, 261). Will's experience with women—mother, sister, and girlfriends—is part of his political education. Such education must be part of the new nation building if the revolution is to create an equitable society.

That Will becomes a writer is Sonny's fault: "What he did—my father—made me a writer" (*MSS*, 277). Early on in the novel Will comments: "I wish I didn't have so much imagination, I wish that other people's lives were closed to me" (*MSS*, 79). Will understands the power of literature to tell a story, to tell "what it was really like." He understands that though the details must be invented, the power of art really lies in what exists beneath the surface. Gordimer states in *Writing and Being* that "the expression in art of *what really exists* beneath the surface is part of the transformation of a society. What is written, painted, sung, cannot be ignored" (*WB*, 131). So the writer helps to transform a society, and it is therefore fitting that the poem that Will the writer sends his father in prison is not Shakespearean. Its themes of prison, violence, and the dream of freedom are decidedly South African,

So, Af
poem
Check

and it grounds both narrator/author Will and author Gordimer firmly as South African writers.

This novel, like the previous novels, includes some of the most sensitive and nuanced descriptions of complicated human interaction. Rather than focusing on the clash of culture and color endemic to South African existence, the narrative picks its way through the entanglement of repressions and deceptions that stress family life, particularly during a time of great social upheaval. Gordimer's choice of a family with no surname and with diminutive first names like Sonny, Baby, and Will signals their representative status as a family. But her use of the Coloureds as representatives of all South Africans creates an awkward tension in the text. The Coloureds, like the white and black South Africans, are a culturally complex and politically varied group whom one would expect to find richly texturized in the novel. But Gordimer's metaphoric need tugs against a richer cultural realism, resulting in a niggling uncertainty for the reader. Gordimer's own uncertainty about her use of the Coloured family emerges when she deemed it necessary to point out their representative status in postpublication interviews. The reader's uncertainty, on the other hand, is echoed by critics like Greenstein, who notes that the novel "offers a minimalist representation of the material, linguistic and political culture in which it is set" and suggests that while some readers may read the novel as "a bold adventure into new territory, others might condemn it as a travesty, a self-conscious *tour de force*, a novel written in blackface" (Greenstein, 194). Most readers will concur, however, with the judgment that in *My Son's Story* Gordimer has ventured into the complicated territory of gender relations more boldly than ever before, signaling the continued growth in consciousness that has been the hallmark of her work since the 1950s.

None to Accompany Me

By its placement on the cusp of the transition to freedom, Gordimer's 1994 novel, *None to Accompany Me,* must be scanned for a shifting focus. Not quite a postapartheid novel, it was written and is set during the time of major political and social transition after Nelson Mandela's release from prison in February 1990 and before free elections in May 1994.

Like all the later novels, *None to Accompany Me* engages quite deliberately with the events of its historical time. With their backs against the wall in a hostile world, with a weakened economy and ungovernable

townships, the white electorate swept President F. W. de Klerk into
power in 1989 on his promise of political reform; he immediately began
consultations with the ANC leadership. Only when all imprisoned ANC
leaders were freed was Nelson Mandela willing to accept his own uncon-
ditional release after 27 years in prison. The regime's ban on political
opponents was finally lifted, legalizing the ANC, the PAC, and other
organizations; and political exiles—like the Maqoma family in the
novel—were allowed to return home. Yet continuing violence among
political rivals and errant and unemployed youth plagued the country,
indicating that the transition of power to a freely elected government
was not going to be easy. The assassination of a young leader that takes
place in the novel recalls the assassination of charismatic ANC youth
leader Chris Hane in 1992. He was gunned down outside his home by a
white extremist, and the novel's description pays tribute to his spirit:
"His presence carried the peculiar authority of the guerrilla past in
working for peace. If men like him wanted it, who could doubt that it
was attainable? If a man like him was there to convince his young fol-
lowers, could they fail to listen to him?"[18]

In the interests of reducing the terrible violence, the ANC reached
out to heal differences with rival movements like the PAC, though they
held firm against giving up their military wing, Umkhonto we Sizwe,
and refused to abandon their demand for continued international sanctions until discriminatory laws were changed. In the novel tribute is also
paid to the integrity of Joe Slovo, longtime head of Umkhonto we
Sizwe, who was named Mandela's minister of Housing after elections.
He was ill with cancer for a long time and died shortly after the ANC
government took over in 1994. Described in the novel as ill with an
incurable disease and often absent from his place on the National Executive, the character named Dave addresses the Patriotic Front conference:

> If we're going to ask our people to put trust in a new constitution we
> have first to put our lives on the table to vow integrity, we have to swear
> publicly, here and now, and entrench this in a constitution, that we will
> not take up with power what the previous regime has taken. . . . Let us
> tell our people, and mean it—we shall not lie, and cheat, and steal from
> them. Without this, I tell you, all the provisions of a constitution we are
> debating so carefully are meaningless! (*NAM,* 234–35)

The negotiating process for a new constitution was pursued through a
multiparty forum, the Convention for a Democratic South Africa
(Codessa), and teams of consultants and experts were engaged. In the

novel, protagonist Vera Stark, a lawyer, is selected to sit on the Technical
Committee on Constitutional Issues, the committee responsible for
drafting the new constitution.

Any temptation to read *None to Accompany Me* as radically different
from her earlier work because of its transitional status is forestalled by
Gordimer's comment in a 1995 interview that "all novelists are in effect
writing one book . . . looking at [similar] themes from a different angle
and from a different stage of knowledge of life" (Bazin interview, 583).
None to Accompany Me certainly revisits the major recurring themes of
Gordimer's work. Predictably present are the private and the political,
the role of sexuality, the place of whites in an independent South Africa,
and the significance of gender relations, though all are contemplated
from a shifted perspective. The novel takes on, as well, concerns that
will dominate the new nation if liberation is to be real: issues of land
redistribution and housing, constitutional guarantees of equity and freedom, and political machinations concomitant with black empowerment
and power sharing. For readers who have wondered what South African
writers will write about once apartheid is over and what form such writing may take, *None to Accompany Me* indicates a cautious shift of focus. It
captures the ambiguities and compromises that each member of the new
majority leadership must face as the ANC emerges from its position of
moral and revolutionary opposition to occupy the legitimate center of
government power.

The political transition that is the setting of the novel is echoed in the
personal transition of the protagonist, an aging woman turning inward
to be more in touch with her self. The central drama of the novel takes
place within the internal life of Vera Stark, who journeys through her
past to arrive—like the country—at an independence, alone, and free to
continue the political work that has become her life's commitment.
Both the personal and the political transitions involve a reassessment of
the past in an attempt to interpret its meaning for the unfolding future.
The novel examines the phenomenon of power, now lost to the white
government, and documents its reemergence in new forms and alliances
within the new ruling community.[19] Implicit in its probe for new forms
and structures particularly suited to the complexities of the South
African situation is a caution to avoid the pitfalls of the authoritarian
past. Gordimer is convinced that stultifying and oppressive patterns
embedded in conventional family structures (explored in all her novels)
echo the patterns of much larger political and economic institutional
structures. This conviction emerges in her focus on two families—one

white and one black, and has clear implications for the model of a new nation. It highlights the irrefutable echo between the private and public patterns.

The novel centers around two families: Didymus and Sibongile (Sally) Maqoma and their teenage daughter, Mpho; and Vera and Bennet Stark and their now adult children, Ivan and Annick. Friends in the early days of political activism, the families lose contact when the Maqomas have to slip into exile, reuniting after 20 years when they return to a changing South Africa in 1990. Didymus, who has been an important figure in the ANC leadership in exile, is shunted to the sidelines in the shuffle for new leadership positions, while Sibongile, the supportive, unquestioning wife during Didy's dangerous missions in exile, rises to prominence as the stylish and assertive head of the placement bureau for returning and unemployed exiles. The couple has some initial difficulty adjusting to the shift in political fortunes, but after Sibongile's name is discovered on a hit list, Didy's survival skills in a menacing environment prove comforting to the family, and they handle their reversal of roles quite gracefully. Born in England, 16 year-old Mpho is more of an English teenager than she is a black South African; she is only now learning to speak an African language. Socially precocious, a schoolgirl who "combined the style of *Vogue* with the assertion of Africa" (*NAM*, 49), she finds herself pregnant by the young married clerk, Oupa, in Vera Stark's office. Her angry parents pressure her into an abortion, ignoring the protests of her Alexandra township grandmother who believes abortions are what white people do. A few years later, Mpho leaves South Africa to study at New York University, where her admission and scholarship has been secured thanks to her mother's influential contacts.

Although the Maqomas' story is viewed externally and forms a pivotal part of the comparative structure, the novel centers predominately on Vera's examination of her interior life: her submerged motivations and partially understood relationships, and her personal evolution in relation to the political situation in the country. The novel describes Vera revisiting her past, for, as Vera observes: "It's some sort of historical process in reverse we're in. The future becomes undoing the past" (*NAM*, 261). She claims that now, in her 60s, she wants "to find out about my life. The truth. In the end. That's all" (*NAM*, 313). Believing the consequences of our choices to be highly instructive in making sense of our lives, Vera explores the breakup of her early first marriage and her love affair with Bennet Stark while her first husband was away at war. She grants sexuality a tremendous shaping power when she admits to

herself the real reason for the failure of her first marriage and her passion
for Bennet:

> She is the one who, she understands, sent her soldier husband a photo-
> graph ringed in revenge—that was it; she has never forgotten or forgiven
> him premature ejaculation. . . . the real reason for the passion for Bennet
> . . . his ability discovered on the mountain holiday to sustain what the
> other had failed at, to stay within her and exchange the burden of self.
> (*NAM*, 161)

The last time she sees the first husband is immediately after their
divorce when he comes to the house to collect some belongings while
Bennet is out. Irrationally they make love for the first time in two years,
probably conceiving Ivan with whom Vera is pregnant when she marries
Bennet, a secret she has kept from everyone.

Bennet, a frustrated sculptor, is a junior English professor at the university. He soon gives up both his art and his teaching to work in the
business world to secure an income and retirement for himself and Vera,
a move that ultimately backfires when his "promotional luggage" business fails. The new family lives in the house Vera gets in the divorce settlement, and she earns her law degree while working for a prosperous
legal firm. When daughter Annick is born, Vera gives up her lucrative
position. She chooses, after the baby, to take a position at the Legal
Foundation, which fights population removals of black communities
and negotiates land redistribution claims. She is tired, she says, of fighting claims for the rich who have lost their jewelry or their Mercedes. She
works at the foundation,

> not out of the white guilt people talked about, but out of a need to take
> up, to balance on her own two feet the time and place to which, by birth,
> she understood she had no choice but to belong. This need must have
> been growing unheeded—seed shat by a bird and germinating, sprout-
> ing, beside a cultivated tree—climbing the branches of passionate
> domesticity. (*NAM*, 20–21)

While her life appears to have two strands—her public work life and
her private and sexual life, the novel makes clear the interplay between
them and the reverberations when one or other strand is drawn too
tensely. The more involved she is with her work, the less need she has of
family life, and conventional views about loyalty and responsibilities
seem increasingly alien to her. Vera recalls her intense affair with a Ger-

man filmmaker, Otto Abarbanel, whom she meets at the foundation
when Annie is a teenager. After their first passionate lovemaking, Vera
was surprised to realize that

> what had happened in the three hours interim was something that con-
> cerned her alone, her sexuality, a private constant in her being, a charac-
> teristic like the colour of the eyes, the shape of the nose, the nature of a
> personal spirit that never could belong to anyone other than the self. . . .
> She lay beside Ben that night with a sense of pride and freedom rather
> than betrayal. (*NAM*, 62–63)

When, much later, she realizes that Annie knew about the affair, she
knows the young girl could never have understood all its implications:
"How can a schoolgirl be expected to know the family never was the
way she's been told families are, to accept that her own father was
'another man', her mother's sexuality something that made a claim
above the love of children?" (*NAM*, 164).

Vera is well respected at the foundation; "no one can imagine the
Foundation running without her" (*NAM*, 12). During the course of the
novel she reviews her growing sense of commitment and dedication to
the work and the people. Witnessing the precariousness of existence, she
is fascinated by the body as a vessel of life or death. During one of her
field trips with the foundation's young clerk, Oupa (who acts as her driver on these occasions), they stop to visit his wife and children in the
countryside. Ambushed by robbers on the way home, Oupa receives a
chest wound that—after an initial recovery—proves fatal, while Vera is
shot in the leg. Her trauma and her distress over Oupa's death lead Vera
to contemplate issues of identity, existence, consciousness, and the randomness of life and death.

On an earlier mission with Oupa to negotiate with an Afrikaans
farmer, Odendaal, about the rights of squatters encamped on his land,
she meets Zeph Rapulana, ex-teacher and spokesperson for the squatters. She and Zeph develop a profound and close relationship over time
as they work together on political matters. Zeph is sought after as an
advisor because of his wisdom and negotiating skills, and he soon sits on
the boards of several financial companies. But Zeph's claim is modest:

> I'm just a schoolmaster who's trying to educate them to diversify their
> excess profits into enterprises that will benefit our people whose labour
> made those profits. That's all. Cheap bonds for housing, technical train-
> ing instead of casinos, backing for blacks to get into setting up our own

financial institutions—and the right kind of co-operation to make sure we don't fail while we're gaining experience. (*NAM*, 259)

He builds a home for his family in Odenville, the reclaimed squatter camp, and secures for himself a house in a modestly affluent suburb previously exclusively white.

Vera's developing friendship with Zeph is unlike any other in her life. While it begins with the same gesture as her affair with Otto began (a hand grasping her arm) it is not sexual; it is something quite different. Her uncluttered connection with Zeph slowly exposes the inadequacy of her relationship with Ben, her growing recognition that Ben lives his life only for her, that he puts on her "the whole weight of his life" (*NAM*, 223). Her revelation that "a self, unlike a bed, cannot be shared, and cannot be shed" (*NAM*, 121) accounts to a large extent for her gradual disengagement from her relationship with Ben, who clings to the family even when he has lost Vera. Ben visits Ivan in England and, knowing he is unlikely to return, Vera sells her house and rents the annex to Zeph's house. Meanwhile, Annie, the lesbian daughter who is now a doctor, is living in fashionable domestic style with her partner and their newly adopted black baby in Cape Town. She is perplexed and upset by her mother's actions, and she pushes Vera to explain what on earth she thinks she is doing: "Vera searched there for something partially, tentatively explanatory that would not make some homely philosophy of a process that must not be looked back upon with the glance of Orpheus.—Working through—what shall I say—dependencies" (*NAM*, 313). For Vera, marriage has been a process of growth.

The novel ends late one winter's night when Vera enters Zeph's house quietly to fetch pliers to turn off a burst water pipe. In order not to wake him she avoids turning on a light, but, in the dark, she accidentally brushes against the warm softness of a young woman exiting the bathroom. Vera has encountered Zeph's young lover. The young woman scuttles back to his bedroom, while Vera goes out into the garden and shuts off the leaking pipe. The scene before her has the stripped, singular clarity that she is achieving at last in her life:

> Cold seared her lips and eyelids; frosted the arrangement of two chairs and table; everything stripped. Not a leaf on the scoured smooth limbs of the trees, and the bushes like tangled wire; dried palmfronds stiff as her fingers . . . under the swing of the sky she stood, feet planted, on the axis of the night world. Vera walked there, for a while. And then she took up her way, breath scrolling out, a signature before her. (*NAM*, 323–24)

free of sexuality

Vera is free of the most powerful dependency of all—sexuality.

That this is a novel of transition, a watershed—for the country, the blacks, the whites, women, and for Vera personally—is affirmed by its three-part structure, the titles of which further reinforce the theme of transition: baggage (what we carry from our past), transit (the process and progress of coming to terms with our actions and their consequences), and arrivals (the plural indicates a choice of possible destinations). All roles are changing and issues are subject to reexamination. The issue now seems less how whites will find a place and role in the new society, and more how each person—black or white—will find a way to fit in. To this end the novel registers the instability of identity, the struggle for self-knowledge, and unpredictability as factors determining the course of our lives. Oupa's life is a case in point. Studying at night to become a lawyer, he previously spent four years on Robben Island as a political prisoner. He tells Vera of the profound sense of brotherhood he had with his comrades. He is perplexed, however, by the fact that

> you suddenly hate someone, you can hardly keep your hands off his throat—and it's over nothing, a piece of string to tie your shoe. . . . And the same two people, when we were on a hunger strike, we'd do anything for each other . . . I can't think it was me. . . . She didn't console, didn't assure him that that individual, that self, no longer existed.—It was you. (*NAM*, 15)

Oupa juggles a series of roles, and after the fateful visit to his family he chats happily to Vera in the car about his son. Vera senses a new harmony in him, an acceptance of the contradictions that are a part of the human condition, though triggered often by economic and social conditions: "To say he was happy: it's to say he was whole. He'd accepted himself again; husband, father, Freedom Fighter, womanizer, and clerk at the Legal Foundation" (*NAM*, 195). Yet the novel draws attention to the inexplicable, the unpredictable events that can throw a life off course in an instant. When Oupa is gunned down minutes later, he ends up lying in hospital, unconscious and dying. He is simply "identified by the mute face. . . . No privacy for that body. On his back, totally exposed" (*NAM*, 208), and Vera speculates on the connection between the body and consciousness: "Must consciousness be receptive, cognitive, responsive for there to be a presence? Didn't the flesh have a consciousness of its own, the body signalling its presence through the lungs struggling to breathe with the help of some machine" (*NAM*, 210). Then, at his funeral in the country, Oupa takes on another identity, one demanded by his family and society. Zeph Rapulana delivers the eulogy on Vera's behalf, and his sense of the community's tradition gives the people the Oupa they need to remember. Vera observes:

> The cadence of [Zeph's] voice, his gestures, transformed a fragmented life into wholeness, he knew exactly how to do it, it came to him from within himself in symbiosis with the murmuring group gathered. . . . It was not true; the son and husband of this place left behind did not think only of his family, he yearned for a girl who had seen things and possessed knowledge he would never have, he did not die peacefully, his body, in attempts made to keep it alive, suffered tortures his interrogators in prison had not thought of. It was not true, in fact, but this stranger she had brought with her made it so beyond evidence. (*NAM*, 216)

But Zeph himself knows that Oupa never wanted to return to the rural family situation. "He was going to disappear and travel the world, he was going to Cuba—to England, China, specially Cuba—everywhere" (*NAM*, 217). The containment that institutions such as family and marriage seek to place on the individual obscures the complexities and contradictions of life, and the negotiation of Oupa's subjectivity, his many selves, emphasizes the fragmentedness and unknowableness of each person, reminding us that truth is always partial and relative. Oupa's history is rewritten in death at the funeral, but it is a reduction of a complex person in a relative universe.

The novel warns against accepting reductive social models as measures for the self, and in its focus on Vera's process of self examination it uncovers the inadequacies and limits of the models that mold our expectations. Vera's quest to read her life is signaled at the beginning of the novel when she turns over an old photograph to read its underside; it is the "lifting of a stone" (*NAM*, 4). Like Rosa Burger she finds she is moved by the misery and suffering of others as she comes to know them through the foundation. Whereas in the past she found the answer to everything to lie with her lover and husband Ben, she recognizes that she increasingly "was finding an answer within herself" (*NAM*, 26). Her need to commit to something outside herself grows slowly, ultimately chafing against the inherent moral contradiction between her job and Ben's job, which aims at producing a profit that will secure their old age. Reuniting with the Maqomas raises for Vera a "sense of confrontation with uninterpreted life kept about her, saddled on her person along with the bulging shoulder bag always on her arm, her briefcase documenting inquiry into other people's lives" (*NAM*, 39). Vera has her own baggage that needs inquiry, and she slowly starts to fulfill that need. When Ben tells her after the shooting that he couldn't live without her, Vera recalls that "the words fell from him with the clatter of a weapon concealed on his person. . . . A jump of fear, of refusal within her. . . . She was not responsible for his existence, no, no, love does not carry that covenant; . . . *What to do with that love.*" (*NAM*, 199–200).

Vera gradually picks herself free from the old, complicated ties of social and personal relationships, distilling her life to a simpler and clearer independence. This process involves a scrutiny of the institutions of marriage and family that has implications for remaking the country as a whole. Conventional bonds will not do. Vera is seeking a new path, just as South Africa must find a new path as well. Her connection with Zeph is portrayed as different to any previous relationship, for when Vera ponders the new type of relationship, she realizes:

> What had disturbed her as a mimesis of the past was the beginning of some new capability in her, something in the chemistry of human contact that she was only now ready for. . . . There was between them a level of knowledge of one another, tranquil, not very deep, but quite apart from those relationships complicated and profound, tangled in their beings, from which each came to it, a level that was neither sexually intuitive nor that of friendship. (*NAM*, 120, 122).

Vera's scrutiny of self and of her newly created relationship with Zeph have metaphorical implications for the future of the country, which Gordimer believes must undergo its own self-scrutiny during this crucial period. The novel, as much as it is about the internal journey of an elderly woman, is also about the internal struggle of a people to create a new, hybrid nation and culture. The idea of a nation, a place, as home to a people is examined in the novel, and its meaning is created by the emotional investment of each individual. When returning exiles arrive at the airport terminal there is joyous celebration, dancing, and singing: "Home: that quiet word: a spectacle, a theatre, a pyrotechnic display of emotion for those who come from wars, banishment, exile, who have forgotten what home was, or suffered not being able to forget" (*NAM*, 44). But the novel ironically contrasts this idea of South Africa as home with the reality of home for many people. Sibongile, preoccupied with bourgeois notions of locking her car against thieves, is stunned to discover that the woman street cleaner who excitedly returns her greeting

turns out to be her mother's cousin, a reminder of Sibongile's connections and responsibilities to the disenfranchised for whom the country is
also home: "Wakened suddenly, shaken alive into another light, another
existence. Sally is drawn over to her other self, standing there, the one
she started out with, this apparition with a plastic bag tied over the
hand with which, deftly, it picks up dirt the broom misses. Home"
(NAM, 52).

Building a nation worthy of being called home is not going to be
easy. Perceptions of land reform, for instance, are very different. The
white farmer for whom land reform means the loss of his fishing retreat
needs to understand that "without reform the tenant-laborers are losing
the mealies and millet they have worked the land for, every day, for generations" (NAM, 163). The bridging of these yawning gulfs will require
tremendous creative energy. Timothy Brennan notes that "the idea of
nationhood is not only a political plea, but a formal binding together of
disparate elements. And out of the multiplicities of culture, race, and
political structures, grows also a repeated dialectic of uniformity and
specificity: of world culture and national culture, of family and people"
(Brennan, 62). The Maqomas' daughter, Mpho, is offered as a
metaphorical hybrid resolution to the nation-building task faced by
South Africa. She is

> a sixteen-year-old beauty of the kind created by the cross-pollination of
> history. Boundaries are changed, ideologies merge, sects, religious and
> philosophical, create new idols out of combinations of belief, scientific
> discoveries link cause and effect between the disparate, ethnically jum-
> bled territorial names make a nationality out of many-tongued peoples of
> different religions, a style of beauty comes out of the clash between dom-
> ination and resistance. Mpho was a resolution—in a time when this had
> not yet been achieved by governments, conferences, negotiations, mass
> action and international monitoring or intervention—of the struggle for
> power in the country which was hers, and yet where, because of that
> power struggle, she had not been born . (NAM, 48–49)

But Vera and Zeph understand that a new nation must be built by hard
and creative work. They understand the necessity for people to believe
in a new and peaceful nation. People must believe that

> elections and the first government in which everyone would have a vote
> would stop the AK-47s and the petrol bombs, defeat the swastika wear-
> ers, accommodate the kinglets clinging to their knobkerries of ethnic

power, master the company at the Drommedaris; no purpose in giving satisfaction to prophets of doom by discussing with them the failure of the mechanisms of democracy, of elections "free and fair", in other countries of the continent. (*NAM*, 294–95)

The question ultimately becomes how to create a new nation. What does a new nation stand for, what does it strive toward? What creates a national essence? Recent theorists who have pondered the nature of a nation point to the role of (national) literature as a significant factor in the formation of nations. Brennan comments that it was especially the novel as a composite but clearly bordered work of art that was crucial in defining the nation as an "imagined community" (Brennan, 48). He adds that race, geography, tradition, language, size, or some combination of these seem finally insufficient for determining national essence, claiming rather that it is the fictive quality that provides the mythical coherence of nationhood. The idea that nations are invented where they previously never existed means that they depend on an "invented" tradition, and literature here plays an important role. Brennan writes, "Nations, then, are imaginary constructs that depend for their existence on an apparatus of cultural fictions in which imaginative literature plays a decisive role. . . . the novel allowed people to imagine the special community that was the nation" (Brennan, 49).

Gordimer is well aware of the role that fiction plays in nation building, and has consciously invoked its power, particularly in *A Sport of Nature*. In *My Son's Story* and *None to Accompany Me*, she is intent on examining and deconstructing the inherent patriarchy within the nation. Patriarchy within the microcosm of the nation, the family, is also examined as a potential pitfall to successful nationhood as Reich would have warned. *None to Accompany Me* tackles the national model obliquely through a critique of the two families, the Maqomas and the Starks. Both start out as conventionally structured families, but end up quite changed from their former patriarchal models. Gordimer restructures alliances and patterns to suggest new familial and—by implication— new national forms that stretch the boundaries of our thinking, our imagination, "seeking a new connection with responses untapped, as there are known to be connections in the brain that may go unused through a lifetime" (*NAM*, 120). Authoritative or patriarchal patterns controlling sexual, spatial, and social spheres give way to more experimental and untried paradigms.

In the Maqoma family we witness a political power shift to Sibongile. The entrenched patriarchy that she must overcome in her new position is clear when Didymus expresses his fear of discrimination against *imp* Sibongile by her male peers. He feels that her self-confident style may threaten some men and impede her advancement in the movement:

> He felt that even her obvious undocile femininity would count against her; the physical disturbance she made no attempt to minimize prefigured the disturbance in the male appropriation of power she seem presumptuous enough to ignore. . . . He was familiar with the way things were done, he was part of them; he could sense how others would feel towards a personality like Sibongile's; and a woman's. (*NAM*, 78)

Didymus admits being a part of this group, though his changed circumstances (and a solid relationship bonded by a common political vision) are educating him to another point of view. He nevertheless finds it hard to shake a protective paternalism. Fearing that Sibongile cannot judge the political climate astutely, he can't help "putting in a word when this *imp* seems appropriate" (*NAM*, 78) when he has a private moment with one or other of the old guard.

The novel's concern for the Maqoma family, however, seems to come more from their alienation from African ways and their easy adoption of western lifestyle and values due to all their years abroad. Sibongile's London boots, her insistence on Mpho's abortion, and her arrangement for Mpho's departure to an American college all sound a warning against a potential mimicry of the west. A reminder of African values comes from the grandmother in the Alexandra township who opposes Mpho's abortion, but she has no power to enforce against Sibongile's wishes what she believes to be the African way. Mpho, daughter of dedicated African activists, seems set on a path that, ironically, leads her away from Africa. In an insightful discussion of spatial control in the novel, critic Dominic Head indicts the Maqomas for their assumption of bourgeois morality, particularly when Sibongile blames Vera for Mpho's pregnancy because Vera had introduced the couple. He points out that the description of the confrontation scene in Oupa's flat uses a theatrical motif, underscoring both the imitative un-African existence the Maqomas are living and Gordimer's broader concern with "Eurocentric artistic forms, as potential limitations on black African experience if not put to some new hybridized purpose."[20] Also troubling is the implication that as gender power relations within the family (and the movement) move toward greater equity and balance, the danger of losing the communal values of their African identity through entrapment in more individualistic bourgeois values becomes the more pressing threat.

The bond that holds Didy and Sally Maqoma together as they each grow and change is their mutual commitment to the political struggle in South Africa. The Starks, on the other hand, seem to lose the possibility of that kind of bond when Ben allows economic insecurity about the future and his all-consuming love for Vera to dictate his choices in life. Vera comments to her son, Ivan:

> —You see, Ben made a great mistake. Choice . . . He gave up everything he needed, in exchange for what he wanted. The sculpture. Even an academic career . . . He put it all on me. . . . The whole weight of his life. That love he had. (*NAM*, 223)

Vera refutes Ben's idea that one can belong to another, claiming that lovemaking is responsible for that illusion, and she rejects the limitations and stasis that such a possessive relationship incurs. For Ben, the breakup of their marriage means it was a failure, whereas Vera "sees it as a stage on the way, along with others, many and different. Everyone ends up moving alone towards the self" (*NAM*, 306). Though Ben is not overtly authoritative and controlling, it is his assumptions about sexual love that confine and restrict. His sculptures of Vera—two headless torsos—are fashioned out of a love and passion for her, but they conjure the image of the crude and plastic torso that the powerful patriarch Vermeulen has in his living room when Rosa Burger meets with him to request help with a passport. The male urge to possess is subtly evident in an early comment about the sculptures: "No one singles out the identity—*sculptor*—of the one who shaped them, only *he* remembers the identity of the missing head, the complex nerve-centre of the woman he lives with and that he had given up (once, long ago) attempting to capture in its material form" (*NAM*, 73). That Ben ends up with international banker Ivan in the imperial metropolis of London is fitting, for father and son (who repeats the cycle of domination and control in *his* marriage and divorce) still manifest mind-sets that align them with the old world patriarchy.

But the Maqomas and the Starks represent a passing generation. The future lies with the next generation, who will build on the foundations laid by their parents. The irony of Mpho heading west as a young internationalist is underscored by the return to South Africa of Ivan's teenage son, Adam, foisted onto his grandparents from England by a disinterested father. Adam settles comfortably into his new way of life, dating young women with no thought to race, hoping particularly to date

Mpho because "she's a damn nice kid. We have a good time together" (*NAM*, 269). He displays few of his father's traits, takes his grandmother Vera's advice, and appears destined to become a good citizen. While the Starks spawned Adam's less-than-admirable father, they also have Annie who—in her domestic arrangement—provides a new and experimental family structure. She and her lesbian partner, Lou, have adopted an black baby girl and are distracted and preoccupied by the pleasures of parenting and sharing all duties. They appropriate Ben's headless torsos, which are now featured in their home as "the expression of desire between woman and woman. In Annie's house the headless torsos were become household gods" (*NAM*, 228). They provide a new definition of home. Vera notes that "somehow, she and Annie have exchanged places. She has left home, and Annie is making home of a new kind entirely" (*NAM*, 314).

Two other familial structures that bear some scrutiny are Oupa and Zeph's arrangements with their families. Though economic need seems a major reason that Oupa's family remained in the country, Zeph's family apparently chooses to remain in the house that Zeph built for them in Odenville. Presented as a comfortable, if not a traditional African arrangement, the novel appears not to question too closely the implications of power imbalance in these families separated from their men. One may argue that, like July's rural wife in *July's People* who was psychologically independent and capable, Oupa's wife (she has no name), also strong and capable, is caught in the vestiges of the old apartheid system. Though these African women function almost entirely autonomously, they remain economically dependent on the men, and what appears in Zeph's case as a mature choice can in fact be read as a perpetuation of an oppressive system. Head's analysis of spatial control is instructive here in its separation of urban and rural space, for we recognize urban space as the area of power (Head 1995, 47). That the wives and families are perforce or by choice outside of the urban centers raises questions about the patriarchal tendencies of these two black men, and therefore about the future. Zeph, in fact, admits to a blindness or insensitivity regarding the conditions of women. When Vera asks him about women on the boards of directors, he can at first recall none. An afterthought turns up one, but he cannot comment on her at all; she has been invisible to him: "I have to admit I didn't notice it, how she was treated. Among us black men, too, it's been usual. I suppose I've been conditioned from boyhood. Although I like to think I've resisted all that!" (260).

One reviewer has commented that *None to Accompany Me* is a novel of strong women and relegated men,[21] but, significantly, not all men are relegated. Zeph is at least conscious of his conditioning, Didymus is coping admirably with his loss of position and power, and Adam seems to hold the potential for more balanced attitudes and relationships than his father's generation. It is true, however, that women are a strong and growing power, though they also have a responsibility to correct the balance of power and work for equity. Despite all her progress toward shedding dependencies, even Vera still displays a whiff of a need for the idealized male in her presentation of Zeph. Her quick endorsement of him as "the least conditioned person I've met" (*NAM,* 260) immediately after he has revealed his gendered blind spot, alerts us to possible flaws in her judgment. Zeph's willingness to compromise (unlike Didymus) with the white businessmen, as well as hints of possible mismanagement in the financial enterprise of empowerment that Zeph directed, further humanize him for the reader. This is a novel with no heroes.

Nevertheless, the novel does propose a strong and empowered line of women as agents of change. The vigilance of the Veras and Sibongiles, the Annies and the Mphos, and the nameless black wives will ensure the equity that must shape the future. Without their equal contribution a creeping authoritarianism will resurface. The novel's rearrangement of patterns of intimacy unravels the conventional family structure, providing an open-endedness that points to new and experimental possibilities for the family, the community, and the nation. This open-endedness stresses the need in the personal lives of all South Africans for a commitment beyond themselves, while at the same time recognizing the autonomy of each person. Family or blood ties ensure no special understanding or connection, and such ties appear to deserve no privileged commitment. The curious detachment Vera experiences when she watches Annie's scene of domestic bliss highlights the randomness of relationship with one's offspring, suggesting that each person will find their own path: "So often Vera had felt like this, far removed from what was steering her daughter's life, further and further, unable to check the remove" (*NAM,* 309). This detachment is also acknowledged as part of a generational shift; the future, unknowable, passes to the young. The older generation knows only that you do what you can, that the individual role is minor, but must be played. Vera, as a white South African, finds her role through her divestment of her personal, psychological baggage and her economic assets gained from a privileged white system on the one hand, and her investment in her all-absorbing humanitarian political work on the other: "She had no thought, no space in herself for anything else" (*NAM*, 164). When Vera tells Zeph that South Africans must believe they can correct the mistakes of the apartheid era, Zeph replies: "A piece here, a piece there. It's all broken up. You do what you can, I do what I can. That's it" (*NAM*, 261). The advantage of broken pieces is that they can be set back together in an entirely new and creative way. Each must find his or her own way to serve, for there are many ways to "arrive" and their discovery lies with the younger generation. The novel implies that cultural and racial interfusion will increasingly take place. Hybridity is an organic process and cannot be stopped. For such national integration to be healthy and harmonious, all issues of equity must be addressed.

The integrative vision toward which *None to Accompany Me* moves is sought not only on the personal and political fronts but also on the cultural. Aesthetically speaking, this novel—while open-ended in its many paths toward resolution—is not as formally experimental as *A Sport of Nature* or *My Son's Story*. Striving to put the broken pieces of the past together in a new way, Gordimer manipulates time. In Proustian fashion the past is present in memory, and time's forward march turns back to retrieve what seems lost: "The past is set down on the streets of the present" (*NAM*, 36). Gordimer chides a cultural elitism practiced in fields like architecture (its structural metaphor being central to the novel) in which considerations are often purely aesthetic and formal, out of time, rather than socially and politically grounded. The social consequences of such elitism are the poverty and misery of the underclasses. She holds that "jagged tin and tattered plastic sheets . . . are the architecture of the late twentieth century as marble was the material of the Renaissance, glass and steel that of Mies van der Rohe; the squatter camps, the real Post-Modernism: of the homeless" (*NAM*, 81). European high culture has produced the third world, but now, seeking redress, the squatter camps speak back.

Linking art with politics, Vera declares them both transcendent as opposed to the transitory nature of personal life, and she poses an evolutionary paradigm of politics: "Politics affects and is evolved endlessly through future generations—the way people are going to live, the way they think further" (*NAM*, 305). The novel's epigraph by Proust echoes this view: "We must never be afraid to go too far, for truth lies beyond." Advancing the need for the individual's commitment to a political life, the novel implies that national and self-integration are sought on the same path. The view of politics as evolutionary rather than cyclical places the reins of the future in the hands of the new generation. With them will evolve a literature of hybridity that unselfconsciously reflects the multifaceted new nation. But like *Sport of Nature* and *My Son's Story, None to Accompany Me* is constrained by a self-consciousness of purpose, both literary and political, that tends to distance the reader from the lives of the characters, making it perhaps less compelling than her earlier work. We are reminded of the descriptive lyricism and the subtly captured nuance of behavior of those earlier novels in a scene where—celebrating her small role in this important evolving human endeavor—Vera dances alone in her living room, unselfconsciously claiming for herself a certain South African hybridity:

> When the news gave way to some piece of popular music revamped from the past, Vera, too old to find a partner, danced alone, no one to witness, in the livingroom of her house, the rock-'n'-roll and pata-pata her body remembered from wartime parties and the Fifties in the Maqomas' Chiawelo house. . . . She would stop: laughing at herself giddily. But the dancing was a rite of passage. An exultation of solitude would come over her. . . . Everyone ends up moving alone towards the self. (*NAM,* 305–6)

Or as the novel's epigraph by seventeenth-century Japanese poet Basho states it:

> None to accompany me on this path:
> Nightfall in Autumn

Chapter Six

The Future Is Another Country:
The House Gun

Gordimer's latest novel, *The House Gun,* was published in January 1998 during the final stages of preparation for this book. Rather than a conventional conclusion that tediously reviews the focus of this study, we can end instead with an analysis of Gordimer's first novelistic move into the new world of postapartheid South Africa. We can end, so to speak, with a new beginning, seeking in our reading those threads that she draws from the past into the new future with her and noting those threads she is content to leave behind. *The House Gun* is the first real test of Gordimer's artistic endurance beyond her political engagement with the apartheid era. Most reviewers agree that it is a gripping novel with little focus on the issues of overt racial discrimination and inequity that dominated much of her previous work. What endures is her interest in the expanding cultural interface in South Africa and its implications for a humane and creative hybrid culture of the future. Gordimer interrogates the persistence of violence in society, and she maintains a watchful eye on pockets of potential oppression as South Africa asserts its new nationhood.

The House Gun is set in early 1996, when the Mandela government was not even two years old. The events of the novel occur against a background of a country with a new and very different constitution from the previous government's, one with commitments to human rights and freedoms never before granted. Of the many new constitutional provisos, two are most relevant to this novel. The South African Constitution, one of the most liberal in the world today, upholds the right of sexual preference and, as such, protects gay citizens from discrimination and abuse. Also, the new constitution enshrines the right to life. The ANC government consequently declared a moratorium on the death penalty, which was still on the books when they came to power. In 1996 the death penalty was being challenged in the highest court of the land, the Constitutional Court, and Gordimer injects the language of the constitution into the novel:

Section 9 guarantees the right to life Section 10 protection of human dignity Section 11 outlaws cruel or degrading treatment or punishment.[1]

While academic debates over ethics and constitutional issues were taking place in the halls of justice, the social climate of 1996 was one of spreading crime and violence. Disillusionment and unemployment proved endemic after unrealistic expectations about redistribution and economic equity wavered. In a culture grown callous to a pain and violence institutionalized by a brutal regime through its police force and against whom retaliatory violence was sanctioned and encouraged, the transference of violence from political targets to anyone standing in the way of some quick gain has been easy. Car jackings, taxi wars, muggings, and break-ins seem often accompanied by unnecessary and brutal acts of violence that comment ironically on the niceties of a court decision aimed at preventing state-sanctioned violence against murderers. As the public continues to clamor for more protection, security companies' profits soar. Installations of electronic alarms, guard dogs, razor wire, and rapid response systems have mushroomed in middle- and upper-class neighborhoods, and road rules have been modified to reduce the risk drivers run when stopping at a red light late at night. Gordimer's ever-present sense of irony makes rich use of the challenging disjunction between the ideal and real life in the mid- to late 1990s.

The novel takes a popular fiction and television genre, the law trial, and—without losing its page-turning quality—redirects it to interrogate the persistence of violence in human affairs. It examines the individual and collective need to come to terms with a certain inevitability, inexplicability, and randomness of it, and emphasizes our responsibility to create a humane and healing social environment in an effort to both de-escalate violence as a solution, and to understand and cope with the chaotic aftermath that violence sows.

Divided into two parts, the novel focuses first on the reaction of Duncan Lindgard's parents, Harald and Claudia, to the shocking news of their son's arrest for murder. We are slowly introduced to Duncan through his stunned parents' attempts to cope with this life-shattering incident as they receive the details of what happened in piecemeal fashion from friends and attorney. Though we glimpse him in court, Duncan is not accessible in the first half of the book. The second half grants us fragmented snatches of his deeper, troubled consciousness. These snatches provide a contrasting perspective to the versions gleaned from the characters around him (parents, girlfriend Natalie, friends, attorney) who, like the reader, are trying (vainly) to construct an identity that will reveal who the murdering Duncan really is. In its concentration on the inadequacy of interpretation and the disorienting reality of the unexplainable, the novel can be considered postmodern. The text self-consciously draws attention to its own lacunae: "Why is Duncan not in the story? He is a vortex from which, flung away, around, are all: Harald, Claudia, Motsamai, Khulu, the girl, and the dead man" (*HG*, 151). And it asks later: "Again, why is Duncan not in the story? He is the vortex from which, flung away, around, is the court. If he cannot understand why he did what he did, there will be the explanations of others" (*HG*, 191).

A 27-year-old middle-class architect in Johannesburg, Duncan lives with his girlfriend, Natalie James, in the garden cottage of a large old house, which is home to his group of gay friends. He has admitted shooting one of the friends, an ex-lover, Carl Jespersen, through the head. Duncan's short affair with Jespersen seems well in the past. Apparently Jespersen had quickly grown tired of his dalliance with the rather intense Duncan, who, it appears, had taken this exceptional (for him) gay affair more seriously than the older Scandinavian man. When the novel opens, Duncan has been living in a troubled relationship with the neurotic Natalie for a while. After an impromptu party in the house late one Thursday night, he stumbles upon Natalie and Jespersen (who has previously avowed a total distaste for women) in the throes of sex on the living room sofa. Distraught and doubly humiliated, Duncan flees back to the cottage to wait for Natalie (she has been with other men periodically before), but she never returns. He hides out at the cottage all of Friday, failing to go to work, and only when his dog clamors for food in the late afternoon does he emerge and wander over to the main house. There he finds Jespersen lolling on the sofa from the night before. Jespersen begins a rambling, lighthearted apology, offering platitudes and a brotherly drink, but the disturbed Duncan picks up the house gun (unfortunately left lying on the coffee table) and shoots him through the head. It is ostensibly this dastardly situation that the novel sets out to unravel. The superb defense mounted by black South African defense attorney Hamilton Motsamai, who pleads "loss of self-control as inability to act in appreciation of wrongfulness" (*HG*, 236), wins Duncan the best deal possible: a short seven-year sentence. But Gordimer sidesteps the sensational and the prurient, as she did in *Occasion for Loving,* and early on deliberately draws attention to the novel's form. The text warns the reader of what it is not—"This is not a detective novel"

(*HG,* 16)—directing focus instead on the inner struggles of both the parents and the son. Rather than a superficial whodunit, Gordimer interrogates the unknown terrors that lie within our unfathomed selves and within those whose selves we think we know.

To shield their lives from increasing societal violence, Duncan's parents, Harald and Claudia, insurance executive and physician, respectively, have recently moved into a security-monitored townhouse. They fear the random brutal acts that are frequently visited on unprotected homeowners and drivers in the city. Yet, ironically, it is in their safe new haven on a cozy and uneventful Friday night as they watch television that a friend of Duncan brings them news of his arrest, news of a violence that reaches past security gates to shatter their protected world. Duncan has requested that they not seek him out or try to take action; he has already hired an attorney. He asks that they wait to see him on Monday in court when he will be committed to trial (he is refused bail) for murder. In the ensuing scramble to make sense of this incredible and frightening situation, the parents—in the weeks that follow—question Duncan's friends; they discreetly check (through Harald's connections) the impeccable reputation of Duncan's counsel, Hamilton Motsamai, a black South African trained and practiced in England; they meet with Motsamai in the advocates' chambers; and Harald meets with Natalie in Motsamai's office. Both parents vainly search their parenting history for clues that may shed light on this inexplicable event. The incongruencies and philosophical differences in their own relationship (Harald's religion and love of literature, particularly Dostoevsky and Thomas Mann; Claudia's trust in science)—so smoothed over by time and accommodation—rise to chafe anew, challenging the marriage to reassess its commitments. Their covenant made to Duncan as a child that "there's nothing you cannot tell us" (*HG,* 159) rings hollow and empty. They find themselves now "on the other side of privilege. Neither whiteness, nor observance of the teachings of Father and Son, nor the pious respectability of liberalism, nor money, that had kept them in safety— that other form of segregation—could change their status" (*HG,* 127).

A central figure in the novel is Hamilton Motsamai, Duncan's defense counsel, for it is upon him that all parties must depend for the outcome of the trial. But Gordimer has made him a key figure for other reasons. It is Motsamai who represents the hope and the new direction for South Africa, his hybrid blend of cultures and his goodwill promise a positive future. It is he who uncovers and uses Natalie's pregnancy (by Jespersen or Duncan?) so skillfully in the trial, but—more than that—

he opens through the child a route to some sort of salvation for Duncan and his parents. This salvation, both personal and political/social, is embodied also in the loyal friendship of one of the house occupants, Nkululeko Dladla (Khulu), who stands by Duncan and his parents throughout the ordeal. That Motsamai and Khulu are black seems to signify that there lies some healing, teaching power within African cultural attitudes for ailing white South Africans. By the time the novel closes Duncan has instructed his parents to assist Natalie's child. He understands that "violence is a repetition we don't seem able to break," (*HG*, 294) asserting nevertheless that he has to find a way. "Carl's death and Natalie's child . . . They become one, for me. It does not matter whether or not anyone else will understand: Carl, Natalie/Nastasya and me, the three of us. I've had to find a way to bring death and life together" (*HG*, 294).

In *The House Gun* the problem of violence is no longer yoked to race. Racism is a receding issue in the novel, a point driven home by Motsamai's ability to define his relationship to the white Lindgards:

> Without bothering to ask permission from them, he [Motsamai] had established first-name terms. The fact that he himself was prepared to address Harald by first name was licence granted. He had the authority. . . . Motsamai, the stranger from the Other Side of the divided past. They are in his pink-palmed black hands. (*HG*, 86)

Duncan's parents—despite their wishy-washy liberalism—are still tainted with old prejudices (they wonder at first whether a Jewish or an Indian lawyer would be better than the black Motsamai, and they must rethink their assumption that gayness is a "disintegration"), but for Duncan and many of his generation, color and sexual orientation seem dead issues. Duncan chooses a black attorney, and his most faithful friend is both black and gay. Yet according to a text that Harald reads late one night when he can't sleep, the lives of this less prejudiced generation are inevitably impregnated with violence:

> "the transition from any value system to a new one must pass through that zero-point of atomic dissolution, must take its way through a generation destitute of any connection with either the old or the new system, a generation whose very detachment, whose almost insane indifference to the suffering of others, whose state of denudation of values proves an ethical and so an historical justification for the ruthless rejection, in times of revolution, of all that is humane." (*HG*, 142)

The theme of random violence, explored in *None to Accompany Me* in the shooting attack on Vera Stark and Oupa, is taken up once again in *The House Gun*. The novel evolves as a profound meditation on the philosophy and nature of violence: its sources, its context, its consequences. Violence is seen as a contamination. It spreads like a disease through close association, and Harald and Claudia have been infected: "The difference between Harald and Claudia as what they used to be, watching the sunset, and what they are now is that they are within the labyrinth [of violence] through intimate contact with a carrier" (*HG*, 141). The Constitutional Court—housed in the building that was the old Fever Hospital—becomes one way that this societal infection of violence is being healed. Another healing influence can be found in the intertextual references to other literary works which call forth various authors' explorations of the topic of violence, and draws—like father and son—on the "substance of writers' imaginative explanations of human mystery" (*HG*, 71). Father and son read works "that are dangerous and indispensable, revealing to you what you are" (*HG*, 292), a claim for the essential need for art in society. Harald's familiarity with the quotation from Thomas Mann's character Naphta in *The Magic Mountain* raises Mann's extended debate between Settembrini's support for the liberal-individualism of our bourgeois humanitarian age and Naphta's much harsher social conceptions, such as the use of the death penalty and corporal punishment for the good of the soul, a debate particularly relevant to the South Africa of 1996. Gordimer's character, Harald, is haunted by Naphta's comments:

> "the man is as he has wished to be, and as, until his last breath, he has never ceased to wish to be. He has revelled in slaying, and does not pay too dear in being slain. Let him die, then, for he has gratified his heart's deepest desire."
> "Deepest desire?"
> "Deepest desire."
> "It is absurd for the murderer to outlive the murdered. They two, alone together—as two beings are together in only one other human relationship, one acting, the other suffering him—share a secret that binds them forever. They belong to each other." (*HG*, 71–72)

Harald is haunted, too, by a quotation from Dostoevsky's *The Idiot*, which is scrawled in a notebook of Duncan's that he finds in the cottage after Duncan's arrest, a quotation that hints of a darker side of the son whose emotional depths are unknown to his parents. The comment is made by Rogozhin about Nastasya Filippovna, whom he later murders in a jealous rage: "She would have drowned herself long ago if she had not had me; that's the truth. She doesn't do that because, perhaps, I am more dreadful than the water" (*HG,* 47).

In jail, Duncan relies on a different book, however, one his father never gave him. He finds that the clue to understanding his own violence lies in the fishmoth-infested copy of *The Odyssey* that he uncovers in the prison library. He quotes from the scene where Odysseus returns after 20 years to challenge the suitors wooing his wife, and he focuses particularly on the part where Odysseus shoots Antinous through the throat with an arrow. He comments about the book:

> But now there's something that's for me, that's been waiting for me, in this place, in my time. Time to read and reread it. "With that he trained a stabbing arrow on Antinous . . . just lifting a gorgeous golden loving-cup in his hands . . . But Odysseus aimed and shot Antinous square in the throat, and the point went stabbing clean through the soft neck and out— / and off to the side he pitched, the cup dropped from his grasp/ as the shaft sank home." (*HG,* 293)

Duncan feels a kinship with Odysseus and Homer; he understands how Odysseus could act this way. He admits, too, that he realizes as illusion the sense of originality of the act of murder:

> The moment when you put your hand out to do it . . . you think it's a *discovery,* it's something that's come to you that has never been known before. But it's always been there, it's been discovered again and again, forever. Again and again, what Odysseus did, and what Homer, whoever he was, knew. (*HG,* 293–94)

But Natalie is no Penelope and, however neurotic and cruel she may seem, she feels trapped and suffocated by the conventional middle-class relationship she perceives Duncan imposing on her. She rants at him late one night: "you plan to save me in the missionary position not only on my back good taste married your babies . . . develop 'careers' you invent for me because that's what a woman you've saved should have you took away from me my death . . ." (*HG,* 153). Natalie's critique of the bourgeois nuclear family model is ironically echoed by Duncan's own description in court of the living arrangements of the friends at the old house: "The house is a place where people just turn up. And often Natalie and I would join the men at the house and we'd eat together at

night. I suppose we were a sort of family. Better than a nuclear family, a
lot of friendship and trust between us" (*HG,* 208).

Gordimer's concern about the restrictive role of the patriarchal
nuclear family as an impediment to the creation of a new and free nation
reasserts itself in this novel. Once more the hope of a successful new
nation is linked in a profound way to the loosening of blind familial and
clan loyalties and the imagining of broader and more principled
alliances. From her early consideration of the formation of a new independent nation in *A Guest of Honour* to her analysis of the narrowness
and self-centeredness of nuclear family loyalties in *None to Accompany Me,*
Gordimer has sought more conscious and politically meaningful connections for her characters. Placing Harald and Claudia "on the other side"
through their misfortune forces them to identify, to empathize, with the
very people they have sought to keep at bay in their lives. Gordimer
shows again that blood ties do not ensure closeness, understanding, or
knowledge. Whether as a result of bourgeois white values of "decency"
and "privacy" or simply of individualistic differences, parents seem not
to know their children. In his attempt to understand what has happened
to their family, Harald comments to Duncan's friend:

> You must understand we've lived, my wife and I, parents and son, as
> three independent adults, we're close but we don't expect to be privy to
> everything in his life. Different relationships. We have ours with him, he
> has his with others. It's been fine. But when something like this falls on
> your head—we understand what this—respect, I suppose, for one
> another, can mean. Just that we don't know anything we need to know.
> (*HG,* 21)

Feeling implicated in and resentful of their son's act of violence generates an alienating sense of shame and guilt in Harald and Claudia, and
prompts "a need to re-conceive, re-gestate the son" (*HG,* 63). Harald's
attempts to understand the possibilities of such violence lead him to
contemplate issues of heredity and culture, to revisit Duncan's upbringing, and to recall the suicide of one of Duncan's schoolmates—an incident that had disturbed them all. This incident was the first that made
the parents realize that

> the unease they felt came from revealed knowledge that there are dan-
> gers, inherent, there in the young; dangers within existence itself. There
> is no segregation from them. And no-one can know, for another, even
> your own child, what these destructives, these primal despairs and drives

are. . . .What came to them was fear—fear that there could be threats to
their son about which they could not know, could do nothing. (*HG*, 69)

It is this sense of a family driven by fear, a family seeking some insurance
against harm or disaster, that is posed in contrast to the large, open-
hearted family of Hamilton Motsamai. When Claudia and Harald visit
the Motsamai family they encounter sprawling children, uncles, nieces,
hangers-on; all are a part of an inclusive and shared benevolence. The
evening ends with Claudia dancing in the Motsamai's living room,
where she has made an affirming human connection:

> Claudia had been found by a man who came from a different experience
> in every other way but this one: the music, its expression on body and
> feet, of the Sixties, it didn't matter where he had performed its rituals in
> shebeen and yards, and she had carried them out in student union halls,
> they assumed the form of an assertion of life that was hidden in each.
> (*HG*, 175)

This sense of a human connection is also driven home to the Lindgards through Khulu's spirit of generosity and warmth. Khulu's
message to Duncan—sent via his parents: "UNGEKE UDLIWE
UMZWANGEDWA SISEKHONA," which means "you will never be
alone because we are alone without you" (*HG*, 249–50), his warm smile
to Duncan across the courtroom when he takes the witness stand, and
his supportive presence throughout the trial for Claudia and Harald
makes him a surrogate son and a true brother to Duncan. Yet the parents still have a lot to learn about love and humanity. Their reluctance
to initiate any connection with Natalie's child, to take on any responsibility for him, is again based in fear. Khulu recognizes that "what
they're appalled by is that they might be expected to prove themselves
as parents to their own son by taking in the kid, themselves. As if—with
his people—this would need a second's thought! Children belong, never
mind any doubts about their origin, in the family" (*HG*, 290). Hamilton
Motsamai assumes that human warmth and caring will eventually triumph. He will "arrange what he calls access. Get to know the small boy.
Have him at the townhouse, watch him play with the dog" (*HG*, 291).

In this way, for Gordimer, a life-affirming spirit grows out of disaster.
Early in the novel Harald had defined love: "Love is life, it's procreative,
can't kill. If it does, it's not love" (*HG*, 76). So, like Hans Castorp in *The
Magic Mountain* (he also spent seven years in confinement, in a sanitar-
ium), Duncan—and his parents—must learn to love not only individu-

ally; they must love all of humanity. Thomas Mann writes that Castorp
finds, or at least divines, the Holy Grail for which he searches. His
understanding of the reverence for humanity is the same understanding
that permeates all of Nadine Gordimer's work as well:

> It is the idea of the human being, the conception of a future humanity
> that has passed through and survived the profoundest knowledge of dis-
> ease and death. The Grail is a mystery, but humanity is a mystery too.
> For man himself is a mystery, and all humanity rests upon reverence
> before the mystery that is man.[2]

sexist

— by Thomas Mann
The Magic Mountain

Notes and References

Preface

1. Interview with Nadine Gordimer by Stephen Clingman, "The Future Is Another Country," *Transition* 56 (1992): 137; hereafter cited in text as Future.

2. Nadine Gordimer, "Turning the Page: African Writers on the Threshold of the Twenty-first Century," *Transition* 56 (1992): 5; hereafter cited in text as Turning.

Chapter 1

1. Nadine Gordimer, *The Essential Gesture: Writing, Politics and Places,* ed. Stephen Clingman (New York: Knopf, 1988), 143; hereafter cited in text as *EG*.

2. Stephen Clingman, *The Novels of Nadine Gordimer: History from the Inside* (London: Allen and Unwin, 1986), 15; hereafter cited in text as Clingman.

3. Nancy Topping Bazin and Marilyn Dallman Seymour, eds., *Conversations with Nadine Gordimer* (Jackson: University Press of Mississippi, 1990), 248; hereafter cited in text as *CNG*.

4. John Cooke, *The Novels of Nadine Gordimer: Private Lives/Public Landscapes* (Baton Rouge: Louisiana State University Press, 1985), 10.

5. David Ward, *Chronicles of Darkness* (London: Routledge, 1989), 26; hereafter cited in text as Ward.

6. Michael Wade, *White on Black South Africa: A Study of English-Language Inscriptions of Skin Colour* (New York: St. Martin's Press, 1993), 150; hereafter cited in text as Wade.

7. Kathrin Wagner, *Rereading Nadine Gordimer* (Bloomington: Indiana University Press, 1994), 2; hereafter cited in text as Wagner.

8. Rowland Smith, ed., introduction to *Critical Essays on Nadine Gordimer* (Boston: G. K. Hall, 1990), 4–8.

9. A. W. Oliphant, "Crash Course in Literary Bulldozing," *Sunday Times* (Sept. 3, 1995), sec. 2, p. 18.

10. Nadine Gordimer, *Writing and Being* (Cambridge, Mass.: Harvard University Press, 1995), 131; hereafter cited in text as *WB*.

11. Nancy Topping Bazin, "An Interview with Nadine Gordimer," *Contemporary Literature* 36, no. 4 (Winter 1995): 573; hereafter cited as Bazin interview.

Chapter 2

1. Nadine Gordimer, *The Lying Days* (New York: Simon and Schuster, 1953), 11; hereafter cited in text as *LD*.

2. Judie Newman, *Nadine Gordimer*, Contemporary Writers Series (London: Routledge, 1988), 22; hereafter cited in text as Newman.

3. Nadine Gordimer, *A World of Strangers* (New York: Simon and Schuster, 1958), 36; hereafter cited in text as *WS*.

4. *Coloured(s)* was the official classificatory term used by the apartheid National government to designate people of mixed racial descent. I retain the term for historical accuracy.

5. Nadine Gordimer, *Occasion for Loving* (New York: Viking, 1963), 278; hereafter cited in text as *OL*.

6. See J. M. Coetzee's article "Man's Fate in the Novels of Alex La Guma," *Studies in Black Literature* 5, no.1 (1974): 16–23. Coetzee states, "Tragedy [in white South African fiction] is typically the tragedy of interracial love: a white man and a black woman, or vice versa, fall foul of the laws against miscegenation, or simply of white prejudice, and are destroyed or driven into exile."

Chapter 3

1. Nadine Gordimer, *The Late Bourgeois World* (New York: Viking, 1966), 8; hereafter cited in text as *LBW*.

2. Nadine Gordimer, *A Guest of Honour* (New York: Viking, 1970), 98; hereafter cited in text as *GH*.

3. Anderson quoted in Timothy Brennan, "The National Longing for Form." In *Nation and Narration,* ed. Homi K. Bhabha (London: Routledge, 1990), 48; hereafter cited in text as Brennan.

4. Frantz Fanon, *Wretched of the Earth,* trans. Constance Farrington (New York: Grove Press, 1963), 145; hereafter cited in text as Fanon 1963.

5. Nadine Gordimer, *The Black Interpreters: Notes on African Writing* (Johannesburg: Spro-Cas/Ravan Press), 5.

6. Frantz Fanon, *Black Skin, White Masks,* trans. Charles Lam Markmann (New York: Grove Press, 1967), 17–18; hereafter cited in text as Fanon 1967.

7. Elaine Fido, "*A Guest of Honour:* A Feminist View of Masculinity." In *Critical Essays on Nadine Gordimer,* ed. Rowland Smith (Boston: G. K. Hall, 1990), 99.

8. Nadine Gordimer, *The Conservationist* (New York: Viking, 1974), 147; hereafter cited in text as *Cons*.

Chapter 4

1. Nadine Gordimer, *Burger's Daughter* (New York: Viking, 1979), 113–14; hereafter cited in text as *BD*.

2. Nadine Gordimer (with others), *What Happened to "Burger's Daughter" or How South African Censorship Works* (Johannesburg: Taurus, 1980), 17.

3. Nadine Gordimer, "The Value of a Conference: Introduction." In *Culture in Another South Africa,* ed. Willem Campschreur and Joost Divendal (New York: Olive Branch Press, 1989), 12.

4. Nadine Gordimer, *July's People* (New York: Viking, 1981), 65; hereafter cited in text as *JP.*

5. Robert Boyers, "A Conversation with Nadine Gordimer," *Salmagundi* 62 (Winter 1984): 28; hereafter cited in text as Boyers.

Chapter 5

1. Nadine Gordimer, "Apprentices of Freedom," *The Arts in Adversity* (supplement to *New Society*) (December 24–31, 1981): v; hereafter cited as Apprentices.

2. Nadine Gordimer, *A Sport of Nature* (New York: Knopf, 1987), 100; hereafter cited in text as *SN.*

3. Epigraph of *A Sport of Nature* credited to the Oxford English Dictionary.

4. Daniel Schwarz, *Rereading Joyce's Ulysses* (New York: St. Martin's, 1987), 14; hereafter cited as Schwarz.

5. J. M.Coetzee, *White Writing: On the Culture of Letters in South Africa* (New Haven: Yale University Press, 1988), 153.

6. Dorothy Driver, "The Politicisation of Women." In *Critical Essays on Nadine Gordimer,* ed. Rowland Smith (Boston: G. K. Hall, 1990), 186; hereafter cited in text as Driver.

7. Richard Peck, "What's a Poor White to Do? White South African Options in *A Sport of Nature.*" In *Critical Essays on Nadine Gordimer,* ed. Roland Smith (Boston: G. K. Hall, 1990), 153.

8. Dominic Head, *Nadine Gordimer* (Cambridge: Cambridge University Press, 1994), 144; hereafter cited as Head 1994.

9. Mamphela Ramphele, Presentation at Women's Caucus Breakfast, African Studies Conference (Atlanta, GA, November 1989), 6.

10. Sheila Roberts, "Nadine Gordimer's Family of Women." In *Critical Essays on Nadine Gordimer,* ed. Rowland Smith (Boston: G. K. Hall, 1990), 179.

11. Karen Lazar, "Feminism as 'Piffling'? Ambiguities in Some of Nadine Gordimer's Short Stories," *Current Writing* 2 (October 1990): 103.

12. Susan Gardner, quoted in Driver, 198.

13. Michel Foucault, *The Archeology of Knowledge and the Discourse on Language* (New York: Pantheon, 1972), 49.

14. Catherine A. Lutz and Lila Abu-Lughod, "Introduction: Emotion, Discourse, and the Politics of Everyday Life." In *Language and the Politics of Emotion: Studies in Emotion and Social Interaction,* ed. Catherine Lutz and Lila Abu-Lughod (Cambridge: Cambridge University Press, 1990), 10; hereafter cited in text as Lutz and Abu-Lughod.

check — in CNG?

15. Interview with Nadine Gordimer by Terry Gross. National Public Radio, Tacoma, Washington (Fall 1992).

16. Nadine Gordimer, *My Son's Story* (New York: Farrar, Straus and Giroux, 1990), 14; hereafter cited in text as *MSS*.

17. Susan M. Greenstein, *"My Son's Story:* Drenching the Censors—the Dilemma of White Writing." In *The Later Fiction of Nadine Gordimer,* ed. Bruce King (New York: St. Martin's Press, 1993), 201; hereafter cited in text as Greenstein.

18. Nadine Gordimer, *None to Accompany Me* (New York: Farrar, Straus and Giroux, 1994), 241; hereafter cited in text as *NAM*.

19. See my discussion of Foucault's concept of power in "Sexuality, Resistance and Power in Nadine Gordimer's Novels." In *Multicultural Literatures through Feminist/Poststructuralist Lenses,* ed. Barbara Frey Waxman (Knoxville: University of Tennessee Press, 1993), 138:

> Foucault describes the conditions from which power arises as "the moving substrate of force relations which, by virtue of their inequality, constantly engender states of power, but the latter are always local and unstable." He emphasises that power is not an institution, nor a structure, but rather the name that one attributes to a complex strategical situation in a particular society. It is exercised from innumerable points, in the interplay of nonegalitarian and mobile relations, and it comes from below through the linking of oppositions that bring about realignments and ultimately convergences of force relations.

20. Dominic Head, "Gordimer's *None to Accompany Me*: Revisionism and Interregnum," *Research in African Literatures* 26 (Winter 1995): 51–52; hereafter cited in text as Head 1995.

21. Rosemary Dinnage, "In a Far-Off Country." Review of *None to Accompany Me* in *Times Literary Supplement* 4771 (September 9, 1994): 20.

Chapter 6

1. Nadine Gordimer, *The House Gun* (New York: Farrar, Straus and Giroux, 1998), 136; hereafter cited in text as *HG*.

2. Thomas Mann, *The Magic Mountain,* trans. H. T. Lowe-Porter (New York: Vintage Books, 1969), 727.

Selected Bibliography

Primary Sources

Novels

The Lying Days. New York: Simon & Schuster, 1953.
A World of Strangers. New York: Simon & Schuster, 1958.
Occasion for Loving. New York: Viking, 1963.
The Late Bourgeois World. New York: Viking, 1966.
A Guest of Honor. New York: Viking, 1970.
The Conservationist. New York: Viking, 1974.
Burger's Daughter. New York: Viking, 1979.
July's People. New York: Viking, 1981.
A Sport of Nature. New York: Knopf, 1987.
My Son's Story. New York: Farrar, Straus & Giroux, 1990.
None to Accompany Me. New York: Farrar, Straus & Giroux, 1994.
The House Gun. New York: Farrar, Straus & Giroux, 1998.

Short-Story Collections

Face to Face. Johannesburg: Silver Leaf, 1949.
The Soft Voice of the Serpent and Other Stories. New York: Simon & Schuster, 1952.
Six Feet of the Country: Fifteen Short Stories. New York: Simon & Schuster, 1956.
Friday's Footprint. New York: Viking, 1960.
Not for Publication and Other Stories. New York: Viking, 1965.
Livingstone's Companions. New York: Viking, 1971.
Selected Stories. New York: Viking, 1975.
Some Monday for Sure. London: Heinemann, 1976.
A Soldier's Embrace: Stories. New York: Viking, 1980.
Town and Country Lovers. Los Angeles: Sylvester, 1980.
Six Feet of the Country. Harmondsworth: Penguin, 1982 (a collection of previously collected stories, different from the 1956 collection with the same title).
Something Out There. New York: Viking, 1984.
Crimes of Conscience. Oxford: Heinemann, 1991.
Jump and Other Stories. New York: Farrar, Straus & Giroux, 1991.
Why Haven't you Written? Selected Stories 1950–1972. London: Penguin, 1992.

Nonfiction

"Apprentices of Freedom." *The Arts in Adversity* (supplement to *New Society*) 24 (December 31, 1981): ii–v.
The Black Interpreters: Notes on African Writing. Johannesburg: Spro-Cas/Ravan Press, 1973.
The Essential Gesture: Writing, Politics and Places. Edited and introduced by Stephen Clingman. New York: Knopf, 1988.
"Turning the Page: African Writers on the Threshold of the Twenty-first Century." *Transition* 56 (1992): 4–10.
What Happened to Burger's Daughter or How South African Censorship Works (with others). Johannesburg: Taurus, 1980.
Writing and Being. Cambridge: Harvard University Press, 1995.

Interviews with Gordimer

Bazin, Nancy Topping, and Marilyn Dallman Seymour, eds. *Conversations with Nadine Gordimer.* Jackson: University Press of Mississippi, 1990. Collection of the bulk of interviews with Gordimer between 1958 and 1989.
Bazin, Nancy Topping. "An Interview with Nadine Gordimer." *Contemporary Literature* 36, no. 4 (Winter 1995): 571–87.
Boyers, Robert. "A Conversation with Nadine Gordimer." *Salmagundi* 62 (Winter 1984): 3–31.
Clingman, Stephen. "The Future is Another Country." *Transition* 56 (1992): 132–50.
Gross, Terry. National Public Radio, Tacoma, Washington. Fall 1992.

Secondary Sources

Bibliographies

Driver, Dorothy, Ann Dry, Craig MacKenzie, and John Read. *Nadine Gordimer: A Bibliography of Primary and Secondary Sources, 1937–1992.* Bibliographical Research in African Literature Series. London: Hans Zell Publishers, 1994.

Books and Parts of Books about Nadine Gordimer

Clingman, Stephen. *The Novels of Nadine Gordimer: History from the Inside.* London: Allen and Unwin, 1986. Traces the novels' engagement with history and the development of Gordimer's historical consciousness as evidenced in her fiction over the years.
Cooke, John. *The Novels of Nadine Gordimer: Private Lives/Public Landscapes.* Baton Rouge: Louisiana State University Press, 1985. Explores the idea that Gordimer's private realm increasingly informs the public themes of her novels.

Ettin, Andrew V. *Betrayals of the Body Politic: The Literary Commitments of Nadine Gordimer.* Charlottesville: University Press of Virginia, 1993.

Head, Dominic. *Nadine Gordimer.* Cambridge: Cambridge University Press, 1994. Traces Gordimer's increasing concern with a the politics of textuality.

King, Bruce, ed. *The Later Fiction of Nadine Gordimer.* New York: St. Martin's Press, 1993.

Newman, Judie. *Nadine Gordimer.* Contemporary Writers Series. London: Routledge. Reassesses Gordimer's work from a poststructuralist approach with an emphasis on issues of gender.

Smith, Rowland, ed. *Critical Essays on Nadine Gordimer.* Boston: G. K. Hall, 1990.

Wade, Michael. *White on Black in South Africa: A Study of English-Language Inscriptions of Skin Colour.* New York: St. Martin's Press, 1993.

Wagner, Kathrin. *Rereading Nadine Gordimer.* Bloomington: Indiana University Press, 1994. Examines the survival and prevalence of subtextual cultural and ethnic stereotypes regarded as undermining the overt idealogical thrust of Gordimer's fiction.

Ward, David. *Chronicles of Darkness.* London: Routledge, 1989. Part of the book addresses Gordimer's narrative strategy in her fiction's shift from chronicle to prophecy.

Articles and Other Critical Sources

Bailey, Nancy. "Living without the Future: Nadine Gordimer's *July's People.*" *World Literature Written in English* 24 (1984): 215–24.

Brennan, Timothy. "The National Longing for Form." In *Nation and Narration,* ed. Homi K. Bhabha. London: Routledge, 1990.

Coetzee, J. M. "Man's Fate in the Novels of Alex La Guma." *Studies in Black Literature* 5, no. 1 (1974): 16–23

———. *White Writing: On the Culture of Letters in South Africa.* New Haven: Yale University Press, 1988.

Dinnage, Rosemary. "In a Far-Off Country." Review of *None to Accompany Me* in *Times Literary Supplement* (4771) September 9, 1994: 20.

Driver, Dorothy. "The Politicisation of Women." In *Critical Essays on Nadine Gordimer.* Ed. Rowland Smith. Boston: G. K. Hall, 1990.

Fanon, Frantz. *The Wretched of the Earth.* Trans. Constance Farrington. New York: Grove Press, 1963.

———. *Black Skin, White Masks.* Trans. Charles Lam Markmann. New York: Grove Press, 1967.

Fido, Elaine. "*A Guest of Honour:* A Feminist View of Masculinity." In *Critical Essays on Nadine Gordimer.* Ed. Rowland Smith. Boston: G. K. Hall, 1990.

Foucault, Michel. *The Archeology of Knowledge and the Discourse on Language.* New York: Pantheon, 1972.

————. *The History of Sexuality: An Introduction,* vol. 1. New York: Vintage Books, 1980.

Gardner, Susan. "Still Waiting for the Great Feminist Novel: Nadine Gordimer's *Burger's Daughter.*" *Hecate* 8 (1982): 61–76.

Gray, Stephen. "Landmark in Fiction." Reprinted in *Conversations with Nadine Gordimer.* Ed. Nancy Topping Bazin and Marilyn Dallman Seymour. Jackson: University Press of Mississippi, 1990.

Greenstein, Susan M. "*My Son's Story:* Drenching the Censors—The Dilemma of White Writing." In *The Later Fiction of Nadine Gordimer.* Ed. Bruce King. New York: St. Martin's Press, 1993.

Head, Dominic. "Gordimer's *None to Accompany Me:* Revisionism and Interregnum." *Research in African Literatures* 26 (Winter 1995): 46–57.

JanMohamed, Abdul. *Manichean Aesthetics: The Politics of Literature in Colonial Africa.* 1983; Amherst: University of Massachusetts Press, 1988.

Lazar, Karen. "Feminism as 'Piffling'? Ambiguities in Some of Nadine Gordimer's Short Stories." *Current Writing* 2 (October 1990): 101–16.

Lutz, Catherine A., and Lila Abu-Lughod. "Introduction: Emotion, Discourse, and the Politics of Everyday Life." In *Language and the Politics of Emotion: Studies in Emotion and Social Interaction.* Ed. Catherine Lutz and Lila Abu-Lughod. Cambridge: Cambridge University Press, 1990.

Mann, Thomas. *The Magic Mountain.* Trans. H. T. Lowe-Porter. New York: Vintage Books, 1969.

Peck, Richard. "What's a Poor White to Do? White South African Options in *A Sport of Nature.*" In *Critical Essays on Nadine Gordimer.* Ed. Roland Smith. Boston: G. K. Hall, 1990.

Ramphele, Mamphela. Lecture. Women's Caucus Breakfast, African Studies Conference. Atlanta, GA. November 1989.

Schreiner, Olive. *The Story of an African Farm.* 1883; Harmondsworth: Penguin, 1971.

Schwarz, Daniel. *Rereading Joyce's Ulysses.* New York: St. Martin's Press, 1887.

Smith, Rowland. "Masters and Servants: Nadine Gordimer's *July's People* and the Themes of her Fiction." *Salmagundi* 62 (Winter 1984): 93–107.

Temple-Thurston, Barbara. "Madam and Boy: A Relationship of Shame in Gordimer's *July's People.*" *World Literature Written in English* 28 (1988): 51–58.

————. "Nadine Gordimer: The Artist as *A Sport of Nature.*" *Studies in Twentieth Century Literature* 15 (1991): 184–92.

————. "Sexuality, Resistance, and Power in Nadine Gordimer's Novels." In *Multicultural Literatures through Feminist/Poststructuralist Lenses.* Ed. Barbara Frey Waxman. Knoxville: University of Tennessee Press, 1993.

Index

The Author

Barbara Temple-Thurston is an associate professor of English at Pacific Lutheran University in Tacoma, Washington, where her teaching and research interests center on African and Caribbean literature. She was born and raised in South Africa, studied as an undergraduate at the University of the Witwatersrand in Johannesburg, where she received her B.A., and then taught high school on the Witwatersrand and in Swaziland for a number of years. She moved to the United States in 1976 where she received her M.S.Ed and her Ph.D. in English from Southern Illinois University at Carbondale. She has taught in South Dakota, Virginia, and North Carolina. Several of her published articles focus on the fiction of Nadine Gordimer.

The Editor

Bernth Lindfors is a professor of English and African literatures at the University of Texas at Austin. He has written and edited more than thirty books, including *Black African Literature in English* (1979, 1986, 1989, 1995), *Popular Literatures in Africa* (1991), *Comparative Approaches to African Literatures* (1994), *Long Drums and Canons: Teaching and Researching African Literatures* (1995), *Loaded Vehicles: Studies in African Literary Media* (1996), and (with Reinhard Sander) *Twentieth-Century Caribbean and Black African Writers* (1992, 1993, 1996). From 1970 to 1989 he was editor of *Research in African Literatures*.

LAW

LD check Paul's job w. Native help organ. to see role of LAW

WSt. p. 20 Anna Louw, an attorney for the Legal Aid Societ
21 - Blacks too, like Toby, can want to NOT be involved in
politics
3 types of law: • white apartheid solidifies racism into
crimes + punishments
• white lawyers (ex. Anna Louw) - She leaves h
own group to work for blacks - a
"frontiersman" Lawyers in Sport + NAM
• new constitution - post apartheid.

p 24 ★ Anna Louw is "just law"?
based on Bettie du Toit, a banned
trade unionist Toby Hood based on Toby Street (street
bet Sophiatown + white area, See Clingman '71.

★ 31-32 LAWS- whites make + change them. Africans not act
excluded by b

LBW

42 Graham (new boyfriend) is a lawyer (inadequate)
49 Courts + law - mother of Max - concerned only w.
self.
44 GRAHAM
44-45 " his "neutral legalistic sense of truth"
Clingman 18

Get essay Joe SLOVO "South Africa - No Middle Groun
1976
109 "laws made of skin + hair"
★116 "Early 1980s, when petty apartheid laws are bein
dismantled"
118 MSS - Will's desire for a blond "brought on
by laws"
121 Law forbids Sonny Hannah

129 LAW in NAM
P 131 LAW in NAM
145 New constitution in 1996 - in HGun.
146 Law trial in HG
147 black lawyer

AUTO
9 X - Autobiog. - what goes unsaid appears in fiction
82 - unhappy marriage. (CNG 30 7 ?)
97 John Cooke says her rebellion ag her overly
possessive mother included rebelling ag
the "d   political order."
31 Auto
p. 24 Anna
"ima
pos
see

35 AUTO fa
36 Bloch
37 NG tra
39 Where a
113 John C
relati
has th
Mich
See 113 -
See 114 -
MSS - u
resp
the
p. 127 - Tim
too -

} not my
aim
not fact
but time
futures

- Yg
way o

eber - d
- bool
tskness

isl
ne).
lack +
utobiog